D1457211

THE FORMAL STRAIN

THE FORMAL STRAIN

Studies in Augustan Imitation and Satire

Howard D. Weinbrot

The University of Chicago Press
Chicago and London

Library of Congress Catalog Card Number: 68-54706
The University of Chicago Press, Chicago 60637
The University of Chicago Press, Ltd., London W.C. 1
© 1969 by The University of Chicago. All rights reserved
Published 1969. Printed in the United States of America

169983

To My Mother and to the Memory of My Father

PREFACE

I have two central aims in this study: to investigate the background and conventions of the "Augustan" Imitation and formal verse satire and, where possible, to suggest ways in which knowledge of these conventions can illuminate the successes and failures of several eighteenth-century poems. Recent editors and critics, notably Reuben Brower,[1] have shown that Pope's poetry "alludes" to classical authors, and that one can better understand Pope with a knowledge of these ancestors. Pope, Johnson, and Young, also "allude" to earlier British and continental literary theory. The pattern of praise and blame in formal verse satire, for example, is surely found—so Dryden and others thought—in the satires of Persius, Juvenal, and Boileau. Furthermore, Horace's distinction between the more acerbic satire and the gentler epistle was noted by several of the major continental Renaissance scholars, was certainly known to Pope and, as examination of the relevant poems shows, influenced his work. Examination of Johnson's verse satires shows that his knowledge of the pattern of satire influenced his work as well. Similarly, the peculiarly post-Restoration form of Imitation demanded that the modern reader be aware of the ancient or foreign poem, and often included the latter in order to facilitate the pleasurable task of comparison. Consequently, the reader cannot regard the appended Latin (or French) as an interesting curiosity; it is part of the poet's conception and can enrich our understanding of the tone, imagery, and structure of the poem.

The main aims of the historical inquiry, then, are to determine the "genealogy" and essential qualities of Augustan Imitation and formal verse satire; the main aims of the literary analysis are to

1. *Alexander Pope: The Poetry of Allusion* (Oxford: Clarendon Press, 1959), *passim.*

determine how these operate in specific works. As will become clear in the following chapters, I believe that past literary criteria can be used as effective tools of analysis in the present. I would like us to assume that if Pope and Johnson knew how poetry affected intelligent readers in their own century, they did so for such readers in subsequent centuries as well; that if historical investigation suggests that such authors chose to write a poem of a particular literary genre, and assumed that genre had certain roughly definable attributes and emotional appeals, it is possible they were right. Accordingly, we might think about incorporating their criteria into ours, instead of merely looking at theirs in an isolated context. Thus viewed, my discussion of the satires of Young, Pope, and Johnson is not historical criticism, but an attempt to write modern criticism based on at least some of our authors' criteria for the work at hand; it is an attempt to make historical criticism part of modern criticism. We have come to grips with the principle of indestructible matter; we have yet to do this with an analogous principle—indestructible, valid, literary criteria.[2] Hence if we apply Dryden's theory of satire to Young's *Love of Fame* and Johnson's *London* and *The Vanity of Human Wishes*, we will be using a critical tool which is well suited to these poems and can, therefore, help to clarify their respective intentions and achievements. Of course incorporation of older critical methods should not cast out the "new"; close analysis of structure, metaphor, rhetoric, and tone—among other things—should be present in discussion of the "generic" qualities of a work. And we should always recall that these qualities often are guidelines and tendencies, not rigidly defined *differentiae*.

I also assume a guideline approach to the difficult question, to what extent can we generalize from poetic theory to poetic practice? Both Pope and Johnson, for instance, condemned puns, but used them successfully. Similarly, Coleridge has shown how Wordsworth neglected to employ the ordinary language of ordinary men in his own poetry. Clearly, a certain degree of scepticism is in order; the student choosing to apply theoretical distinctions must carefully

---

2. Of course I exclude such aberrations as an obsessive demand for the three unities.

avoid "finding" what he is looking for merely because it is "supposed" to be in the poem. I hope to have avoided this error in part by showing that the conventions discussed were widespread, respected, and known to the poets at the time they wrote their satires. It is no less likely that Pope would apply his understanding of, say, epistolary satire in *Arbuthnot* than his understanding of epic traditions in *The Dunciad*. Moreover, the poems themselves suggest that this is likely. The theory of Imitation that Pope received demanded that the reader be made aware of the original poem. Pope puts this into practice very effectively by not only reproducing that original, but also by placing certain of its particularly important words or phrases in distinctive type. Thus, though theory and practice often diverge, they often blend as well, and the latter may be clarified when guided—not restricted by—the former.

As a reader I too often overlook those sections where the apparently dull duty of an acknowledger breaks out; as an author I find this the pleasantest of tasks. I began my research at the University of Chicago and Newberry Libraries and completed much of it at the Sterling and Beinecke Libraries of Yale University. I also made substantial use of the Henry E. Huntington Library and visited the William Andrews Clark and University of California, Riverside, Libraries for finishing touches; my sincerest thanks to the staff (and *collections*!) of these institutions. In an earlier and very different form my study was read by Arthur Friedman and directed by Gwin J. Kolb. Somewhat later, individual chapters were read by Frederick W. Hilles, William K. Wimsatt, Jr., Martin Price, Louis A. Landa, Aubrey L. Williams, Earl R. Wasserman, Ernest H. Lockridge, Michael J. K. O'Loughlin, and C. Earl Ramsey. Robert F. Gleckner read several chapters, and Paul K. Alkon, Edward W. Rosenheim, Jr., Donald J. Greene, and Kathleen Williams, read the entire manuscript. I owe particular debts to the friendship of Paul K. Alkon, to Gwin J. Kolb's numerous and extraordinary acts of kindness over a period of several years, and to Donald J. Greene, whose sympathetic rigor addressed to the first and to a final draft has been of immense value. Stanley N. Stewart, David A. Hansen, and Susan L. Hawk provided useful discussion of particular points.

In many cases these readers forced me to clarify, retract, or add to certain sections; of course they are not responsible for any errors of commission or omission. Professor John Oates translated the Latin in chapter 5; Robert F. Gleckner aided this with research funds; George A. Knox kindly coerced his departmental secretaries into typing much of the manuscript; and James Stauffer, Beverly Kasper and Andrew Richter aided with preparation of the manuscript for the press. To these and other friends, colleagues, assistants, and students, as well as for the University of California's Inter-Campus, Intramural, and Summer Faculty Fellowships, I am grateful. Part II of chapter 1 first appeared in *ELH*, chapter 2 in *PMLA*, and an earlier version of chapter 5 was read before the Comparative Literature Colloquium of the University of California, Riverside. Each chapter has been altered in its present form; my thanks to the editors of the journals for permission to reprint the essays.

CONTENTS

1

The Imitation: The General Matrix and the Immediate Genealogy

I The Background of the Imitation: The General Matrix

The English Imitation is largely a post-Restoration form.[1] There are few examples of it before 1660, and there is apparently no dictionary definition of it until 1755. The Imitation reaches its qualitative peak in Pope's *Imitations of Horace* (1733–38), and has its last major display in Johnson's *Vanity of Human Wishes* (1749). Through much of the later eighteenth century the form loses its strength, and some of its attraction;[2] but between about 1660 and 1750 this important genre attracted such poets as Cowley, Rochester, Dryden, Oldham, Congreve, Swift, Prior, Rowe, Pope and Johnson. In 1738 and again in 1749 Johnson chose Imitation as the vehicle for a major poem and, according to Boswell, he "had the originals and correspondent allusions [of Juvenal's satires] floating in his mind, which he could, when he pleased, embody and render permanent without much labour."[3] What, one wonders, were

1. Throughout this study the genre of Imitation has been capitalized in order to distinguish it from imitation as borrowing.
2. "There was an increase in modernizations between 1700 and 1750, but between 1750 and 1800 there was a diminution in the number of adaptations and a corresponding falling off in the ability of the imitators. No artist approaching the importance of Pope and Dryden devoted any attention to systematic imitation after Johnson's *Vanity of Human Wishes* in 1749" (William Francis Gallaway, "English Adaptations of Roman Satire, 1660–1800" [unpublished Ph.D. diss., University of Michigan, 1937], p. 219). Gallaway's essay contains several valuable references, and is the most thorough, if not the most satisfying, study of the Imitation.
3. *Boswell's Life of Johnson: Together with Boswell's Journey of a Tour to*

the traditions that helped to initiate so popular a form? Why should different kinds of Imitation flourish during this period, and why should so many poets find it a sympathetic vehicle for their genius? We can, I think, find several minor and two major sources behind the form, both a general matrix and an immediate genealogy.

The concept of general nature, a commonplace during the Restoration and the eighteenth century, was one part of the matrix of the Imitation. If the sins and sinners of Augustan Rome are similar to the sins and sinners of "Augustan" London, then certainly the terms of castigation may also be similar. The belief in general nature is found in classical literature as well, and is exemplified in Juvenal's well-known first satire: "To these ways of ours posterity will have nothing to add; our grandchildren will do the same things, and desire the same things that we do."[4] After quoting his own version of these lines (1647) Sir Robert Stapylton says that the value of reading Juvenal cannot be "limited within the narrow bounds of his owne age, or climate, but [is] communicated and alike usefull to all Ages, to all Nations, for the sad cause which he himself foretold."[5] In his *Modern Essay on the Thirteenth Satyr of*

the Hebrides and Johnson's Diary of a Journey into North Wales, ed. George Birkbeck Hill, and rev. L. F. Powell (Oxford: Clarendon Press, 1934–50), 1: 193.

4. *Juvenal and Persius*, Loeb Classical Library, trans. G. G. Ramsay (London: Wm. Heinemann, 1930), p. 15, ll. 147-49.

5. *Juvenal's Sixteen Satyrs, or A Survey of the Manners and Actions of Mankind* (London, 1647), sig. A4ʳ. The subject of the uniformity of nature has been dealt with in several studies. See Arthur O. Lovejoy, "Nature as an Aesthetic Norm," *MLN*, 42 (1927): 444-50, and *The Great Chain of Being* (Cambridge, Mass.: Harvard University Press, 1936), pp. 288-93; Francis Gallaway, *Reason, Rule, and Revolt in English Classicism* (New York: Charles Scribner's Sons, 1940), pp. 132-37; Walter Jackson Bate, *From Classic to Romantic* (Cambridge, Mass.: Harvard University Press, 1946), pp. 59-92 (but, on Bate's own admission, in *The Achievement of Samuel Johnson*, p. 240, n. 30, this chapter is faulty and should be corrected by chapter 1 of Hagstrum, below), and *The Achievement of Samuel Johnson* (New York: Oxford University Press, 1955), pp. 198-99; Scott Elledge, "The Background and Development in English Criticism of the Theories of Generality and Particularity," *PMLA*, 62 (1947): 147-82; W. R. Keast's review of Elledge's article, in *PQ*, 27 (1948): 130-32, and Keast, "The Theoretical Foundations of Johnson's Criticism," in *Critics and Criticism*, ed. R. S. Crane (Chicago: University of Chicago Press, 1952), pp. 389-407; Jean H. Hagstrum, *Samuel Johnson's Literary Criticism* (Minneapolis: University of Minnesota Press, 1952), pp. 14, 56-75; M. H. Abrams, *The Mirror and the*

Juvenal (1686) Henry Higden similarly observes: "the vices here taxed by our Satyrist, are not so antiquated, but a slight Inquisition may discover them amongst our selves, though perhaps something altered in Dress and Fashion."[6] Shortly thereafter, Dryden uses general nature as the basis for a critical system. He remarks that "Nature is still the same in all ages, and can never be contrary to herself. Thus from the practise of Aeschylus, Sophocles, and Euripides, Aristotle drew his rules for tragedy; and Philostratus for painting."[7] Johnson uses the same concept as the basis for evaluation of both subject matter and the possibility of qualitative progress in poetry. Hence in the *Rambler,* no. 36 (1750), he observes that the pastorals of antiquity cannot be much changed or improved, for poetry deals with the unchanging passions of men.[8] These remarks suggest that "nature" in man is both internally and externally uniform. Both aspects are neatly summed up in Richard Hurd's *Discourse concerning Poetical Imitation* (1751). *"Similarity of mind,"* he says ". . . like that of outward *form* and *make"* has been given to "the whole species. We are all furnished with the same original *properties and affections,* as with the same stock of *perceptions and ideas."*[9] Borrowing from past writers is therefore not only legitimate, but necessary. Since much of what the moderns say must be similar to what the ancients have said, we may certainly reinforce our utterance with their wisdom and style, particularly since imitation of the ancients—who were unencumbered by modern "art"—is imitation of nature. Accordingly, Pope tells the

Lamp (New York: Oxford University Press, 1953), pp. 38-42; and Paul Fussell, *The Rhetorical World of Augustan Humanism* (New York: Oxford University Press, 1965), pp. 54-69.

6. (London, 1686), sig. b2ʳ (this part of the original is italicized throughout).

7. "A Parallel of Poetry and Painting: Prefixed to the Version of Du Fresnoy, *De Arte Graphica"* (1695), in *The Essays of John Dryden,* ed. W. P. Ker (Oxford: Clarendon Press, 1926) (referred to hereafter as *Essays*), 2:134.

8. *The Works of Samuel Johnson* (Oxford, 1825), 2:180. (Unless otherwise specified, subsequent references are to this edition.) Johnson frequently discusses unchanging nature. See, for example, the *Adventurer,* no. 108 (1753); the *Idler,* no. 94 (1760); chap. 10 of *Rasselas* (1759); the "Preface" to *Shakespeare* (1765), as in Johnson's *Works,* 5:105-6.

9. *Q. Horatii Flacci Epistola ad Augustum. With an English Commentary and Notes. To which is added a Discourse concerning Poetical Imitation* (London, 1751), p. 123.

readers of his *Imitations of Horace* that an Horatian answer to his detractors "was both more full, and of more Dignity, than any I cou'd have made in my own person."[10] Dryden before Pope and Johnson after him also discuss the community of thought between modern and ancient authors. In the *Rambler,* no. 143 (1751), for instance, Johnson insists that the ancients have planted "flowers of fiction" in the "open road of poetry for the accommodation of their successors," and that these flowers belong to "every one that has art to pluck them without injuring their colours or their fragrance."[11]

Clearly, Imitation as modernization is latent within the theory of uniform nature; all the poet need do is modernize allusions, change Roman names to English, alter a few trivial manners, and an ancient poem is available to the understanding of modern Englishmen. Thus Higden feels that the reader of his version of Juvenal's thirteenth satire will "find little other than the *Old Stock* [of vices] new Trim'd,"[12] and John Oldham, explaining his method of imitating Horace's *Ars poetica* (1681), remarks: "I . . . resolved to alter the Scene from *Rome* to *London,* and to make use of *English* Names of Men, Places, and Customs, . . . which I conceived would . . . render it more agreeable to the relish of the present Age."[13]

The concept of general nature, then, both fosters literary borrowing and encourages modernization of ancient names, places, and so on; but it also suggests the modern reader's awareness of that

10. *Alexander Pope: Imitations of Horace,* The Twickenham Edition of the Poems of Alexander Pope, vol. 4, ed. John Butt, 2d ed. (London: Methuen & Co., 1953), p. 3.
11. *Works,* 3: 181. For Dryden's remark, see *Essays,* 2: 198. Fielding defends borrowing in *Tom Jones* (1749), 12: i; and Reynolds defends it in *Discourses* 2 (1769), 6 (1774), and 12 (1784): see Sir Joshua Reynolds, *Discourses on Art,* ed. Robert R. Wark (San Marino, Calif.: Huntington Library, 1959). Several of his major points are summarized by R. Wittkower in "Imitation, Eclecticism, and Genius," in *Aspects of the Eighteenth Century,* ed. Earl R. Wasserman (Baltimore: Johns Hopkins Press, 1965), pp. 153-54. For further discussion of Reynolds and imitation, see Harvey D. Goldstein, "*Ut Poesis Pictura:* Reynolds on Imitation and Imagination," *ECS,* 1 (1968): 213-35.
12. *Modern Essay,* sig. b2ʳ (italics and Roman type inverted in text).
13. *The Works of Mr. John Oldham, Together with his Remains* (London, 1684); new pagination and title page after p. 148: *Some New Pieces* (London, 1684), sig. aᵛ (italics and Roman type inverted in text).

similarity. Dryden's observation, for instance, makes explicit his desire for recognition of his borrowings. In the Preface to *Annus Mirabilis* (1666) Dryden tells Sir Robert Howard that he has followed Virgil "everywhere" in his poem, and that his images and expressions are copied from him. "In some places," he continues, "where either the fancy or the words were his, or any other's, I have noted it in the margin, that I might not seem a plagiary" (*Essays*, 1: 17–18). For Pope imitation as borrowing also requires a response similar to imitation of complete poems. In a letter to Steele (1712) he says of his "Dying Christian to his Soul": "You have it (as Cowley calls it) just warm from the brain. It came to me the first moment I waked this morning: Yet you'll see it was not so absolutely inspiration, but that I had in my head not only the verses of Adrian, but the fine fragments of Sapho."[14] Indeed, some years later Pope supplies an explicit connection between imitation as borrowing of selected phrases or passages, and Imitation as a genre. He tells Spence that as a boy he would attempt to imitate or translate several pleasing passages among the English, French, Italian, Latin, or Greek poets at hand, and this, he says, "was the cause of my Imitations published so long after."[15] In 1713 Pope, or perhaps Steele, provides a psychological explanation of the reader's delight in recognition of borrowed images or thoughts; the kind of pleasure described is similar to the pleasure evoked by a completely imitated poem:

> over and above a just painting of nature, a learned reader will find a new beauty superadded in a happy imitation of some famous ancient, as it revives in his mind the pleasure he took in his first reading such an author. Such copyings as these give that kind of double delight which we perceive when we look upon the children of a beautiful couple; where the eye is not more charmed with the symmetry of the parts, than the mind by observing the resemblance transmitted from par-

14. *The Correspondence of Alexander Pope*, ed. George Sherburn (Oxford: Clarendon Press, 1956), 1: 159-60.
15. *Anecdotes . . . of Books and Men. By Joseph Spence*, ed. James M. Osborne (Oxford: Clarendon Press, 1966), 1:20.

ents to their offspring, and the mingled features of the father and the mother.[16]

As early as 1666, then, there was distinguished precedent for the principle of recognition of an original; its transference to entire modernized poems would be an easy transition for the Restoration or eighteenth-century reader.

The native English tradition was not the only force encouraging the rise of the Imitation. The conceptions of Imitation as borrowing phrases or sentiments to improve one's own style, as working within established genres, and even Imitation as refining and modernizing, were buttressed by similar practices in the exalted Roman and Greek authors. Here too, as George Converse Fiske has noted, we find that the work of one's predecessor is common property. "The general trend of ancient literary tradition," he says, ". . . was to regard the subject matter of an earlier master in any given genre as the common property of posterity." The poet, "working in the spirit of generous rivalry," is obliged "to follow in the steps of his master, to preserve unimpaired the essentials of the great tradition, to perpetuate that ordered freedom which conditioned the growth in Greece and the continuation in Rome of all the literary genres."[17] Thus Horace frequently states that he is the follower of Lucilius, and also justifies his variation from Lucilian satire by citing the latter's own practice, for he found things "to change in the tragedies of Accius." Properly conceived, the spirit of imitation leads not to stagnation, but to growth and refinement and, in Fiske's term, the source of which we will see shortly, "generous rivalry." Horace therefore freely says that Lucilius wrote too quickly, and should not be considered a perfect model.[18] In a famous section of

16. *The Guardian*, no. 12, in *The British Classics* (London, 1804), 13: 63.
17. *Lucilius and Horace: A Study in the Classical Theory of Imitation*, University of Wisconsin Studies in Language and Literature, no. 7 (Madison, Wisconsin: University of Wisconsin Press, 1920), p. 27. Fiske's opening chapter, "The Classical Theory of Imitation," pp. 25-63, is an excellent introduction to its subject.
18. *Horace: Satires, Epistles and Ars poetica*, Loeb Classical Library, trans. H. Rushton Fairclough (Cambridge, Mass.: Harvard University Press, 1926), p. 121, *Satires*, i, 10, ll. 50-71. See also *Satires*, i, 10, ll. 1-4 (p. 114), ll. 16-17, 28-34 (p. 128), ll. 62-78 (pp. 130-32).

the *Ars poetica* Horace also observes the difference between honest
and dishonest borrowers:

> It is hard to treat in your own way what is common: and
> more properly are you spinning into acts a song of Troy than
> if, for the first time, you were giving the world a theme un-
> known and unsung. In ground open to all you will win pri-
> vate rights, if you do not linger along the easy and open path-
> way, if you do not seek to render word for word as a slavish
> translator, and if in your copying you do not leap into the
> narrow well, out of which either shame or the laws of your task
> will keep you from stirring a step. (ll. 128–35)[19]

For Horace as well as (say) Dryden, even imitation as random
borrowing demands recognition of the original and a certain amount
of conscious rivalry with the parent-poet. Horace's plea for moderation in borrowing, however, was more than matched by the pleas
of the rhetoricians, who advised their students to imitate in order
to gain the graces and perception of great "classical" authors and
—obviously—thereby encouraged recognition of the original.
Through reading great authors, Dionysius of Halicarnassus says,
the student gains a "spiritual foundation for imitation," for his
soul "absorbs a stylistic affinity by continual association."[20] Quintilian, in the *Institutio oratoria,* stresses borrowing which not only
copies a model but attempts to excel it (x, 2, 10). Only the best
parts of the best authors may be accepted as models (x, 2, 14) ;
this extends, Quintilian says, not merely to imitation of the words
of these authors, but also their propriety in selection of persons
and things, and their judgment and arrangement of all things which
help the success of their cause (x, 2, 27). In an earlier passage
Quintilian also suggests that modernization, or at the very least
"correction," had earlier Greek precedent:

> Aeschylus was the first to bring tragedy into prominence: he

19. *Ibid.,* pp. 461-63. This section contains the important *"Nec verbum verbo
curabis reddere fidus / interpres"* (l. 133). For examples of Latin modernizing and adapting, see Fiske, *Lucilius and Horace,* pp. 27-31, and 59, n. 7.
20. Fiske, *Lucilius and Horace,* p. 36. Fiske is paraphrasing Dionysius of
Halicarnassus.

is lofty, dignified, grandiloquent often to a fault, but frequently uncouth and inharmonious. Consequently, the Athenians allowed later poets to revise his tragedies and to produce them in the dramatic contests, and many succeeded in winning the prize by such means. (x, 1, 66)[21]

Close imitation of models was similarly urged throughout the Italian Renaissance. For example, in 1596 Lorenzo Giacomini praised Tasso's use of this method. Part of the pleasure evoked by Pope's later use of the genre of Imitation was this delightful recognition of borrowing as Giacomini described it.

> And if we recognize in his works many beauties transported, as he imitates, from the works of others, we shall see nonetheless the imitation either improved by the addition of new graces or mingled with variety; so that to the delight in the recognition of the lovely expressions is added the delight in the competition.[22]

English authors frequently referred to several of these precedents —particularly the Roman—to justify their own practice. In the Account prefaced to *Annus Mirabilis* Dryden defends his anglicizing of Virgil's Latin through an appeal to the dictum of Horace and the practice of Virgil himself. He tells Sir Robert Howard:

> Upon your first perusal of this poem, you have taken notice of some words, which I have innovated (if it be too bold for

21. *The Institutio oratoria of Quintilian*, Loeb Classical Library, trans. H. E. Butler (London: Wm. Heinemann, 1936), 4: 39.

22. "Oratione in lode di Torquato Tasso," read to the Accademia degli Alterati, as quoted in Bernard Weinberg, *A History of Literary Criticism in the Italian Renaissance* (Chicago: University of Chicago Press, 1961), 2: 1059. Of course imitation was urged during the English Renaissance as well. Roger Ascham's *The Scholemaster* (1570) was influential in encouraging imitation as close translation, while Ben Jonson's comedies were often cited as containing characters and scenes from Roman plays. For Ascham, see *The Scholemaster*, ed. Edward Arber (London, 1870), pp. 26, 93, 114-15; and for Jonson, see n. 25, below, and Gerard Langbaine, *Account of the English Dramatic Poets* (Oxford, 1691), pp. 145-46. For extensive and interesting eighteenth-century remarks on Renaissance imitation as borrowing, copying, adapting, improving, and translating, see both volumes of Thomas Warton's *Observations on the Fairy Queene of Spenser*, 2d ed. (London, 1762).

The Imitation

me to say refined) upon [Virgil's] Latin; which, as I offer
not to introduce into English prose, so I hope they are neither
improper, nor altogether unelegant in verse; and in this
Horace will again defend me—

> Et nova, fictaque nuper, habebunt verba fidem, si
> Graeco fonte cadant, parce detorta.

The inference is exceedingly plain; for, if a Roman poet
might have liberty to coin a word, supposing only that it was
derived from the Greek, was put into a Latin termination, and
that he used this liberty but seldom, and with modesty; how
much more justly may I challenge that privilege to do it with
the same prerequisites from the best and most judicious of
Latin writers. (*Essays*, 1: 17–18) [23]

Similarly, Tom Brown, translating Dacier's "Essay on Satyr," refers
to Horace as a refiner of Lucilius;[24] a few years later, in the
Preface to his translation of Boileau's *Le Lutrin* (1708), John Ozell
defends his own "adaptation" of Boileau by reference to the practice of Terence, Horace, and Ben Jonson, all of whom borrowed
from earlier masters;[25] and in his *Polymetis* (1747) Joseph Spence
praises Virgil's "judgment, in omitting such circumstances in his
imitations of Homer, as would have clashed with the taste and customs of the Romans."[26]

Longinus' *On the Sublime* was also important as an example of
the wisdom of the ancients and a spur to imitation. Boileau's translation of it into French (1674) placed great new authority behind
Longinus, and he was soon coupled with Aristotle and Horace as
one of the foremost ancient critics. For our purposes, xiii, 2–4,
and xiv, 1–2, are significant. Plato, Longinus says, shows us an

23. Dryden is cleverly adapting *Ars poetica*, ll. 52-53.
24. *The Works of Mr. Thomas Brown, Serious and Comical*, 4th ed. (London,
1715), 1: 20. Brown adds that "Horace has no less refin'd the satires of
Lucilius, than he has those of *Ennius and Pacuvius*." For information regarding the "Essay," see Benjamin Boyce, *Tom Brown of Facetious Memory*
(Cambridge, Mass.: Harvard University Press, 1939), p. 38.
25. *Le Lutrin* (London, 1708), sigs. *2v–*3r.
26. *Polymetis* (London, 1747), p. 361. Spence refers the reader to pp. 53 and
210 for examples of this "judgment," and on p. 22 refers to Horace as a
refiner of Lucilius.

important path "which will carry [us] to the true sublime." And what is this path?

Why, an Imitation and Emulation of the greatest Orators and Poets that ever flourished. And let this, my Friend, be our Ambition; be this the fix'd and lasting Scope of all our Labours.

For hence it is, that numbers of Imitators are ravish'd and transported by a Spirit not their own, like the *Pythian* Priestess, when she approaches the sacred Tripod. There is, if Fame speaks true, a Chasm in the Earth, *from whence exhale divine Evaporations*, which impregnate her on a sudden with the Inspiration of her God, and cause in her the Utterance of Oracles and Predictions. So, from the sublime Spirit of the Ancients, there arise some fine Effluvia, like Vapours from the sacred Vents, which work themselves insensibly into the Breasts of Imitators, and fill those, who naturally are not of a tow'ring Genius, with the lofty Ideas and Fire of others. Was *Herodotus* alone the constant Imitator of *Homer*? No: *Stesichorus* and *Archilochus* imitated him more than *Herodotus*; but *Plato* more than all of them; who, from the copious *Homeric* Fountain, has drawn a thousand Rivulets to cherish and improve his own Productions. . . .

Nor is such proceeding to be look'd upon as Plagiarism but, in Methods consistent with the nicest Honour, an Imitation of the finest Pieces, or copying out those bright Originals. Neither do I think, that *Plato* would have so much embellished his Philosophical Tenets with the florid Expressions of Poetry, had he not been ambitious of entering the Lists, like a youthful Champion, and ardently contending for the Prize with *Homer*, who had a long time engros'd the Admiration of the World. The Attack was perhaps too rash, the Opposition perhaps had too much the Air of Enmity, but yet could not fail of some Advantage; for, as *Hesiod* says,

Such brave Contention works the Good of Men.

A greater Prize than the Glory and Renown of the Ancients

can never be contended for, where Victory crowns with never-dying Applause, when even a Defeat, in such a competition, is attended with Honour.

SECTION XIV

IF ever therefore we are engaged in a Work, which requires a Grandeur of Stile and exalted Sentiments, would it not then be of use to raise in ourselves such Reflexions as these?—How in this case would *Homer*, or *Plato*, or *Demosthenes*, have raised their Thoughts? Or if it be historical,—How would *Thucydides*? For these celebrated Persons, being proposed by us for our Pattern and Imitation, will in some degree lift up our Souls to the Standard of their own Genius. [2] It will be yet of greater use, if to the preceding Reflexions we add these.—What would *Homer* or *Demosthenes* have thought of this Piece? or, what Judgment would they have pass'd upon it?[27]

These passages were frequently echoed by the English Augustans. Dryden, for one, states that his adaptation of the scene between Troilus and Hector in *Troilus and Cressida* was based upon Euripides' "excellent example in his *Iphigenia*, between Agamemnon and Menelaus" (*Essays*, 1: 205). He defends his practice with a quotation from section xiii, 4, above, in which Longinus images Plato as the young athlete emulating Homer. In chapter ix of the *Peri Bathos* Pope parodies Longinus when he says that we must ask ourselves, "how would Sir Richard have said this? do I express myself simply as Ambrose Philips? or flow my numbers with the

27. *Dionysius Longinus on the Sublime*, trans. William Smith, 2d ed. (London, 1742), pp. 36-39. For a modern version, see *Longinus on the Sublime*, trans. W. Rhys Roberts, 2d ed. (Cambridge, 1907), pp. 79-83. There are several major studies of the sublime. See, for example, Samuel Holt Monk, *The Sublime: A Study of Critical Theories in XVIII-Century England* (New York: Modern Language Association of America, 1935); Walter J. Hipple, *The Beautiful, the Sublime, and the Picturesque* (Carbondale, Illinois: Southern Illinois University Press, 1957); J. T. Boulton's edition of Edmund Burke's *A Philosophical Enquiry into the Origin of our Ideas of the Sublime and Beautiful* (London: Routledge and Kegan Paul, 1958); and Marjorie Nicolson, *Mountain Gloom and Mountain Glory* (Ithaca, New York: Cornell University Press, 1959).

quiet thoughtlessness of Mr. Welsted?" Addison, in the *Spectator*, no. 339 (1712), insists that Milton "has doubtless very much raised and ennobled his Conceptions, by such an Imitation as that which *Longinus* has recommended." Moreover, Dr. John Douglas, in the *Monthly Review* for December 10, 1750, uses Longinus' distinction between plagiarism and imitation to defend *Paradise Lost* against Lauder's attacks, and Joseph Warton, in the *Adventurer*, no. 89 (1753), echoes both the sections on the Pythian inspiration and on emulation of the ancients.[28] In his *Conjectures on Original Composition* (1759) Edward Young praises Longinus' notion of emulation, of the battle between younger and older poets as the key to successful imitation.[29] And across the Channel in France, the author of the article on "Imitation" in Diderot and D'Alembert's *Encyclopédie* also echoes Longinus when he insists that Boileau, in his imitations of Horace, "n'a pas traduit le poëte latin, mais il a joûté contre lui, parce que dans ce genre de combat, on peut être vaincu sans honte."[30]

Any form of imitation, whether borrowing, modernization, use of genre, or Longinian emulation, ultimately depends upon a respect for ancient thought and literature. This respect was both exhibited and solidified in contemporary education. For instance, St. Evremond reports that the Latin poets studied by Rochester at Oxford "made such a deep impression on him that he never lost a true taste of any Sovereign Beauty of those great Authors."[31] Bishop Hurd later remarks that "the most universal cause, inducing *imitation* [as borrowing] in great writers, is the force of early discipline and education." He continues:

28. For these references, see Elizabeth Nitchie, "Longinus and the Theory of Poetic Imitation in Seventeenth and Eighteenth-Century England," *SP*, 32 (1935) : 590-92.
29. Edith J. Morley, ed. (Manchester: University of Manchester Press, 1918), pp. 29-30.
30. *Encyclopédie, ou dictionnaire raisonné des sciences, des arts et des métiers, par une société de gens de lettres* (Neuchâtel, 1765), 8: 568. The article is signed "D.J."; he is probably "M. le Chevalier de Jaucourt," who is praised for his "solicitations tendres" to the editors: see 8: i.
31. St. Evremond's authority—seconded by Anthony Wood, Robert Whitehall, and Bishop Burnet—is accepted by John Hayward. See his edition of *Rochester's Collected Works* (London: Nonesuch Press, 1926), p. xxi.

We are habituated to a survey of this *secondary and derivative nature*, as presented in the admired works of *art*, thro' the intire course of our education. . . . When the poet, thus tutored in the works of *imitation*, comes to address himself to *invention*, these familiar images, which he hath so often and so fondly admired, immediately step in and intercept his observation of their great *original*. Or, if he has power to hold them off, and turn his eye directly on the *primary object*, he still inclines to view it only on that side and in those *lights*, in which he has been accustomed to study it. Nor let it be said, that this is the *infirmity* only, of weak minds. It belongs to our very natures, and the utmost vigour of genius is no security against it.[32]

Even students in the later eighteenth-century felt the force of a classical education. Coleridge and Wordsworth understood that a key aspect of Gray's poetic method—borrowing from Shakespeare and Milton—"had been kept up, if it did not wholly arise from, the custom of writing Latin verses, and the great importance attached to those exercises in our public schools."[33]

Quite naturally, if respect for a classical education encouraged the positive use of a model, resentment of the model would encourage burlesque of it. Hence we hear John Phillips, in his *Maronides: or Virgil Travesty* (1673) insist: "I leave the world to determine whether it be not reason, that he that has caused us so often to cry when we were Boys, ought not now to make us laugh as much now we are men. Our School Masters were *Aeneas* our Tayles were

32. *Poetical Imitation*, p. 191.
33. As quoted in A. R. Humphreys, "A Classical Education and Eighteenth-Century Poetry," *Scrutiny*, 8 (1939) : 195. Humphreys regards the classical education as responsible for the "devitalization" (p. 205) and "flaccidity" (p. 206) of much eighteenth-century poetry. For more information regarding contemporary education, see Christopher Wordsworth, *Scholae Academicae: Some Account of the Studies at the English Universities in the Eighteenth Century* (Cambridge, 1910) ; Hayward, n. 31, above; Charles Edward Mallet, *A History of the University of Oxford* (London: Methuen & Co., 1927), 3: 127-28; Alice Stayert Brandenburg, "English Education and Neo-Classical Taste in the Eighteenth Century," *MLQ*, 8 (1947) : 174-93; James Sutherland, *Preface to Eighteenth-Century Poetry* (Oxford: Clarendon Press, 1948), p. 52; Fussell, *Rhetorical World*, p. 11.

Turnus. Turnus had the worst on't."[34] As I will show later, in either a "serious" or "comic" work the presence of the poem imitated is essential.

The concept of general nature, a classical education, and the many favorable uses of the term *imitation,* all created a favorable context for the Imitation.[35] The new genre with the familiar name would easily be accepted, for, as we have seen, it expected a response similar to the recognition of the borrowed phrase or style. Indeed, the difference between borrowing and adapting of entire poems is one of degree, not of essence. The varied but ancient and venerated tradition of imitation thus lent support in many ways for the emerging genre of Imitation.

This support, however, is only a partial explanation of its rise. Further inquiry into the Imitation's background will suggest two other important sources: the acceptance of a free theory of translation, and the development of the Restoration burlesque.

II. Translation and Parody: The Immediate Genealogy of the Imitation

In his *Dictionary* (1755), Johnson defines Imitation as "a method of translating looser than paraphrase, in which modern examples

34. *Maronides: or, Virgil Travesty, Being a New Paraphrase Upon the Sixth Book of Virgil's Aeneids in Burlesque Verse* (London, 1673), sig. A1ᵛ (italics and Roman type inverted; what I call A1ᵛ is unsigned and precedes B1ʳ by two pages).
35. I have omitted the term *mimesis,* as the mutations of its meaning are too complex to discuss here. John Draper, however, summarizes one broadly accepted eighteenth-century meaning: " 'Imitation' in the sense of copying was the common conception that the age gleaned from its dictionaries and rhetorics, as well as from the commentators and translators of Aristotle. The rhetoricians, moreover, regularly accepted it as a copy of models, enjoined it in the schoolroom, and so moulded the taste and the creative production of the age" ("Aristotelian 'Mimesis' in Eighteenth-Century England," *PMLA,* 36 [1921]: 375). For other discussions of the meaning of the term, see Abrams, *Mirror and the Lamp,* pp. 8-14; Richard McKeon, "Literary Criticism and the Concept of Imitation in Antiquity," in *Critics and Criticism,* pp. 160-68; Harvey D. Goldstein, "Mimesis and Catharsis Reexamined," *Journal of Aesthetics and Art Criticism,* 24 (1966) : 567-77. For a broader discussion of the concept of representation of reality, see Erich Auerbach's *Mimesis,* trans. Willard Trask (Princeton: Princeton University Press, 1953).

The Imitation

and illustrations are used for ancient, or domestick for foreign."[36] Johnson is right in regarding the Imitation as a species of translation; it seems in part to be an outgrowth of the theory of free translation made popular by Denham and Cowley. Though often discussed, however, the similarity between the two forms has not been adequately documented;[37] nor do students of the period make clear that free translation accounts only for the kind of Imitation defined by Johnson, that which is basically a modernized work largely faithful to the original author. The theory of translation does not account for one of the peculiar traits of the greater Augustan Imitation, the insistence that recognition of the poem imitated is necessary for the modern reader's pleasure. In this form the poet incorporates much or all of a specific older model into his own poem, one in which the focus is on the living (or domestic) rather than the dead (or foreign) author.[38] There is, in short, an Imitative spectrum on

36. *A Dictionary of the English Language* (London, 1755). All subsequent references are to this edition.
37. The most distinguished discussion of the Imitation is Harold F. Brooks' "The 'Imitation' in English Poetry, Especially in Formal Satire, Before the Age of Pope," *RES*, 25 (1949): 124-40. See also R. S. Crane, "Imitation of Spenser and Milton in the Early Eighteenth Century: A New Document," *SP*, 15 (1918): 195-206; W. K. Wimsatt, Jr., "Rhetoric and Poems: The Example of Pope," in *English Institute Essays 1948* (New York: Columbia University Press, 1949), p. 183; John Butt, *Imitations of Horace*, pp. xxvi-xxx; Butt, "Johnson's Practice in the Poetical Imitation," in *New Light on Dr. Johnson*, ed. Frederick W. Hilles (New Haven: Yale University Press, 1959), pp. 19-20. For relevant articles concerning Augustan translation, see John W. Draper, "The Theory of Translation in the Eighteenth Century," *Neophilologus*, 6 (1921): 241-54; Constance B. West, "La Théorie de la traduction au XVIIIe siècle par rapport surtout aux traductions françaises d'ouvrages anglais," *Revue de littérature comparée*, 12 (1932): 330-55; Douglas Knight, *Pope and the Heroic Tradition: A Critical Study of his Iliad* (New Haven: Yale University Press, 1951); William Frost, *Dryden and the Art of Translation* (New Haven: Yale University Press, 1955); Douglas Knight, "Translation: The Augustan Mode," in *On Translation*, ed. Reuben A. Brower (Cambridge, Mass.: Harvard University Press, 1959), pp. 196-204.
38. The self-conscious use and alteration of the ancient poet's meaning has been discussed by Aubrey L. Williams, "Pope and Horace: *The Second Epistle of the Second Book*," in *Restoration and Eighteenth-Century Literature: Essays in Honor of Alan Dugald McKillop*, ed. Carroll Camden (Chicago: University of Chicago Press, 1963), pp. 309-21. See also Reuben A. Brower, *Alexander Pope: The Poetry of Allusion* (Oxford: Clarendon Press, 1959); G. K. Hunter, "The 'Romanticism' of Pope's Horace," *Essays in Criticism*, 10 (1960): 390-404; John M. Aden, "Pope and the Satiric Adver-

which recognition of the poem imitated acts as a dividing line. On the one side we see the pure translator and the Imitator who is generally faithful to his author's sense and meaning, but modernizes allusions, places, and names. They are alike in wanting to approach their master and pass his thoughts to the audience. On the other side we see the "independent" Imitator who, depending upon his aims, may either parallel or differ from an acknowledged model which he subordinates to a new poetic intention. The translator and Imitator as modernizer normally direct their work towards an audience substantially unfamiliar with the original; the more "creative" Imitator demands familiarity with his source and believes that much of the reader's pleasure comes from an active comparison of the two texts. For example, no reader innocent of Latin would turn to Pope's *Epistle to Augustus* (1737) to understand Horace's poem of that name; and no reader of Pope's *Epistle* can fully understand it without Horace in mind. Pope, indeed, was both a free translator and an Imitator, and exemplifies the focus of each genre. In his Preface to Homer's *Iliad*, he insists that "it is the first grand duty of an interpreter to give his author entire and unmaimed," and in his Postscript to the *Odyssey*, he observes that as a translator he "in some measure takes the place of *Homer*." In the 1735 Advertisement of his *Imitations*, however, Pope says:

> The Occasion of publishing these *Imitations* was the Clamour raised on some of my *Epistles*. An Answer from *Horace* was both more full, and of more Dignity, than any I cou'd have made in my own person; and the Example of much greater Freedom in so eminent a Divine as Dr. *Donne* seem'd a proof with what Indignation and contempt a Christian may treat Vice or Folly, in ever so low, or ever so high, a Station.

sary," *SEL*, 2 (1962) : 267-86; Thomas E. Maresca, "Pope's Defense of Satire: *The First Satire of the Second Book of Horace Imitated*," *ELH*, 31 (1964) : 366-94 (reprinted in his *Pope's Horatian Poems* [Columbus, Ohio: Ohio State University Press, 1966], pp. 37-72). Pope's Imitations of Donne have been studied by Ian Jack, "Pope and 'The Weighty Bullion of Dr. Donne's Satire,'" *PMLA*, 66 (1951) : 1009-22; and William Youngren, "Generality in Augustan Satire," in *In Defense of Reading*, ed. Reuben A. Brower and Richard Poirer (New York: E. P. Dutton & Co., 1962), pp. 207-23.

Both these Authors were acceptable to the Princes and Ministers under whom they lived.

In translation and, in all likelihood, in Imitation as a translated but modernized poem, Pope stresses his author's achievement; in original Imitation Pope insists that Horace and Donne are allies in *his* battle and, therefore, reinforce *his* satiric mask of the *vir bonus*.[39]

Since the theory of translation offers no precedent for this principle of recognition we should look for another "source" for the Augustan Imitation. It is likely that the Restoration parody is such a source: like the Imitation the parody both demanded knowledge of the parent-poem and often printed extensive quotations from it. Moreover, the parody anticipates the Imitation by about twenty years, and was associated with it through the theory of free translation and use of the word *parody* as Imitation.

In his poem *"To Sir* Richard Fanshaw *upon his Translation of* Pastor Fido" (1648), Denham makes what appears to be the first important pronouncement favoring the Imitation. He rejects literal translation and insists that ancient thoughts be adapted to modern times. Following one's author "word by word, and line by line" is "servile" and a poor way to represent an older author. Fanshawe "wisely" restored "whatsoever grace/ [*Pastor Fido*] lost by change of Times, or Tongues, or Place." Though Denham does not here counsel the complete adaptation to modern dress that is a part of the Imitation, he does suggest how this adaptation might affect the translation, for "New names, new dressings, and the modern cast,"

39. For the remarks on translation, see Joseph Warton, ed., *The Works of Alexander Pope, Esq.* (London, 1797), 4: 406, 438; and for the Advertisement, see Butt, *Imitations of Horace*, p. 3 (italics and Roman type are inverted in the text). Williams notes that the Latin texts which Pope printed facing his own Imitations "are studded with italicized words or phrases, which are obviously designed for the reader's particular attention and which seem to have had one of two purposes: first, they signal moments when Pope apparently wishes it remarked that he is following hard upon Horace, perhaps in order to gain consent to what in the *Imitation* might seem a novel idea or phrasing; second, but equally important, the italics signal moments when Pope wishes it to be noticed that he has deliberately forsaken the original" (*Restoration and Eighteenth-Century Literature*, p. 311).

together with the alteration of "Some Scenes [and] some persons," could convince the world that it was Fanshawe's work.[40] A few years later, in the Preface to *The Destruction of Troy* (1656), Denham elaborates on his suggestion regarding the "modern cast" and employs a figure basic to the free translators, the Imitators, and—as we will later see—the parodists: namely, that the original author must be dressed in new clothes in the English style: "And as speech is the apparel of our thoughts, so are there certain Garbs and Modes of speaking, which vary with the times; the fashion of our clothes being not more subject to alteration, than that of our speech . . . and therefore if *Virgil* must needs speak English, it were fit he should speak not only as a man of this Nation, but as a man of this age."[41] In the same year, perhaps, as Dryden thought, because of his association with Denham, Cowley adapts the manners of the ancients to see how they "will look in an *English habit*." In the Preface to his *Pindarique Odes* Cowley insists upon the differences between modern and ancient customs, and remarks that there are a "thousand particularities of places, persons, and manners, which do but confusedly appear to our Eyes at so great a distance" and which, consequently, must be modernized.[42] Later in the Preface, Cowley attempts to name his new method of translating. Though grammarians may object to his "libertine way," he is "not so much enamoured of the *Name Translator*, as not to wish rather to be *Something Better*, though it want yet a *Name*." He then speaks about his "manner of *Translating*, or *Imitating* . . . the two ensuing *Odes* of *Pindar*" not so much to defend it, as "to rectifie the opinion of divers men upon this matter" of proper translation.[43]

40. *The Poetical Works of Sir John Denham*, ed. Theodore Howard Banks, Jr. (New Haven: Yale University Press, 1928), pp. 143-44. Pope knew both Guarini's poem and Fanshawe's translation; see Nicholas J. Perella, "Pope's Judgment on the *Pastor Fido* and a Case of Plagiarism," *PQ*, 40 (1961): 444-48.
41. Banks, *Poetical Works*, p. 160. For Dryden's use of this remark see his "Preface to the Translation of Ovid's *Epistles*" (1680), in *Essays*, 1:239; "*Sylvae: or The Second Part of Poetical Miscellanies*" (1685), *Essays*, 1: 252; "Dedication of the *Aeneas*" (1697), *Essays*, 2:228.
42. *The Works of Mr. Abraham Cowley* (London, 1668), sig. T3ʳ.
43. *Ibid.*, sig. T3ᵛ. Brooks traces the rise of the Imitation to the theory of

The Imitation

The theory of free translation soon became entrenched, and along with it the demand for modernization of "dress"—that is, of language, place, and names. Elkanah Settle, for example, praises Henry Higden's *Modern Essay* [or Imitation] *on the Tenth Satyr of Juvenal* (1687) because Higden naturalizes his author and turns *"Classick Roman"* into *"Modern State."* Juvenal is now "Sprightly and Gay . . ./Drest *Al-a mode,* and speaks en *Cavalier."*[44] Similarly, John Oldham, in his Imitation—in this case a modernized translation—of the *Ars poetica,* remarks that he will put Horace "into a more modern dress, than hitherto he has appeared in, that is by making him speak, as if he were living, and writing now."[45]

Though Dryden distinguished between metaphrase, paraphrase, and imitation, other translators and Imitators often blur the distinction between these terms, thereby further showing the intimate connection between their arts. For instance, in many cases *translation, paraphrase,* and *imitation* were used synonymously. One sees this synonymy when Alexander Brome refers to his edition of Horace as a translation, though the volume consists of literal trans-

Denham and the theory and practice of Cowley and his circle. See Brooks, "The 'Imitation,' " pp. 129-34.
44. (London, 1687) sig. a3ʳ (italics and Roman type inverted). Higden's method was similar in his earlier "essay" of Juvenal's Thirteenth Satire: "I have aimed to abate something of his serious Rigour, and expressed his sense in a sort of Verse more apt for Raillery, without debasing the dignity of the Author" (sig. b2ᵛ; original is italicized throughout). In the same remarks to the reader, Higden, like Denham before him, tentatively expresses the dual nature of his genre. "Well then, A *Modern Essay* let it be; for as a *Translation* I could not, and as a *Paraphrase* I would not own it: If I have ventured at something between both, I hope I may be the less censured, since the Vices here taxed by our Satyrist, are not so antiquated, but a slight Inquisition may discover them amongst ourselves, though perhaps something altered in Dress and Fashion. As near therefore as I could, I have equipp'd them *Al-a-mode;* though nevertheless you'll find little other than the *Old Stock new Trim'd,* and that our present Age comes not much behind our Author's, in all sorts of Gentil Vice and Debauchery" (sig. b2ʳ; italics and Roman type inverted).
45. *Works of Mr. John Oldham; Some New Pieces,* sig. aᵛ (this part of the original is italicized throughout). According to Brooks ("The 'Imitation,' " pp. 137-38), Oldham inspired the subsequent Imitations of Juvenal by Wood (1683), Higden (1686, 1687), and Matthew Prior (1694). For other references, see *The Diary of Samuel Pepys,* ed. Henry B. Wheatley (New York, 1898), 6: 335; Higden, *Tenth Satire,* sig. a4ᵛ; Francis Willis, *Anacreon done into English* (Oxford, 1683), sigs. a2ʳ–a3ʳ. Willis is admittedly indebted to Cowley's method.

lations, modernized Imitations, paraphrases, and poems which preserve some of their Latin allusions and change others to English counterparts.[46] In 1673 Dryden calls Etherege's modernization of Boileau's First Satire a translation,[47] and in the Preface to Horace's "Art of Poetry, Imitated in *English*," Oldham fears that the reader will think him guilty of "high presumption in the adventuring upon a Translation of *The Art of Poetry*" after the versions of Ben Jonson and Roscommon.[48]

In the preceding cases *translation* and *imitation* generally denoted either a modernized poem or a free translation; but *translation* and *Imitation* were also used synonymously for Imitations which were original works, for in March, 1743, Pope observes that "Rochester has very bad versification sometimes," after which Spence records: "He instanced this from his translation of the tenth satire of Horace, his full rhymes, etc."[49] This translation, however—the "Allusion to Horace"—is a free Imitation which alters Horace's examples and, at certain times, his meaning to suit Rochester's purposes. Shortly thereafter, Pope tells Spence that Bolingbroke "observed how well that [*First Satire of Horace's Second Book*] would hit my case, if I were to imitate it in English. After he was gone, I read it over; translated it in a morning or two, and sent it to the press in a week or fortnight after."[50]

The prestige of Denham and Cowley undoubtedly reinforced the influence of the theory of translation upon Imitation; however, another influence of importance was a relevant remark in Horace's

46. *The Poems of Horace . . . Rendred in English Verse by Several Persons* (London, 1666), *passim*; and see Brooks, "The 'Imitation,'" p. 130, n. 2. Pope may have known this edition: see G. K. Hunter, "Pope's Imitation of Fanshawe," *N&Q*, 204 (1959): 193-94.
47. *The Works of John Dryden*, ed. Sir Walter Scott, and rev. George Saintsbury (Edinburgh, 1882–92), 18: 94.
48. *Works of Mr. John Oldham; Some New Pieces*, sig. a^r (italics and Roman type inverted). See also John Ozell's translation of *Le Lutrin* (London, 1708), sigs. *1^r–*3^v, and Warton, *Works of Alexander Pope*, 4: 437.
49. Spence, *Anecdotes*, 1: 202. Note, too, that the term "allusion" was also used as a synonym for Imitation as modernization. See Rochester's "Allusion to Horace" (1680), and *Thomas Dilke's XXV Select Allusions to Several Places of Horace, Martial, and Petron. Arbiter* (London, 1698), sig. A2^v.
50. Spence, *Anecdotes*, 1: 143.

Ars poetica. *"Nec verbum verbo curabis reddere fidus/interpres"* was known and echoed at least from George Chapman to Edward Burnaby Greene.[51] During the Restoration period Brome observes that all of the translators he selected for his *Horace* "studied to shun a nice *Pedantical Translation,* which *Horace* could not abide."[52] In 1680 the Earl of Roscommon criticizes Ben Jonson's literal translation of the *Ars poetica* because *"Horace* in this Book declares himself an Enemy" to it,[53] and Oldham—an Imitator as modernizer—similarly says that he has not been "over-nice in keeping to the words" of the *Ars poetica,* "for that were to transgress a Rule therein contained."[54]

The use of Horace's remark by both Imitators and free translators again suggests that it is only Imitation as modernization that stems from free translation. In his version of the *Ars poetica,* for example, Oldham modernizes Horace's allusions, is largely faithful to his author's intention, and avoids intruding his own opinions upon Horace's. In their Imitations, however, Swift, Pope, and Johnson demand that the reader both recognize the poem's model, and be aware of how it has been changed; this demand was generally absent in modernization and pure translation. Perhaps the inadequacy of resting on translation as the sole source for the more creative form of Imitation will be clearer still if one reads the first verse paragraph of Boileau's Eighth Satire (1667), and Rochester's (1679) and Oldham's (1682) versions of it. Oldham's is a modernized translation which directs the reader's attention towards Boileau's rather than Oldham's meaning. Rochester's, however, is an original effort,[55] and, though too far from the parent-poem for

51. For Chapman's remark, see *Chapman's Homer,* Bollingen Series, vol. 41, ed. Allardyce Nicoll (New York: Pantheon Books, 1956), 1: 17; and for Greene, see *The Satires of Juvenal Paraphrastically Imitated and Adapted to the Times* (London, 1763), p. xv. See also, Dryden, Preface to Ovid's *Epistles, Essays,* 1: 237-38; and Henry Ames, *A New Translation of Horace's Art of Poetry, Attempted in Rhyme* (London, 1727), p. iv.
52. *The Poems of Horace,* 2d ed. (London, 1671), sig. A5ᵛ (italics and Roman type inverted).
53. *Horace's Art of Poetry Made English,* 2d ed. (London, 1684), sig. A2ʳ.
54. *Works of Mr. John Oldham; Some New Pieces,* sig. aᵛ (this part of the original is italicized throughout).
55. For the relevant works, see *Oeuvres de Boileau,* ed. A. Charles Gidel, with

the pleasure of closer parallel that Pope or Johnson sought, is a key forerunner of the kind of Imitation they wrote—the kind in which the earlier author's meaning is part of a new work, and the very contrast which translation or Imitation as modernization seeks to avoid is essential to full appreciation of the new author's intention and achievement.

The desire for recognition of the original points up still another way in which free translation is unsatisfactory as a single "source" for all kinds of Imitation: it does not adequately explain one of the most distinctive *differentiae* of the genre, the Imitator's frequent requirement that extensive parallels be printed on the same or facing page. Perhaps, since the form is related to translation, it grew out of the common practice of printing bi-lingual texts; but most pure translation was meant for the mere English reader and did not include knowledge of the original as one of its legitimate pleasures.[56] I should, therefore, like to discuss another aspect of the rise of the Imitation:[57] the Restoration and eighteenth-century parody or trav-

a Preface and Notes by Georges Mongrédien (Paris: Garnier Frères, 1928), p. 49; *Rochester's Poems on Several Occasions*, ed. James Thorpe (Princeton: Princeton University Press, 1950), pp. 6-7 (or *Poems by John Wilmot Earl of Rochester*, ed. V. de Sola Pinto [London: Routledge and Kegan Paul, 1953], pp. 118-19); *Works of Mr. John Oldham; Poems and Translations*, pp. 1-2 (or *Poems of John Oldham*, with introduction by Bonamy Dobrée [London: Centaur Press, 1960]), p. 203. For a sampling of contemporary and modern opinion regarding the relationship between Boileau's and Rochester's poems, see John F. Moore, "The Originality of Rochester's *Satyr Against Mankind*," *PMLA*, 58 (1943): 393 and n. 1. Dryden's well-known strictures on Imitation in the Preface to Ovid's *Epistles* also emphasize the proper focus of translation, for Dryden there insists that the imitative method of Denham and Cowley invited infidelity to the author's intention. This is "the greatest wrong which can be done to the memory and reputation of the dead" (*Essays*, 1:240). The translator must communicate his author's thoughts, not his own (*Essays*, 1:237-43).

56. For example, Nicholas Rowe observes that Ozell is right to change French to English names in his translation of *Le Lutrin*, since the poem is now "intended for *English* Readers, and more especially for those who don't understand *French*" (London, 1708), sig. A7[r]; and John Stevens, in the Dedication to his *Comical Works . . . of Quevedo*, 2d ed. (London, 1709), says: "I own Translations are not fit to appear before those who understand, and have the Authors in their native Tongue . . . . Here is something that I hope may please such as cannot be acquainted with the Author himself" (sig. A3[v]).

57. For discussions of burlesque, see Paul Morillot, *Scarron et le genre Burlesque* (Paris, 1888); Sturgis E. Leavitt, "Paul Scarron and English Trav-

esty was also related to the theory of free translation; it was born in England some years before the earliest formal Imitations and was associated with them; it provides ample precedent for the use of on-page parallels, and, therefore, also demands recognition of the original author's work.

A similarity in conception between the Imitation and the parody may be seen in the parodists' use of the metaphors of modernization and changed clothing which, we know, were widely used by the free translators and adapted by the Imitators. In 1664, for instance, James Scudamore, in his *Homer A la Mode*, says that Homer is now "dressed in the new mode" (Oxford, sig. A3v). John Phillips uses the image of dress when, in the Preface to his *Maronides* (1673) he tells Dr. Valentine Oldis that he has "stript [Virgil in Book VI] out of his old *Roman* dress, and put him into the fashion Ala-mode."[58] Moreover, numerous eighteenth-century parodists use the same image. In their *Homerides: or, Homer's First Book Moderniz'd* (1716), Sir Thomas Burnet and George Duckett ironically remark that they had previously advised Pope "to brush up the old-fashion'd *Greek* Bard, and give him the *English* Air as well as Tongue." Since Pope had not modernized Homer, the burlesque authors decided to do the job themselves.[59] A few years later Charles Cornwall, in his

esty," *SP*, 16 (1919): 108-20; George Kitchin, *A Survey of Burlesque and Parody in English* (Edinburgh: Oliver and Boyd, 1931); Albert H. West, *L'Influence française dans la poésie Burlesque en Angleterre entre 1660 et 1700* (Paris: H. Champion, 1931); Richmond P. Bond, *English Burlesque Poetry 1700–1750* (Cambridge, Mass.: Harvard University Press, 1932); Edward Ames Richards, *Hudibras in the Burlesque Tradition* (New York: Columbia University Press, 1937); V. C. Clinton-Baddeley, *The Burlesque Tradition in the English Theatre after 1660* (London: Methuen & Co., 1952); Bonamy Dobrée, *English Literature in the Early Eighteenth Century* (New York: Oxford University Press, 1959), pp. 128-32; Francis Bar, *Le Genre Burlesque en France au XVIIIe siècle: Étude de style* (Paris: D'Artrey, 1960); H. Gaston Hall, "Scarron and the Travesty of Virgil," *Yale French Studies: The Classical Line: Essays in Honor of Henri Peyre*, 38 (1967): 115-27. For other essays relevant to Scarron, see Hall, pp. 115-17, and nn. 1-4.

58. *Maronides: or, Virgil Travesty*, sig. A1v (italics and Roman type inverted).
59. (London, 1716), pp. iv-v (italics and Roman type inverted). This work and the earlier *Letter to Mr. Pope* are mentioned frequently in *The Letters of Thomas Burnet to George Duckett 1712–1722*, ed. D. Nichol Smith

Homeros, Homoros (1722), a parody of the third book of the Iliad, says that "it seems evident to me, that *Homer* would look as handsome in a Burlesque Dress, as in any" (London, sig. B3ʳ).

Several of the remarks cited above—Burnet and Duckett's, for one—suggest that the parody, like the Imitation, stems in part from the theory of free translation. This suggestion is confirmed when we see that the parodists "Nickydemus Ninnyhammer," in *Homer in a Nut-Shell* (1715), and John Ellis, in *The Canto Added by Mapheus* (1758), both use Horace's *"Nec verbum verbo curabis reddere fidus/interpres"* as title-page mottoes. Ninnyhammer also humorously tells the reader that although he hoped to *"Translate all Homer's Works,"* he found himself anticipated by Pope and Tickell, and so published "this small Specimen of Homer's Iliad" in hopes of gaining favor for a translation of the *"Batrachomuomachia,* to the Tune of Chivy-Chase" (London, sigs. A6ʳ⁻ᵛ). Burnet and Duckett, in their ironic *Homerides: or, a Letter to Mr. Pope,* advise Pope not to follow "any of those Translators, that pin themselves down to the Sense of their Author, but follow the glorious Example of Mr. Cotton, who in his *Heroi-Comical* Translation of *Virgil,* has never baulk'd a Jest, because it was not in the Original" (London, 1715, p. 9). The same authors later refer to burlesque as modernized translation, and "Henry Fitzcotton" and John Ellis (tongue in cheek) similarly regard comic burlesque as a form of free translation.[60]

The Imitation, then, would have been associated with the parody by means of a common source, the theory of free translation. How-

(Oxford: Oxford University Press, 1914); see especially pp. 81, 85, 99. For other remarks on the image of dress, see Denham's Preface to *The Destruction of Troy* (*Poetical Works,* Banks), p. 160; the anonymous *The Wits Paraphrased . . . A Burlesque on the Several Late Translations of Ovid's Epistles* (London, 1680), sigs. A2ᵛ–A3ʳ; Alexander Radcliffe, *Ovid Travestie, A Burlesque upon Several of Ovid's Epistles* (London, 1680), sigs. *2ᵛ–*3ʳ; James Miller, *Harlequin Horace* (London, 1731), sig. b3ᵛ; Henry Fitzcotton, *A New and Accurate Translation of the First Book of Homer's Iliad* (Dublin, 1749), p. vii; John Ellis, *The Canto Added by Mapheus to Virgil's Twelve Books of the Aeneas* (London, 1758), p. x. Bond, *English Burlesque Poetry,* p. 443, suggests that Fitzcotton is "probably a pseudonym."

60. For Burnet and Duckett see *Homerides: or Homer's First Book Moderniz'd,* pp. iv-v; Fitzcotton, *A New and Accurate Translation of the First Book of Homer's Iliad,* p. v; Ellis, *The Canto Added by Mapheus,* pp. ix-x.

ever, they were also associated through the contemporary use of the term *parody* to refer to both Imitation and translation. For example, in a letter quoted by Johnson for his *Dictionary* illustration of the verb *parody*, Pope writes to Swift: "I have translated, or rather parody'd, another of Horace's [satires], in which I introduce you advising me about my expences, housekeeping, &c."[61] Pope here alludes to his Imitation of *The Second Satire of the Second Book of Horace* (to Bethel). In 1733 Pope tells Swift that he has sent him "another thing of mine, which is a parody from Horace, writ in two mornings" (*Correspond.*, 3:348). This parody is *The First Satire of the Second Book of Horace* (to Fortescue), in which Pope ardently defends his right to attack vice in high places. Bishop Warburton, in his remarks (1751) on this Imitation, says: "this sort of Imitations, which are of the nature of *Parodies*, add reflected grace and splendor on original wit."[62] Similarly, the first editor of Johnson's poems insists that *The Vanity of Human Wishes*, "being an imitation of the tenth Satire of Juvenal . . . has always been esteemed a fine parody on the force and spirit of the original,"[63] and in *The Gray's Inn Journal*, no. 50 (Sept. 6, 1754), p. 298, Arthur Murphy reminds his readers that "Parody does not always carry with it any Sneer at the Author parodied. The quaint things in *Virgil* may be aptly applied to other objects without his being burlesqued."[64]

Pope's use of (free) *translation, parody,* and *imitation,* again suggests overlapping between these genres: all three require freedom towards their author, and all three use the metaphor of dress and Horace's *Nec verbum verbo.* But, the frequent synonymy of the latter two terms is of even greater importance, for one detects in

61. *Correspondence of Alexander Pope*, Sherburn, 3: 366. For similar allusions, see Howard D. Weinbrot, "Parody as Imitation in the Eighteenth Century," *AN&Q*, 2 (1964) : 133-34, n. 6.

62. Warburton, *Works of Alexander Pope*, 4: 51.

63. *The Poetical Works of Samuel Johnson* (London, 1785), p. v. George Kearsley published the volume; the editor may have been William Cooke, who edited other writings of Johnson for Kearsley. I am indebted to Donald J. Greene for this suggestion.

64. For a remark concerning the date and number of this issue, see Bond, *English Burlesque Poetry*, p. 55, n. 1.

them a clear, if partial, similarity in conception. In both cases the reader's pleasure depends upon knowledge of the original; accordingly, both forms often printed the lines imitated along with the adaptation. Indeed, the formal parody not only demands knowledge of the parent-poem, but anticipates the "original" Imitation by, perhaps, almost twenty years, and probably points the way to the physical make-up of the page of this kind of Imitation.[65]

Early in the Restoration English parodists began to print the passages burlesqued along with the burlesque itself. The printed form of Charles Cotton's *Scarronides: or Virgile Travestie* (1664), for instance, amply signifies his aim. The relevant Latin from the first book of the *Aeneid* is italicized at the foot of the page, and "the reader is desired for the better comparing of the *Latin* and *English* together, to read on forward to the ensuing Letter of Direction," before he compares the two.[66] In the same year, James Scudamore also uses "letters of direction"—footnote letters—which point to the Greek text at the bottom of the page of his *Homer A la Mode*. In his Preface, moreover, he too anticipates the Imitation's parallel of ancient and modern: "The Learned Reader, that thinketh it worth his while to observe the correspondence betwixt this Translation and the Text, is desired to compare them, as well for the Illustration of the one, as the other."[67]

Throughout the Restoration and well into the eighteenth century, comic parodists either use printed parallels to enhance the burlesque or clearly suggest that they expect knowledge of the original. The author of *Homer Alamode, The Second Part*, a burlesque upon the ninth book of the *Iliad*, remarks that his poem will "savour best with them, who have had Experience in" Homer. He has, therefore,

65. There were, of course, travesties before Cotton's *Scarronides* in 1664, but he popularized the form and established the trend. For an earlier parody, see James Smith's scurrilous travesty of Ovid's *Loves of Hero and Leander* (London, 1651). This work is discussed in West's *L'Influence française*, pp. 86, 173-81; see also Kitchin, *A Survey of Burlesque*, pp. 1-90. For what may be the earliest Imitation, see n. 71, below.
66. (London, 1664), unsigned verso page preceding sig. B1r (italics and Roman type inverted).
67. *Homer A la Mode: A Mock Poem upon the First and Second Books of Homer's Iliad*, sigs. A3r-v.

made "Some Citations" in the margin, "that you might at least see the connexion of things" (London, 1681, sig. A3ʳ⁻ᵛ). Tom D'Urfey, in his *Butler's Ghost: or Hudibras. The Fourth Part* (1682), does not burlesque a specific work; but he does use a form which requires knowledge of its origin, and so apologizes for the demands of the genre. "This poem," he admits, "will suffer by a number of people, it being not easily to be understood, but by such as have read and are acquainted with the other Three parts."[68] James Farewell—the author of *The Irish Hudibras, or Fingallian Prince* (1689), an adaptation of the Sixth Book of the *Aeneid*—also prints imitated passages and so exhorts his reader "to cast his Eye now and then upon the Latin, at the end of every Page, mark'd with the Alphabetical Letters all along, to direct him from the *Translation* to the Original."[69] Finally, we hear a similar remark from John Smith, who burlesques the Second Book of the *Aeneid* in his *Scarronides: or Virgile Travestie* (1692). He asks of the reader "first and foremost that thou would'st be pleas'd for the better comparing the Latin and English together, to reade on to the ensuing letter of direction" before comparing the latter "with the original."[70]

Significantly, we find the same demand for recognition of the original in the earliest formal Imitations demanding knowledge of a classical satire. For instance, in Thomas Wood's *Juvenal Redivivus, or The First Satyr of Juvenal Taught to Speak Plain English* (1683), as in the English burlesque poems dating from 1664, the Latin parallels are printed at the bottom of the page. Wood uses the genre's requirement of knowledge of the original to discourage female critics

68. (London, 1682), sig. A3ᵛ (3d page, verso, preceding B1ʳ) (italics and Roman type inverted).
69. (London, 1689), sig. A4ᵛ (italics and Roman type inverted).
70. Second ed. (London, 1717), sig. A8ʳ (the original is italicized throughout). See also Alexander Radcliffe, *Ovidius Exulans* (London, 1673), sig. A3ᵛ; Charles Kenneth Eves, *Matthew Prior: Poet and Diplomatist* (New York: Columbia University Press, 1939), p. 97; Samuel Wesley's translation of the *Batrachomuomachia, The Iliad in a Nutshell* (London, 1726), sig. A2ᵛ. For later evidence of the similarity between Imitation and comic parody, see the remarks of Mrs. Thrale and Susan Burney in *The Poems of Samuel Johnson*, ed. D. Nichol Smith and Edward L. McAdam (Oxford: Clarendon Press, 1941), pp. 191-92. Both women discuss Johnson's burlesques of the style of Robert Potter's Aeschylus.

from attacking his work. "If there is any *Genius*" in it, he says, "it appears as being somewhat like a parallel to the Latin, and built upon old *Juvenal's* foundation; which I must crave leave to suppose [the ladies] to be wholly ignorant of." Wood is confident that "the more [the reader] understands the Latin, the farther he searches, I am sure it will be so much the more to my advantage," for he will thus see that Juvenal is made more mannerly, less scolding and unnatural than he seems in Latin.[71] We hear similar remarks in the early eighteenth century as well: in two of his Imitations—neither of which burlesques the parent-poem—Dr. William King prints the relevant Latin at the foot of the page, and indicates certain disadvantages to the modern author. Hence in his *Art of Love: In Imitation of Ovid de Arte Amandi*, King complains that the Imitator "lies under this Misfortune, that the Faults are all his own; and if there is any thing that may seem pardonable, the *Latin* at the bottom shews to whom he is engag'd for it" (London, 1709, p. xxxix).[72]

Dependence upon the original for the effect of a modern poem is also expressed in the entry in Swift's *Journal to Stella* for July 1, 1712. He refers to his lampoon upon the Earl of Nottingham, in Imitation of Horace, *Epistles* l. 5, and asks: "Have you seen Toland's Invitation to Dismal? How do you like it? But it is an imitation of Horace, and perhaps you don't understand Horace."[73] Johnson also shows his understanding of the principle of recognition. In 1738 he wrote to his publisher Cave demanding that the Latin quotations in his *London*, an Imitation of Juvenal's Third Satire, "be subjoined at the bottom of the Page, part of the beauty of the performance (if

71. (London, 1683), sig. A3ʳ (italics and Roman type inverted). So far as I can tell, Wood's poem is the earliest Restoration Imitation to print the relevant lines imitated; it is also the earliest example of the form cited by Brooks ("The 'Imitation,'" p. 139, n. 2). Wood was a collaborator in Willis's *Anacreon*: see Samuel Halkett and John Laing, *Dictionary of Anonymous and Pseudonymous Literature*, rev. James Kennedy, *et. al.* (Edinburgh and London: Oliver and Boyd, 1926), 1: 70. It is impossible to say whether this is, in fact, the first formal Imitation. If, as may be likely, there were Imitations prior to Wood's, and even if they appeared at about the same time as the parodies, the parody would have enhanced the growth of the form.

72. See also King's *Art of Cookery* (London, 1708), pp. 20-21.

73. Quoted from *The Poems of Jonathan Swift*, ed. Harold Williams, 2d ed. (Oxford: Clarendon Press, 1958), 1: 161.

any beauty be allow'd it) consisting in adapting Juvenal's Sentiments to modern facts and Persons."[74] Johnson's comments in the lives of Pope and West also note the necessary dependence of the Imitator upon his author. He says, for example, in "West" (1781) that "an Imitation of Spenser is nothing to a reader, however acute, by whom Spenser has never been perused."[75] Comparison of Johnson's remark with James Beattie's in an essay "Of Ludicrous Composition" (1778) shows the partial similarity in conception between the parody and the Imitation:

> Parodies produce their full effect on those only who can trace the imitation to its original. Clarissa's harangue, in the fifth canto of [*The Rape of the Lock*], gives pleasure to every reader; but to those who recollect that divine speech of Sarpedon [*Iliad,* xii, 310–28], whereof this is an exact parody, it must be entertaining in the highest degree.—Hence it is, that writers of the greatest merit are liable to be parodied; for if the reader perceive not the relation between the copy and its archetype, the humour of the parody is lost; and this relation he will not perceive, unless the original be familiar to him.[76]

74. *The Letters of Samuel Johnson,* ed. R. W. Chapman (Oxford: Clarendon Press, 1952), 1: 11.
75. "Life of West," in *Lives of the English Poets,* ed. G. Birkbeck Hill (Oxford: Clarendon Press, 1905), 3: 332. See also "Life of Pope," *ibid.,* 3: 176, 246-47. Johnson is referring to the "metre, the language, and the fiction" of West's imitations of Spenser, but it is clear from the context, and the similarity of these remarks to those in the "Life of Pope," that the statement is applicable to the Imitation of entire specific works as well.
76. *Essays on the Nature and Immutability of Truth* (Dublin, 1778), 2: 346. See also Thomas Warton's *History of English Poetry,* ed. W. Carew Hazlitt (London, 1871), 4: 386. Beattie's remark also suggests that much of the pleasure of reading mock-heroics consists in recognition of both epic forms in general, and specific lines, episodes, or conventions in particular. Many editions (*e.g.,* Bologna, 1651 and 1670) of Tassoni's *La Secchia rapita* (Paris, 1622) include the *dichiarazioni* of Gasparo Salviani which point out Tassoni's borrowings from serious epics; Saint-Marc performs a similar task for Boileau's *Le Lutrin* (Paris, 1674) (*Oeuvres de M. Boileau Despréaux,* ed. M. de Saint-Marc [Paris, 1747], 2: 184-280); Pope brings the reader's attention to several of his own borrowings in *The Rape of the Lock* (London, 1714). Contemporary and later commentators have appreciated Pope's clues to his intention. See, for example, Aubrey L. Williams, "The 'Fall' of China and *The Rape of the Lock,*" *PQ,* 41 (1962): 418-25; and Martin Price, *To the Palace of Wisdom* (New York: Doubleday & Co.,

We may say, then, that there is little doubt that the Imitation sprang from the theory of free translation made popular by Denham and Cowley and reinforced by Horace's famous demand not to translate word for word. *Imitation* and *translation* were often used synonymously, and in both forms the writer modernized his author and put him into English dress. Translation, however, serves as a sole source for Imitation as modernized translation, and not for Imitation which requires knowledge of the original poem. It is likely, therefore, that the comic burlesque of specific works also fostered the rise of the Imitation. It too was associated with the theory of free translation and, accordingly, with an argument familiar to Imitators of all kinds; and, like Imitators, some parodists used Horace's "*Nec verbum verbo*" remark as a "justification" for their method. The synonymous use of *Imitation* and *parody* again associates the two genres and argues for at least partial similarity of conception. This similarity is based upon the parody's need for conscious parallel of ancient and modern; by placing these parallels on the same page several years before the earliest Imitation demanding knowledge of the parent-poem, the parodists established a precedent which was followed by many of the best Augustan Imitators, for—unlike translation—both forms depend for success upon the reader's awareness of the original. Since this argument is based on analogy rather than explicit evidence it is not altogether conclusive; but it does make defensible the hypothesis that the Augustan Imitation in its most significant form is the offspring not only of a theory of free translation, but of the Restoration parody as well.

1964), p. 152. For further information regarding Pope and *The Rape of the Lock* as mock-heroic, see *Alexander Pope: The Rape of the Lock and Other Poems*, The Twickenham Edition of the Poems of Alexander Pope, vol. 4, ed. Geoffrey Tillotson, 2d ed. (London: Methuen & Co., 1954), pp. 106-12.

2
Three Early Modes of the Imitation

I The Theory and Practice
of Denham and Cowley

Modernization and adaptation in some form appeared long before the Restoration. Chaucer put Boccaccio into a contemporary setting, and Wyatt changed Alamanni's Provence to Kent. Several years later Spenser's readers were aware of his version of the classical pastoral; Shakespeare's audience heard bells chime the hour in *Julius Caesar*; and the more learned of Ben Jonson's followers noticed his extensive borrowing from Roman plays.[1] In his Fourth Satire Donne transplants the "impertinent" of Horace's *Satires*, i. 9, while somewhat earlier Hall frequently imitated his Roman masters. Thomas Warton observes:

> Hall's acknowledged patterns are Juvenal and Persius, not without some touches of the urbanity of Horace. His parodies of these poets, or rather his adaptations of ancient to modern manners, a mode of imitation not unhappily practised by Oldham, Rochester, and Pope, discover great facility and dexterity of invention.[2]

Warton overstates; there is little real precedent for Imitation as practiced by Oldham, Rochester, or Pope. That is—if we except

1. For Jonson's comments upon imitation, see his *Timber: or Discoveries* (1641), in *Ben Jonson*, ed. C. H. Herford, Percy Simpson, and Evelyn Simpson (Oxford: Clarendon Press, 1947), 8: 638-39.
2. W. Carew Hazlitt, ed., *History of English Poetry* (London, 1871), 4: 367-68.

Wyatt's First Satire and, perhaps, Donne's Fourth—we are still dealing with a form of literary borrowing rather than an independent genre.[3] For example, one of the traits of Oldham's Imitation is consistent modernization of ancient circumstances, but Hall begins the Third Satire of his Fourth Book by adapting part of Juvenal's Eighth Satire while keeping the Roman name "Pontice" and juxtaposing it with "The wars in Turwin, or in Turney field."[4] Similarly, he begins 4:vi with part of Juvenal's Tenth Satire and combines "Fond Caenis" with "pinn'd ruffs, and fans, and partlet strips" (pp. 110-11). Inconsistency of modernization is common to Hall and his contemporaries, so that, as A. F. B. Clark observes, "we are never sure in what *milieu* their satire is proceeding."[5] A hallmark of Pope's mode of Imitation is its demand that the reader recognize the original; to insure this the poet often printed the lines imitated or overtly pointed to the parent-poem in some other way. But Hall does not do this, and Warton, in commenting on the passage from 4: iii above, is forced to say that "the humour is half lost, unless by recollecting the Roman original, the reader perceives the unexpected parallel";[6] the later Imitator would not leave the matter to chance recollection. Imitation in the Renaissance is largely casual modernization and the old practice of borrowing; it anticipates but does not include the later seventeenth and eighteenth-century concept.

Modernization was probably suggested by the new Elizabethan theory of translation which insisted that the old work be made a

3. H. J. C. Grierson observes: "This satire, like several of the period, is based on Horace's *Ibam forte via Sacra (Sat. i. 9)*, but Donne follows a quite independent line. Horace's theme is at bottom a contrast between his own friendship with Maecenas and 'the way in which vulgar and pushing people sought, and sought in vain, to obtain an introduction.' Donne, like Horace, describes a bore, but makes this the occasion for a general picture of the hangers-on at Court. A more veiled thread running through the poem is an attack on the ways and tricks of informers" (*The Poems of John Donne* [Oxford: Oxford University Press, 1912], 2: 117).
4. *The Satires of Joseph Hall, with the Illustrations of . . . Thomas Warton. And additional Notes by Samuel Weller Singer* (Chiswick, 1824), pp. 90-91.
5. *Boileau and the French Classical Critics in England (1660–1830)*, Bibliothèque de la revue de littérature comparée, 19 (Paris: E. Champion, 1925): 434. Nicholas Rowe makes a similar criticism of Ozell's translation of *Le Lutrin (Boileau's Lutrin* [London, 1708], sigs. A6ᵛ–7ʳ).
6. Hazlitt, *History of English Poetry*, 4: 386.

poem for English readers;[7] and so, when Denham and Cowley amplified the need for free translation, they spoke to an audience initiated into their ideas but still attracted to their relative newness. Thus Sprat—in his *Life of Cowley* (1668)—insists:

> This way of leaving Verbal Translations, and chiefly regarding the Sense and Genius of the Author, was scarce heard of in *England* before this present Age. I will not presume to say that Mr. *Cowley* was the absolute Inventor of it. Nay, I know that others had the good luck to recommend it first in Print.[8]

Chapman, Fowldes, and Howell, among others, "recommend it" before Cowley, but Sprat is apparently referring to Denham's remarks prefixed to Fanshawe's *Pastor Fido* in 1647.[9] Later references to Denham and Cowley's discussion of the free theory of translation again suggest that it is to them that much of the credit for establishing the theory belongs.[10] As we have seen, modernization of the ancient text to fit modern circumstances was inherent in this theory; however, examination of Denham's translations will show that they are paraphrases rather than Imitations, and that his theory, not his practice, influenced the rise of the form. Denham neither consistently modernizes, nor changes his author's conception while keeping it before the reader.

For example, in the Preface to *The Destruction of Troy* (1656) Denham insists that he has not "any where offered such violence to

---

7. See, for instance, Joel E. Spingarn, *Critical Essays of the Seventeenth Century* (Bloomington, Ind.: Indiana University Press, 1957), 1: xlviii-lviii; F. O. Matthieson, *Translation an Elizabethan Art* (Cambridge, Mass.: Harvard University Press, 1931).
8. Spingarn, *Critical Essays*, 2: 132.
9. See *Chapman's Homer*, Bollingen Series, vol. 41, ed. Allardyce Nicoll (New York: Pantheon Books, 1956), 1: 9-10, 16-17; William Fowldes, trans., *The Strange, Wonderful and Bloudy Battel betweene Frogs and Mise* (London, 1603), sig. B2ʳ; James Howell, *Familiar Letters*, in *Epistolae Ho-Eleiana, The Familiar Letters*, ed. Joseph Jacobs (London, 1892), 1: 171, 329 (1645); 2: 544-45 (1650).
10. For example, see Francis Willis, *Anacreon done into English* (Oxford, 1683), sigs. a2ʳ-3ʳ; Dryden, Preface to Ovid's *Epistles, Essays of John Dryden*, ed. W. P. Ker (Oxford: Clarendon Press, 1926), 1: 237, 240; Johnson, the *Idler*, no. 69 (1759).

[Virgil's] sense, as to make it seem mine, and not his";[11] there are no modernizations in "Sarpedon's Speech to Glaucus in the 12th of Homer"; "The Passion of Dido for Aeneas" adds one couplet not in the original and omits about 150 lines, but it is clearly a translation,[12] and "Of Prudence" and "Of Justice" (1668) from Dominicus Mancinus are merely translated into contemporary English. Denham makes his aim in this poem explicit when he says that he attempts to change the language, not the allusions. He "undertook to redeem [Mancinus' work] from an obsolete English disguise, wherein an old *Monk* had cloathed it, and to make as becoming a new Vest for it, as I could."[13]

Only in *Cato Major* (1669) are there many serious changes, and these are generally related to paraphrastic translation rather than Imitation. By versifying the prose of the original, Denham argues, some of its "severer Arguments may receive a more mild and pleasant taste." Though his version is a new creation, it is not a modern adaptation but, according to Denham, the faithful transposition of Cato himself to seventeenth-century England. Hence it is Cato rather than Cicero or Denham who is speaking in the contemporary idiom. In the Preface Denham declares that he "took the liberty to leave out what was only necessary to that Age, and Place, and to take, or add what was proper to this present Age, and occasion; by laying his sense closer, and in fewer words, according to the style and ear of these times."[14] In spite of this remark, Denham preserves the poem's ancient setting and references not only to Themistocles, Cato, and Scipio, but to such places as Tarentum, Cannae, and Carthage as well. Since the only real addition is that of the modern meter lacking in the original, we may call this negative imitation; that is, the poem does not include allusions to the immediate present but is, rather, an adaptation through exclusion of a few references to archaic subjects.

11. *The Poetical Works of Sir John Denham*, ed. Theodore Howard Banks, Jr. (New Haven: Yale University Press, 1928), p. 160.

12. *Ibid.*, pp. 184-89, nn. 4, 7, 10, 12, 16. I am indebted to the editor's notes for information regarding Denham's condensations.

13. *Ibid.*, p. 190. Denham's original is *Libellus de quattuor virtutibus et omnibus officiis ad bene beateque vivendum* (Paris, 1488).

14. *Ibid.*, pp. 202-3 (original of the Preface is in italics).

For example, in the First Part Denham omits thirteen references to Greek poets and philosophers (p. 211, n. 13) ; in the Second Part he condenses three forgotten Greek names into "Our gallant Ancestors" (p. 212, n. 15) ; and in the Fourth Part he changes an illustration of old age from Arganthonius, King of Tartessus, to Nestor, and thereby makes the allusion comprehensible to his audience (p. 225, n. 37). Denham paraphrases, condenses, and makes minor changes in the original's allusions, but he does not extensively modernize those allusions or use other devices peculiar to the Imitation.[15]

Cowley, however, applies his theory in his practice, and as examples of the Imitation his few poems in the genre are seminal. But we must distinguish between his Imitations as modernizing and adapting, and his Imitations of Pindar; for our purposes, it is the remarks about translation in the Preface to the Pindarique Odes, not the Odes themselves, that were influential. The latter, indeed, are free paraphrases which omit some references but do not include modernization; the poems were conceived for an audience that did not know the original. In the general Preface of the Author to the 1668 folio of his *Poems*, Cowley expresses the fear that the Pindarics would not be understood because of their boldness and strangeness;[16] hence the Arguments preceding the Imitations carefully explain to the new reader some of Pindar's apparent irregularities and digressions. In the Preface to the Odes themselves Cowley says: "I have in these two *Odes* of *Pindar* taken, left out, and added what I please; nor make it so much my aim to let the Reader know precisely what he spoke, as what was his *way* and *manner* of speaking."[17] Cowley thus makes clear both that his imitation is of style, and that his work is directed at an English-speaking audience. The effect of the poem would depend upon its own merit and upon whatever authority the ancient name of Pindar might lend it; accordingly, there is no at-

---

15. Banks comes to a similar conclusion. He remarks: "In theory, . . . Denham is an 'imitator,' but in practice he is more moderate, and departs no farther from his original than paraphrase. Indeed, his changes consist for the most part in condensing and focusing the thought, a characteristic of his original poems" (*ibid.*, p. 43).
16. *Abraham Cowley: Poems*, ed. A. R. Waller (Cambridge, 1905), pp. 10-11.
17. *Ibid.*, p. 156.

tempt to comment upon a present situation through contrast with the past, to rely in any way upon the reader's knowledge of the original or, language excepted, to place Pindar in a modern setting.

Cowley's Imitations of Martial, like some of Denham's translations, are negative imitation; they eliminate ancient place names or proper names in order to give the poem a more modern cast. Though he preserves the sense of the original, he drops allusions to Postumus, Parthians, Armenia, Priam, Nestor, and Quintilian. Cowley's method is different in "*The Praise of* Pindar. In Imitation of *Horace* his second *Ode*, B. 4." He not only eliminates allusions to the Centaurs, the Chimaera, the Tibur, Orcus, and the Sygambri; he also changes the structure of the original poem. Horace's Ode is addressed to Iulus Antonius, Mark Antony's son, Octavia's step-son, and thus Augustus' "nephew." Horace praises the heroic qualities of Pindar's verse, modestly discusses his own inferior lyric talents, leaves the heroic manner of writing to Iulus, praises Augustus, and concludes with two polished lyric stanzas describing the calf he will offer to the gods in honor of Augustus' triumph. The poem has several functions other than providing an example of Horace's skill in his own *métier*: it provides an excuse for him to maintain his more modest lyric muse rather than the muse of heroic poetry; it flatters Augustus; and, by implication, it ironically counsels Iulus not to attempt to sing with Pindar's voice. In his Imitation Cowley also praises Pindar, declares him inimitable, and briefly describes his own "*tim'erous Muse*" in Horace's metaphor of a bee laboring for honey.

> Lo, how th'obsequious *Wind*, and swelling *Ayr*
>   The *Theban Swan* does upwards bear
> Into the *walks* of *Clouds*, where he does play,
> And with extended *Wings* opens his liquid way.
>   Whilst, alas, my *tim'erous Muse*
>   *Unambitious* tracks pursues;
>   Does with weak unballast wings,
>   About the *mossy Brooks* and *Springs*;
>   About the *Trees* new-blossom'ed *Heads*,
>   About the *Gardens* painted *Beds*,

About the *Fields* and flowry *Meads,*
And all *inferior beauteous things*
Like the laborious *Bee,*
For little drops of *Honey* flee,
And there with *Humble Sweets* contents her *Industrie.*[18]

For Horace the metaphor signals—among other things—a transition to Iulus' poetic concerns: "Thou, a poet of loftier strain, shalt sing of Caesar, when, honoured with the well-earned garland, he shall lead in his train along the Sacred Slope the wild Sygambri" (ll.33–36).[19] But Cowley's principal aim is the glorification of Pindar. Thus he discards much of Horace's intention, excludes the young poet and the implied advice to him, the praise of Augustus, the final lyric description of the calf, and ends his poem with the contrast of Pindar's soaring and his own lowly flights. This dependence upon part of a Latin source, together with an overt indication of that source and alteration of its basic structure, is one major form of Imitation.

Cowley also provides an important example of adaptation of ancient to modern circumstances in his "Ode. In Imitation of Horace *Ode . . .* Lib. I, Od. 5" (1656). In his poem Horace asks Pyrrha who her new lover is and for whom she will dress her golden hair. The youth, he says, is new to the tricky breezes of her love and will soon be confounded when her apparent calm turns into winds and heavy seas. But Horace, perhaps once Pyrrha's victim himself, but certainly "love's" victim, has escaped from the storm of love, and so "the temple wall with its votive tablet shows I have hung up my dripping garments to the god who is master of the sea" (ll.13–16).[20] Cowley maintains Horace's image of Pyrrha (by extension, love in general), as the unpredictable sea; since he also describes her as beautiful, tempting, and dangerous, he imitates his original fairly closely. However, in the final paragraph we see an important change: Horace placed a plaque and his wet clothes in Neptune's temple; the lover in Cowley's ode also makes an offering, but one that ironically alters Horace's implication of age:

18. *Ibid.,* p. 179.
19. *Horace: The Odes and Epodes,* Loeb Classical Library, trans. C. E. Bennett (Cambridge, Mass.: Harvard University Press, 1934), p. 289.
20. *Ibid.,* p. 19.

> But there's no danger now for *Me*,
>   Since o're *Loretto*'s *Shrine*
>   In witness of the *Shipwrack* past
> My consecrated *Vessel* hangs at last.[21]

Loretto's Shrine refers to the house in which Mary was born, and which was thought to be miraculously transported from Nazareth to Ancona. This conscious parallel as an example of adaptation in the same volume as the Preface to the *Pindarique Odes* and "The Praise of Pindar," would not have gone unnoticed by a contemporary reader. This method of modernization of an entire poem—here one allusion—rather than elimination of allusions, is an early example of a second major kind of Imitation.

The 1668 folio edition of Cowley's *Works* prints one other important example of both alteration of the original poem's meaning and of modernization. Cowley's version of Horace's "Epodon" (Epode II) is similar in kind to his adaptation of "The Praise of Pindar." In Horace's poem Alfius, an usurer, relates the glories of the country life to which he intends to retire, and, along the way, celebrates the fertility of the fields, the beauty of the country, the pleasures of hunting, and the virtues of a humble, chaste wife who prepares wholesome native dishes. When this speech is over, Horace comments not only upon Alfius, but also upon the nature of man's wishes and accomplishments: "When the usurer Alfius had uttered this, on the very point of beginning the farmer's life, he called in all his funds upon the Ides—and on the Kalends seeks to put them out again."[22]

21. *Poems*, Waller, p. 38. The popularity of Cowley, and Dryden's discussion of his method of Imitation make it likely that this poem was noticed. For example, the anonymous author of *A Short Dissertation upon Horace, with the Fifth Ode* (London, 1708) observes that he has "pitch'd upon" it as "a Specimen" of his own translation because "Scaliger ranks it amongst the darling Lyricks of this Author, and the beloved *Cowley* has not disdained to bind it up amongst his Flowers" (p. 9). Milton's literal translation of this same poem offers a nice contrast to Cowley's relative freedom: see "*The Fifth Ode of* Horace *Lib.* I. Quis multa gracilis te puer in Rosa, *Rendred almost word for word without Rhyme according to the Latin Measure, as near as the Language will permit*": The *Works of John Milton*, ed. Frank Allen Patterson *et al.* (New York: Columbia University Press, 1931), 1:69-70.
22. *Horace*, Bennett, p. 369.

Cowley's version is fairly close to Horace's; but he excludes the speaker's profession and the final ironic stanza, thereby changes the tone and "moral" of his original, makes his Imitation bluntly didactic and a consistently developed discourse on its opening couplet: "Happy the Man whom bounteous Gods allow/ With his own Hands Paternal Grounds to Plough!"[23]

In "The Country Mouse. *A Paraphrase upon* Horace 2 Book, Satyr 6," published first in 1663 and later in the 1668 folio, Cowley introduces modernization more extensive than that in the "Epodon." His paraphrase consists only of the final part of Horace's poem, the fable of the mice. The modernization is apparent when we hear that the country mouse's meagre *"haut-guest"* is unacceptable to the city mouse, who despises the country feast, and still thinks "Upon the *cakes* and *pies* of *London* wrought." He persuades the country mouse to come to the city and seek his pleasure. We hear an English allusion once more when the two mice feast themselves at a rich city-dweller's house behind drapes, "The richest work of *Mortelacks* noble Loom."[24]

Perhaps of even greater importance, however, is Thomas Sprat's Imitation of the opening two-thirds of the satire which was affixed to the poem in Alexander Brome's edition of Horace (1666). Sprat, a friend, biographer, and disciple of Cowley, makes several more modernizations whose topical nature makes it possible to give an approximate date to the work.[25] Brome's Horace also includes poems combining Roman and English allusions, Sprat's unsigned Imitation of *Satires* i. 9, and other modernizations of *Odes* i. 27, and *Satires* ii.

23. Cowley's Imitation is reprinted in his *Essays, Plays, and Sundry Verses*, ed. A. R. Waller (Cambridge, 1906), pp. 412-13. For extensive treatment of the period's theme of retirement, see Maren-Sofie Røstvig, *The Happy Man: Studies in the Metamorphoses of a Classical Ideal 1660–1700* (Oslo, Oxford: Basil Blackwell, 1954); and for a thorough study of Cowley's poetry and thought, see Robert B. Hinman, *Abraham Cowley's World of Order* (Cambridge, Mass.: Harvard University Press, 1960).

24. *The Poems of Horace*, ed. Alexander Brome, 2d ed. (London, 1671), pp. 287, 289. The poem is reprinted in *Essays, Plays, and Sundry Verses*, pp. 414-16.

25. "The date is some time between 30 January and 14 May 1662": see Harold F. Brooks' essential article on "The 'Imitation' in English Poetry," *RES*, 25 (1949): 129. I am indebted to Brooks throughout this chapter.

4. In the second edition, of 1671, moreover, there was a definite rise in the number of Imitations: Flatman has five new Imitations, Brome one, and R.N.—either Robert Napier or Richard Newcourt—has seven; all of these authors were disciples of Cowley.[26] Fairly soon thereafter, in his *Poems* (1677), Nahum Tate also turns to modernization for his Imitations of Martial,[27] and one year later London probably first saw Rochester's popular "Allusion to Horace," perhaps written as early as the spring of 1675,[28] an Imitation of Horace, *Satires* i. 10, which announces its source and freely paraphrases and modernizes each consecutive passage of it. Burnet, in *Some Passages of the Life and Death of . . . Rochester* (1680), relates that "*Boileau* among the *French,* and *Cowley* among the *English* Wits were those" whom Rochester most admired,[29] and it is probably Cowley's influence that Rochester here shows.

In the later 1660's, then, Imitation began in earnest, and it would seem to be due to an outgrowth of certain cultural commonplaces of the age, the theory of translation popularized by Denham and Cowley, the Restoration parody, and the varied practices of Cowley and his circle. Changing the original poet's structure and meaning, as Cowley did in "The Praise of Pindar," and adapting suitable parts of the poem to modern circumstances, as Sprat and Cowley did in Horace, *Satires* ii. 6, were to be two of the basic forms of the eighteenth-century Imitation. But Cowley's was not the only influence on the form. His limited practice needed the help of other important writers at home and abroad before it became not only familiar, but a widely accepted mode of discourse.

II *Boileau, Rochester, Oldham, and Swift*

Boileau published his first seven satires in 1666, at about the time of the rise of the English Imitation. His method of Imitation, how-

---

26. *Ibid.*, p. 130.
27. *Ibid.*, p. 131, n. 2.
28. *Poems by John Wilmot Earl of Rochester,* ed. V. de Sola Pinto (London: Routledge and Kegan Paul, 1953), p. 192. I use this text throughout.
29. (London, 1680), p. 8.

ever, was more eclectic and "original" than that of the early English school. Thus he never titles any of his satires or epistles "An Imitation of" any other work. He differs from Cowley's methods in not announcing his source, in using part of that source in an overtly new way, in depending less upon it, and in avoiding the generally sequential movement of Cowley's imitation—that is, "The Praise of Pindar" begins at the beginning of Horace's poem and stops about halfway through; Boileau's Sixth Satire adapts the latter part of Juvenal's Third Satire and puts it in a somewhat new context. Moreover, as we will see, Boileau may also borrow from more than one classical model. In spite of this greater freedom Boileau's practice is, in fact, imitative in conception and, accordingly depends upon the reader's awareness of his models. For instance, Boileau initially intended his First Satire as a more obvious Imitation of Juvenal's Third, since he planned to include more of Damon's difficulties in Paris as a parallel to those of Umbricius. But, Le Verrier reports, with Boileau's own corrections incorporated in his remarks, "l'auteur aiant reconnu qu'un trop long détail des embarras de Paris languissoit, il résolut d'en faire une satire à part."[30] Boileau's pride in his conscious borrowing appears when, at the end of his Préface to the editions of his satires between 1666 and 1669, he scorns defending himself from charges of "plagiarism": "Il y auroit aussi plusieurs choses à dire touchant le reproche qu'on fait à l'auteur d'avoir pris ses pensées dans Juvénal et dans Horace: mais, tout bien considéré, il trouve l'objection si honorable pour lui, qu'il croiroit se faire tort d'y répondre."[31] Boileau, that is, expects his readers to know the sources of his satires, and finds it "si honorable pour lui." The French encyclopedists, we have seen, agreed entirely.

Other readers sympathetic to Boileau were also aware of the imitative quality of his satire. On July 6, 1700, Brosette wrote to Boileau

30. *Les Satires de Boileau commentées par lui-même et publiées avec des notes par Fréderic Lachèvre: Reproduction du commentaire inédit de Pierre le Verrier avec les corrections autographes de Despréaux* (Courménil, 1906), p. 55. Boileau's satires, we might add, are always geographically, chronologically, and culturally of a piece—he is clearly Parisian, Louis XIV.
31. *Oeuvres de Boileau*, ed. A. Charles Gidel, with a Preface and Notes by Georges Mongrédien (Paris: Garnier Frères, 1928), p. 3.

informing him of a projected Amsterdam edition of his works, "avec des notes, et surtout avec la conférence, et le parallèl des endroits d'Horace et de Juvénal, que vous avez imités." Brosette goes on to make a classical statement concerning the Imitation and the particular kind of pleasure it was meant to evoke:

> A l'égard des passages que vous avez imités, cette comparaison ne peut qu'être bien reçue, parce qu'il est toujours agréable de voir comment deux esprits se recontrent, et les différens tours qu'ils donnent à la même pensée. D'ailleurs, cette comparaison vous fera beaucoup d'honneur, en faisant voir que vous avez partout surpassé vos modèles, et que vous êtes toujours original, lors même que vous imitez.[32]

Numerous eighteenth-century editions of Boileau cite examples of these imitations, and Saint-Marc refers to the First and Sixth Satires as "une imitation de la troisième *Satire* de *Juvénal*."[33]

In England we hear a mixed reaction to this method. Nicholas Rowe observes that Boileau has "the finest and the truest Taste of the best Authors of Antiquity," and that "it is very certain that he had 'em so perpetually in his Eye, that he form'd most of his Poetical Writings so closely after their Models, that in many of 'em especially his *Satyrs*, he can hardly pretend to the Honour of any thing more, than having barely translated them well."[34] Boileau's Epistles were also imitative in conception. In his life of Boileau, Des Maizeaux observes that Boileau's "Epistle address'd *to his Book*, wherein he

32. *Correspondence entre Boileau Despréaux et Brosette*, ed. Auguste Laverdet (Paris, 1858), pp. 47-48. This is letter 13, from Lyons. Brosette attempted a similar task in his edition of the *Satyrs et autres oeuvres de Regnier* (London, 1733). He observes that Regnier borrowed liberally from other authors and that those critics who contrast Regnier's "originality" with Boileau's "plagiarism" are mistaken (pp. v-vi). Moreover, Brosette continues, the notes for this edition are not as full as those for his volumes of Boileau: "L'Auteur de celles-ci a eu le bonheur de travailler sous les yeux de Mr. Despréaux lui-même, & de concert avec lui" (p. vi), whereas he often was forced to conjecture regarding Regnier's borrowing. Imitation, Brosette implies, is part of the good poet's standard operating procedure.

33. *Oeuvres de Boileau Despréaux . . . rédigés par M. Brosette . . . , avec des Remarques & des Dissertations Critiques*, ed. M. de Saint-Marc (Paris, 1747), 1: 24, 96.

34. *Boileau's Lutrin*, sigs. A4ᵛ-5ʳ.

Accounts for his Life and Works . . . is . . . an Imitation of one of the most beautiful Pieces in *Horace*." Shortly thereafter he says that Boileau also "compos'd a new *Epistle*, directed to *his Gardener*," and in a note reminds his readers that "Horace, directed one of his Epistles to his Farmer; it is the XIVth Epistle of the first Book: Villice Silvarum, & mihi me reddentis agelli, &c."[35] Similarly, in the 1729 edition of *The Dunciad* Pope observes that he is adding certain "*Imitations* of the Ancients" for the gratification of his readers. If any man thinks the poem "too much a *Cento*," he continues, "our Poet will but appear to have done the same thing in jest, which *Boileau* did in earnest."[36] Some years later Warburton amplifies this remark about Boileau. Pope, he says, "deem'd it more modest to give the name of Imitations to his Satires, than, like Despreaux, to give the name of Satires to Imitations."[37] We may say, then, that Boileau's conception of his satires and their reception by his audience, place them within the tradition of the Imitation. His general method may be seen in his First and Sixth Satires.

In his First Satire Boileau freely adapts the "plot" of Juvenal's Third Satire: the persecuted good man forced to leave his native city for the country. Boileau employs the typically Juvenalian complaint concerning honesty unrewarded, the rich persecuting the poor, and the prevalence of upstart nobles (compare Juvenal, *Satires*, iii, 21–89, and Boileau, *Satires*, i, 21–80). But Boileau's freedom toward his source may be seen in his adaptation of the Codrus scene. Juvenal's Codrus (ll. 203–11) is rejected by the world after his meager possessions are destroyed by fire; Boileau's Saint-Amant sells his little *héritage*, seeks his fortune through verses at court, and, because he is not poetically "à la mode," is laughed out of court and dies of a fever partially induced by hunger (ll. 97–108). Indeed, for Boileau Paris is so bad that only an adaptation of a famous thought from

---

35. *The Works of Monsieur Boileau made English from the last Paris Edition By Several Hands. To which is prefix'd His Life, . . . By Mr. Des Maizeaux* (London, 1712), 1:cvii-cviii; cxi; cxi, n.
36. *Alexander Pope: The Dunciad*, The Twickenham Edition of the poems of Alexander Pope, vol. 5, ed. James Sutherland, 3d ed. (London: Methuen & Co., 1963), p. 9 (italics and Roman type inverted).
37. *The Works of Alexander Pope*, ed. William Warburton (London, 1751), 4:51.

Juvenal's First Satire can adequately express his state of mind—if nature fails me then indignation will make my verse (ll. 79–80): "La colère suffit et vaut un Appollon" (l. 144).

Boileau is not only eclectic in his use of texts: he knows that he is writing a poem in which modern circumstances will not always parallel the ancient. Accordingly, he adds a Christian conclusion which bolsters his own *ethos* and further blackens that of his opponents who advise him to peddle his sermons at an appropriate pulpit:

> Ainsi parle un esprit qu'irrite la satire,
> Qui contre ses défauts croit être en sûreté,
> En raillant d'un censeur la triste austérité;
> Qui fait l'homme intrépide, et, tremblant de foiblesse,
> Attend pour croire en Dieu que la fièvre le presse;
> Et, toujours dans l'orage au ciel levant les mains,
> Dès que l'air est calmé, rit des foibles humains.
> Car de penser alors qu'un Dieu tourne le monde,
> Et règle les ressorts de la machine ronde,
> Ou qu'il est une vie au delà du trépas,
> C'est là, tout haut du moins, ce qu'il n'avouera pas.
> Pour moi, qu'en santé même un autre monde étonne,
> Qui crois l'âme immortelle, et que c'est Dieu qui tonne,
> Il vaut mieux pour jamais me bannir de ce lieu.
> Je me retire donc. Adieu, Paris, adieu. (ll. 150–64)

Interspersed in this satire are generous portions or suggestions from Juvenal's Seventh Satire, an attack on the persecution of men of learning and letters. Hence Boileau's speaker, Damon, is a poet who shares some of Juvenal's anger regarding his impoverished peers. Boileau omitted or altered about half of the Third Satire, and so he does not scruple at altering the Seventh as well. For Juvenal the lawyer is a virtuous, humble, and persecuted man of learning (ll. 139–49); for Boileau he is a despicable wretch who traps the innocent and turns white to black. Thus the world will have to turn topsy-turvy before Damon becomes a lawyer:

> Avant qu'un tel dessein m'entre dans la pensée,
> On pourra voir la Seine a la Saint-Jean glacée;

Arnauld à Charenton devenir huguenot,
Saint-Sorlin janséniste, et Saint-Pavin bigot. (ll. 125–28)

The omitted half of Juvenal's Third Satire motivates much of Boileau's Sixth, but here too Boileau's originality and wit emerge. In lines 232-314 Juvenal discusses the dangers and discomforts of twenty-four hours of life in Rome;[38] each section either includes or suggests unnatural death, and so the reader is convinced that Umbricius' departure and plea for universal return to the country life is justified. Boileau's speaker, however, neither leaves the city, nor paints it in such grim colors, nor presents a plan for curing the ills of the poor. We are asked, instead, to see the hardships of city life, and to realize that without riches one must endure and thank God for what he has; the counsel of resignation is directly opposed to the Juvenalian scheme, in which the satirist demands not only recognition of evil, but its eradication. For Juvenal life in Rome is a contradiction in terms; for Boileau life in Paris is uncomfortable but—apparently—preferable to life anywhere else, for he is willing to stay and be stoical. Hence Juvenal's distant pastoral retreat is altered to an enclosed garden in which the rich enjoy the virtues of both the country and the city:

Paris est pour un riche un pays de Cocagne.
Sans sortir de la ville, il trouve la campagne:
Il peut dans son jardin, tout peuplé d'arbres verts,
Recéler le printemps au milieu des hivers;
Et, foulant le parfum de ses plantes fleuries,
Aller entretenir ses douces rêveries.
Mais moi, grâce au destin, qui n'ai ni feu ni lieu,
Je me loge où je puis, et comme il plâit à Dieu. (ll. 119–26)

Nevertheless, Boileau's satire clearly follows the structure of Juvenal's: the chronology and many of the examples are at least as Ro-

38. See Gilbert Highet, *Juvenal the Satirist* (Oxford: Oxford University Press, 1954), pp. 75, and 256, n. 22. The second part of the poem may be divided accordingly: early hours, ll. 232-38; morning, ll. 239-48; luncheon, ll. 249-53; afternoon traffic, ll. 254-61; bath and dinner, ll. 261-67; after dinner, ll. 268-301; night, ll. 302 ff.

man as Parisian. We move from the impossibility of sleep in the small hours (ll. 1–26), through the morning and afternoon crowds and the dangers of a rainstorm (ll. 27–82), to the terrors of the night, where thieves reign, one may be murdered in his own home, or subjected to having his *quartier* made a second Troy, open to the plunders of Paris' equivalent of roguish Argives (ll. 83–112). We then return to the early hours and come full cycle in the difficulties of life in Paris (ll. 113–18).

As is clear from these examples, Boileau's eclectic method of adapting and modernizing Roman satire was different from Cowley's, and, in all likelihood, would help to produce a different kind of English Imitation, one that was freer and, though depending upon a specific source or sources, not so overt in announcing it.

The earliest recorded English reference of indebtedness to Boileau is in a letter from Dryden to Rochester in July of 1673. Etherege, Dryden relates, translated Boileau's First Satire and, "changing the French names for English, read it so often that it came to their ears who were concern'd, and forc'd him to leave off the design, ere it were half finish'd." And Samuel Butler, according to Brooks, translated Boileau's Second Satire sometime around 1673.[39] These versions of Boileau were in the English tradition of relatively close adherence to the original's meaning. In 1674, however, Rochester probably wrote his "Timon,"[40] a free Imitation of Boileau's Third Satire which, in turn, is a free Imitation of Horace, *Satires*, ii. 8. The central action of each poem is the dinner. Horace parodies the excessive cost, self-consciousness, and concern associated with *haut-cuisine*; Nasidienus, his host, is too refined and exotic in his culinary taste and too gross in his intellectual taste. The only conversation stems from Nasidienus' instructions concerning recipes and Balatro's mock sermon on the miseries of the human situation. The pretensions of Boileau's host are more genteel intellectually and less genteel culinarily; the dinner thus becomes one aspect, rather than the central aspect, of characterization. The host tricks the poet into thinking not only that the

39. As in Brooks, "The 'Imitation,'" p. 132.
40. See Harold F. Brooks, "The Date of Rochester's Timon," *N&Q*, 174 (1938) : 384; and *Poems by . . . Rochester*, Pinto, p. 197.

celebrated gourmet the Marquis de Villandri will be present, but that Molière and the musician Lambert have promised to come. The real dinner includes mediocre gustatory sensations; the guests are rustics and boors whose conversation mirrors both unthinking clichés and contemporary failures in taste. In Horace's dinner all the guests leave; at Boileau's only the poet himself is victimized and he "gagné doucement la porte sans rien dire" (1. 230).

The example of such freedom was not wasted on Rochester who is equally casual towards his own source. Perhaps Rochester's chief alteration is his use of a certain vulgar sexual interest in the person of the host's wife, a character not in Boileau. This aging beauty persists in talking about sexual love and Louis' two mistresses (ll. 46–64), and introduces the "literary" discussion by alluding to Falkland and "easie" Suckling (1. 105). The rougher English poem includes references to mistresses, castration, adultery, an ample "C**t," whores, venereal disease, and intrigues. In this curious world of female sexual freedom, it is no wonder that the fight, which in Boileau's poem starts over the merits of Quinault, in Rochester's starts when an Englishman defends the valor of the French (ll. 163–67)! By not closely following his original's structure, then, Rochester does closely follow its imitative method.

In his *Satyr Against Mankind,* an Imitation of Boileau's Eighth Satire written early in 1676, Rochester approaches even closer to Boileau's own freeness of Imitation.[41] Burnet's remark regarding Rochester's admiration for Boileau was seconded by John Dennis. In

---

41. Brooks, "The 'Imitation,' " p. 133. Note that poets and readers of the period were aware both of Boileau's attitude towards his source and of the precedent this set for them. The author of the dedicatory poem "To his Ingenious Friend the Author of the following POEMS," says:

> Artfull *Boileau* with such a Genius writes,
>> As tickles us at once and bites:
> In the *Venusian's* footsteps walking; fools,
> Whom the morose Wou'd lash, he ridicules.
>> Yet tho' he oft does imitate,
>> Too mean he thinks it to translate,
> So you his thoughts have always in your view,
> And as his Master *He,* You him pursue.

See the anonymous *Second, Fourth, and Seventh Satyrs of Monsieur Boileau Imitated, With some other Poems and Translations Written upon several occasions* (London, 1696), sig. A6^v (italics and Roman type inverted).

the Preface to his *Miscellanies in Verse and Prose* (1693), he notes
that Rochester was "very well acquainted with *Boileau,* and . . . de-
fer'd very much to his Judgment."[42] Thus instead of a mere close
adaptation of the poem to English circumstances, he only adapts some
of Boileau's ideas while, by preserving certain familiar themes, nevertheless keeps the reader aware of Boileau's presence; contemporary
readers therefore regarded the poem as an Imitation. John F. Moore,
however, has cogently argued that in the *Satyr* Boileau's ideas, rather
than his method of Imitation, "should surely be described by no
stronger phrase than 'partially suggestive.' " Rochester's poem, he
continues, lacks "any sustained verbal parallels" with Boileau's and,
"not one idea" in Boileau's Eighth Satire "has been used by Rochester without important alterations."[43] Moore is right, but we must
realize that for Rochester's readers recognition of the alteration was
part of the beauty of the poem and Rochester's mode of Imitation.

There is still another indication of the "originality" of Rochester's
poem. In October of 1682 John Oldham wrote "The Eighth Satyr of

42. (London, 1693), sig. A6ʳ. Reprinted in *The Critical Works of John Dennis,*
   ed. E. N. Hooker (Baltimore: Johns Hopkins Press, 1939), 1: 8.
43. "The Originality of Rochester's *Satyr Against Mankind,*" *PMLA,* 58
   (1943) : 398-99. For other discussions of the poem and Rochester's poetry, see
   Johannes Prinz, *John Wilmot Earl of Rochester* (Leipzig: Mayer & Muller,
   1927), pp. 122-26; V. de Sola Pinto, *Rochester: Portrait of a Restoration
   Poet* (London: John Lane, 1935), pp. 174-81; Francis Whitfield, *Beast in
   View* (Cambridge, Mass.: Harvard University Press, 1936), pp. 50-54; S. F.
   Crocker, "Rochester's *Satire Against Mankind*: A Study of Certain Aspects
   of the Background," *West Virginia University Studies,* 3 (1937) : 57-73;
   Pinto, "John Wilmot, Earl of Rochester, and the Right Veine of Satire," in
   Essays and Studies by Members of the English Association, collected by
   Geoffrey Bullough, n. s. vol. 6 (London: John Murray, 1953), 56-70; Thomas
   H. Fujimura, "Rochester's 'Satyr Against Mankind': An Analysis," *SP,* 55
   (1958) : 576-90; C. F. Main, "The Right Vein of Rochester's *Satyr,*" in
   Essays in Literary History Presented to J. Milton French, ed. Rudolf Kirk
   and C. F. Main (New Brunswick, N. J.: Rutgers University Press, 1960),
   pp. 93-112; Howard Erskine-Hill, "Rochester: Augustan or Explorer," in
   Renaissance and Modern Essays Presented to Vivian de Sola Pinto, ed. G. R.
   Hibbard (New York: Barnes and Noble, 1966), pp. 51-64. Note that in his
   "Life of Rochester" Johnson observes both the presence of the original and
   Rochester's alterations. By this point in his career, however, Johnson deni-
   grates even so free a form of Imitation: "Of the *Satire against Man* Roches-
   ter can only claim what remains when all Boileau's part is taken away"
   (*Lives of the English Poets,* ed. G. Birkbeck Hill [Oxford: Clarendon Press,
   1905], 1: 226.

Monsieur Boileau, Imitated," which is essentially a modernized translation. Oldham was a great admirer of Rochester,[44] and it seems reasonable to suppose that if he felt that the poem had already been imitated (in his sense) he would not have chosen to do the job again. Furthermore, as he shows in the Preface to his Imitation of the *Ars poetica* (1681), Oldham was aware of the individuality of his kind of adaptation and differentiated it from other forms of translation. Apparently Rochester's poem was so different from Boileau's that Oldham did not think that his new attempt needed any justification. As I have suggested earlier, one sees the great difference between the two methods by comparing the opening lines of each poem: the closeness of Oldham's poem to Boileau's original is as obvious as the differences between Boileau and Rochester in the latter's *Satyr*. Rochester borrows Boileau's independence toward his original, while Oldham adheres to the closer, more conservative English method of line-by-line adaptation.

We have, then, three different modes of Imitation: (1) Cowley's, in which the original is overtly cited, freely translated and truncated, thereby altering the meaning of the poem; (2) Cowley's second mode of paraphrase and consistent modernization of an announced model; (3) extremely free Imitation of an unannounced source which, nevertheless, the poet expected the reader to know; Boileau often imitated more than one source, whereas Rochester generally used a single poem as his guide.

Cowley's first mode is important in its implications as well as its literal influence; it reinforced the notion of pointing to a specific model and of altering its meaning in some way. Both aspects of this kind of Imitation appear in such later poems as *London* and the *Epistle to Augustus*. But this mode—or a variation upon it—was also seen at work in Swift's Imitations; often he might either imitate part of a poem and alter its meaning or tone, or, upon occasion, imitate part of it and largely preserve its meaning.

44. See, for example, his *"Bion: A Pastoral in Imitation of the Greek of Moschus*, bewailing the Death of the Earl of *Rochester,"* published in *The Works of Mr. John Oldham* (London, 1684); new pagination and title page after p. 148: *Some New Pieces* (1681).

He does the former in *Part of the Seventh Epistle of the First Book of Horace Imitated* (1713), where he adapts and prints the relevant parallels from half of Horace's poem.[45] In the omitted part Horace tells Maecenas that he will not be coming to town to see him this winter, since at this point in his life he needs rest and warmth rather than excitement and pleasure. Horace is always respectful towards his patron, always grateful for the wealth he has given him, but, at the same time, gently reminds Maecenas both that he cannot give the essential gifts of youth and vigor and that his own "ease and . . . freedom" (ll. 35–36) are not for sale: "Try me, whether I can restore your gifts, and cheerfully too" (l. 39). He then cites Telemachus' sensible rejection of a gift of horses inappropriate for Ithaca and concludes that "small things befit small folk" (l. 44): and so he prefers "peaceful Tarentum" to "queenly Rome" (ll. 44–45). Horace then relates the story of Philippus who seduces the modest and virtuous Vulteius Mena from a carefree life to a life of professional farming and frequent worries. Vulteius finally implores Philippus to "put me back in my former life" (l. 95) and Horace, in his "own" voice, concludes: "Tis right that each should measure himself by his own rule and standard" (l. 98).[46] The complete poem is not only Horace's excuse to his patron for refusing to join him, but also his way of saying—thank you for helping me, but however much I respect you and am grateful for your favors, I am entirely capable of returning them if your demands are too great. Philippus and Vulteius Mena are thus projections of an undesirable relationship between Horace and Maecenas; by way of masks, the situation shows what might occur if the client does not measure his own needs.

In his Imitation, an adaptation of the tale, Swift develops the device of the thinly disguised mask, for he has his patron Harley spy "Dr. *S--T*:/A Clergyman of special Note,/ For shunning those of his own Coat" (ll. 26–28). But Swift the author is overtly, where Horace was covertly, biographical; "Swift" the character in the poem re-

---

45. *The Poems of Jonathan Swift*, ed. Harold Williams, 2d ed. (Oxford: Clarendon Press, 1958), 1: 169-75. Subsequent references are cited in the text.
46. All quotations are from *Horace: Satires, Epistles, and Ars poetica*, Loeb Classical Library, trans. H. Rushton Fairclough (Cambridge, Mass.: Harvard University Press, 1926), pp. 297-303.

ceives both more praise and more mockery than Vulteius; Swift's tale is self-contained, related directly to Harley and himself, and only peripherally to the human condition, for Swift not only omits the first section, but the final generalizing paragraph as well. Nor is there any of the vigor of independence that motivates Horace's epistle, since Swift merely says "Pray leave me where you found me first" (l. 138), whereas in his opening section Horace in his "own" voice openly offers to return his patron's gift, and in the final lines repeats this sentiment, if not its original language.

This "partial Imitation" seemed congenial to Swift. We recall that Cowley imitated only the country mouse section of Horace, *Satires*, ii. 6, and that Sprat imitated the first part. Swift performed a similar task, writing his "Horace, Lib. 2 Sat. 6 [The First] Part of it imitated" in 1714 (1: 197–202), while, in 1728, Pope added the fable of the mice. Both Swift and Pope are largely faithful to Horace's tone and content, so that this poem, unlike the preceding Imitation, is roughly within the class of translation. Swift returns to partial Imitation and alteration of meaning in "To the Earl of Oxford . . . Out of Horace. Written in the year 1716" (1: 209). He imitates something over half of *Odes*, iii. 2, and in so doing, omits Horace's opening account of the virtues of a brave military life: Swift's poem is addressed to the virtues of a brave political life and is meant, in part, to show that the political leader of contemporary England must be as courageous and virtuous as the military leader of ancient Rome. The form appears again in "Part of the 9th Ode of the 4th Book of Horace" (1721) in which the poet makes clear that Lollius will be celebrated with other great men because he will have a "sacred poet" to sing his name. Swift, on the other hand, excludes the self-conscious and implicitly self-congratulatory poet, and lauds only Archbishop King himself (1: 242–43). There are numerous other examples of this popular form of Cowleyan partial Imitation—it was important through much of the seventeenth, eighteenth, and even early nineteenth centuries.[47]

47. For example, see Tom Brown's "Part of the 2d Ode in *Horace*, l. 4, translated; beginning at: *Dignum laude virum*," in *The Works of Mr. Thomas Brown, Serious and Comical*, 4th ed. (London, 1715), 4: 1-2; *London Maga-*

Cowley's second mode of Imitation as modernization and reasonably close translation was to set the pattern for much Imitation in the Restoration and the earlier eighteenth century, and it was this mode that influenced even the form of Pope and Johnson. As Johnson observed in his "Life of Pope," however, it is to Oldham that we must turn as the poet who reinforces and drives home the value of modernization.[48]

Oldham certainly knew and admired the Imitations of Cowley, Boileau, and Rochester "several years before he wrote any himself"; hence, as Brooks insists, the immediate impetus for his kind of Imitation must be given to Dryden's theory of translation rather than to any of these other authors.[49] In the Preface to his version of *Ovid's Epistles,* Dryden rejects literal translation and reviews the arguments of Denham and Cowley for free translation, which includes modernization as a natural outgrowth. Cowley's method, he says, is unsound for a translator of lesser abilities than Cowley or an author of more regular style than Pindar. Dryden does credit Denham's theory of modernizing an author's thoughts, since the volatile essence of poetry will be lost if new spirit is not infused into the old author; but, says Dryden, Denham's theory argues against literal translation without arguing for imitation. The expression must be changed to accommodate the new language and the new age, but the original sense must also be held sacred and inviolable. For Dryden, his own middle way of paraphrase accomplishes both ends of adherence to sense and the preservation of poetry (*Essays,* 1: 240).

In 1680 Oldham attempted a paraphrase of "The Passion of Byblis out of Ovid's Metamorphosis." In the Advertisement he expresses his dissatisfaction with this "Trifle" and in the process points directly to Dryden's *Ovid* as a source of inspiration for his work: it was "occasioned upon reading the late Translations of *Ovid's Epistles,* which

zine, 7 (April, 1738): 165-66; Francis Hodgson's alteration of Martial, v. 59, because the epigram "encourages instead of checking present enjoyment," in *Lady Jane Grey, A Tale, in Two Books; with Miscellaneous Poems, in English and Latin* (London, 1809), p. 332, note d.

48. *Lives of the English Poets,* Hill, 3: 176. Imitation, Johnson says, "was first practised in the reign of Charles the Second by Oldham and Rochester, at least I remember no instances more ancient."

49. Brooks, "The 'Imitation,' " p. 135.

gave him a mind to try what he could do upon a like Subject." This, he says, is "the first attempt, he ever made in this kind, and likely enough to be the last, his vein (if he may be thought to have any) lying another way";[50] that way was Imitation as modernization of a closely paraphrased poem. In his Imitation of the *Ars poetica* in 1681, he thus wholly accepts Dryden's demands for fidelity to the original (a demand that Dryden makes in several remarks about translation),[51] by implication denies Cowley's claims for the translator's right to add or subtract what he pleases, and adds immediacy through the exchange of classical for English names and settings. In so doing, as Johnson's and Warton's testimony suggests, Oldham firmly established this second Cowleyian mode of Imitation as modernization. It was more conservative than Cowley's first mode, which changed the meaning of the ancient poem, and far less original than those of Boileau and Rochester. In the Advertisement to *Some New Pieces*, Oldham describes his method of imitating the *Ars poetica*, in which he modernizes but refuses to imitate too freely. He also employs the translator's traditional simile of putting the ancient into modern dress, a simile we have already seen in Denham, Cowley, Higden, Settle, and Dryden. The Imitation, he says, was forced upon him, for though Ben Jonson and Roscommon had excellently translated the work, they had not exhausted the possibilities of translation. He hopes to find certain "Advantages" which his predecessors "have either not minded, or scrupulously abridged themselves of." This, he supposes, "was to be effected by putting *Horace* into a more modern dress, than hitherto he has appeared in, that is by making him speak, as if he were living, and writing now." Accordingly, he "resolved to alter the Scene from *Rome* to *London*, and make use of *English* Names of Men, Places, and Customs, where the Parallel would decently permit, which I conceived would give a kind of new Air to the Poem, and render it more agreeable to the rellish of the present Age." He admits that he has not "been over-nice in keeping to the words

50. *Works of Oldham*, new title page: *Satyrs upon the Jesuits . . . and some other Pieces*, sig. A2ᵛ (italics and Roman type inverted).
51. See, for example, the Preface to *Sylvae* (1685), in *Essays*, 1: 252; Dedication of *Examen Poeticum* (1693), in *Essays*, 2: 9-10. See also J. McG. Bottkol, "Dryden's Latin Scholarship," *MP*, 40 (1943): 241-54.

of the Original, for that were to transgress a Rule therein contained [*Nec verbum verbo* . . . .]"; but he has been "religiously strict to its sense, and express'd it in as plain, and intelligible a manner, as the Subject would bear." He has not varied from his text more than "once or twice, and in Passages not much material," and even here, he says, "the skilful Reader will perceive 'twas necessary for carrying on my proposed design."[52]

These remarks not only suggest that Oldham conceived of himself as a translator as well as imitator; they also suggest that he had Dryden's Preface to *Ovid* in mind, for Dryden both mentions Jonson's translation of the *Art of Poetry* as an example of literal translation, and praises Roscommon's rendering of Horace's *Nec verbum verbo*. Oldham's desire to make Horace speak "as if he were living, and writing now" paraphrases Dryden's remark that the translator is to make his author speak "as he supposes that author would have done, had he lived in our age, and in our country," and Dryden and Oldham both use Horace's *Nec verbum verbo* to warn against literal translation. (*Essays*, 1: 237, 239). However, he does refer to his work as an Imitation, and in the remark about the "skilful Reader" we detect a hint of the greater Augustan Imitators' conscious use of parallels to enhance the reader's pleasure. Among other changes, this reader would have noticed that Oldham reverses Horace's discussion of the use of music and dance in drama. For Horace the clarity of the flute and the dance's movements have been lost, so that the thought behind them became unclear and "attuned to the oracles of Delphi" (l. 219) ; for Oldham, "our Monarch by kind Heaven sent,/ Brought back the Arts with him from Banishment,"[53] and so all the theatrical arts have flourished. Thus Oldham generally follows his original closely, and where possible adapts lines and sections to a modern parallel, so that the pre-tunic days of Cethegus become the English age of Chaucer: the closeness, we may say, comes from Dryden's theory of translation, the adaptation probably from Cowley's.

This method quickly spread, for shortly afterward, in 1682 or 1683, Dryden uses it when he substitutes the relevant English names in

52. *Works of Oldham: Some New Pieces*, sigs. a^(r-v) of the Advertisement (italics and Roman type inverted).
53. *Ibid.*, p. 18.

Soame's translation of Boileau's *L'Art poétique.*[54] Similarly, in "The Original and Progress of Satyr" he says that upon occasion he and his colleagues "make [Juvenal] express the customs and manners of our native country rather than of Rome," because there was either "some kind of analogy betwixt their customs and ours" or because "to make him more easy to vulgar understandings we gave him those manners which are familiar to us" (*Essays,* 2: 114). And in 1708 Rowe observes that alteration of French to English names is permissible in Ozell's version of *Le Lutrin,* otherwise it "would be but an odd Entertainment to People here, who never heard of [dull French authors] before; besides it must be allow'd, that one may very easily apprehend the Plaisantry of the Satyr in the Original, by the Translator's mustering up a Set of *English* Authors of equal Degree and like kind of Dulness with those mention'd by M. *Boileau.*"[55] In all of these examples, let us remember, the focus is on the ancient (or foreign), not the modern (or domestic) author, and so we are still dealing with Imitation as a form of translation.

But this form was solidified by Oldham's theory and practice. The substance of Rowe's remarks is similar to Oldham's in the Preface to his *Ars poetica,* while several Restoration Imitations bear distinct traces of Oldham's influence: there are direct borrowings in Wood's *Juvenalis Redivivus* (1683), Higden's Imitations of the Tenth (1686) and Thirteenth (1687) Satires of Juvenal, and in Prior's "A Satyr upon the Poets, being a Translation out of the 7th Satyr of Juvenal" (1694). Pope knew the Imitations of Oldham so well that there are twenty-five passages in the *Ars poetica* alone to which he is indebted. He also echoes Oldham in the Fourth Pastoral, the Saint Cecelia Ode,

---

54. See Tonson's Advertisement to *The Art of Poetry, Written in French by the Sieur de Boileau. Made English by Sir William Soame, Bart. And Revis'd and Alter'd by Mr. John Dryden*: "I saw the Manuscript lye in Mr. Dryden's Hands for about Six Months, who made very considerable Alterations in it, particularly, the beginning of the 4th *Canto*; and it being his Opinion that it would be better to apply the Poem to *English* Writers than to keep to the French Names, as it was first Translated, Sir William desired he would take the Pains to make that Alteration, and accordingly that was entirely done by Mr. Dryden" (quoted from *The Annual Miscellany: for the Year 1694,* 2d ed. [London, 1708], sig. A2ʳ; and see Brooks, "The 'Imitation,'" p. 137).
55. *Boileau's Lutrin,* Ozell, sig. A7ʳ⁻ᵛ.

the epistle of Sapho to Phaon, the *Epistle to Dr. Arbuthnot*, and several of the *Imitations of Horace*.[56] Oldham, then, probably with Cowley's second practice of Imitation and Dryden's theory of translation behind him, substantially helped to establish the English Imitation in its form closest to translation.

The paradigm poems of these three modes of Imitation do not include the printing of extensive parallels on the same or facing page, and Rochester's popular "Allusion to Horace" was not published with the relevant text until 1714. The virtual absence of an early form of Imitation which used extensive on-page parallels reinforces the importance of the Restoration parody; by 1664 this form had established a precedent for comparison of ancient and modern texts, and it was conscious parallel that the major Augustan imitators wanted in their poems. In general, therefore, the Imitations had these traits: they include recognition and publication of the original and adequate closeness to it, so that appreciation of parallels and insights into significant differences could be made more easily than in the case of Rochester's *Satyr*. Swift, Pope, and Johnson neither boggled at changing their Roman masters where necessary, nor accused themselves of "copying" when paralleling them. They accepted Cowley's and Oldham's modernization but, instead of their line-by-line correspondence to the original in both form and content, they followed Rochester's slightly freer practice in the "Allusion" and supplied a section-by-section correspondence; but unlike Rochester they pointed to the sections imitated and used even more originality in treating their poet's themes. For example, in *The Vanity of Human Wishes* Johnson follows Juvenal by including a long section on military pride and substitutes Charles XII for Hannibal; but the uses to which each is put, the way in which the author treats his subject, and the ultimate role of the character in the poem are all quite different. Johnson draws these differences to our attention by including the relevant line-numbers to Juvenal's Tenth Satire. Fully to appreciate these differences, to read the poem as Johnson hoped we would, we must be willing to compare the ancient and modern portraits.

56. Brooks, "The 'Imitation,'" pp. 137-38; for Brooks' discussion of Pope's familiarity with Oldham, see "The Imitation,'" p. 124, n. 3.

Similarly, in Swift's earlier work *T--l--nd's* Invitation to *Dismal*, to Dine with the Calves-Head Club. *Imitated from* Horace, *Epist. 5. Lib. I* (1712; *Poems*, 1:161–66) the reader's pleasure is lessened unless he reads the Latin footnotes, sees Horace adapted, and thereby sees the contrast between true and false fellowship, unity and disunity, friendship and treachery, and a straightforward and ironic method in the ancient and modern poems. We recall, as well, that Swift wrote to Stella regarding this poem: "Have you seen Toland's Invitation to Dismal? How do you like it? But it is an imitation of Horace, and perhaps you don't understand Horace." The extraordinary self-consciousness of the Imitation—as well as part of its roots in translation—can again be seen in another work of Swift's, "On Noisy Tom," a lampoon against Sir Thomas Prendergast, written in 1736. It stems from Horace, *Satires*, i. 6, 34–39, begins by printing and identifying the Latin lines imitated, and then adds a paragraph "Translated literally" with explanatory footnotes. Immediately thereafter Swift includes the same lines "Paraphrased," as he calls it, and generously annotates them so that his readers will both understand his English references and more easily compare them to the Latin (3: 825–26). An anonymous correspondent to *The Gentleman's Magazine* for November, 1770, records the Janus-like reaction necessary for the Imitation. Pope's Horace and Johnson's Juvenal, he says, are "in everybody's mouth"; but "these are not translations, they are something much better, they are English originals in the manner of Horace and Juvenal."[57] In order to appreciate the "original" quality, one must also know the classical "manner."

There are, then, three earlier English modes of Imitation, and all rest in part on the commonplaces and theory of free translation discussed in chapter 1: paraphrase and use of part of the poem, consecutive modernization of a complete poem, and very free adaptation of the content and form of one poem. The first two modes (Oldham's in particular) are basically translations rather than original poems, and the third mode, Rochester's in the *Satyr*, was too far from its original to supply enough of the pleasure of comparison. The first two forms suggested a muted awareness of the original text;

57. 40: 511.

the second suggested modernization; the first and third suggested treating the text with liberty. The Restoration parody was related to the theory of free translation and, perhaps in conjunction with the practice of printing bi-lingual translations, probably suggested the use of on-page parallels. The form of Pope and Johnson was thus firmly anchored in earlier imitative traditions. However, these different traditions should not be rigidly compartmentalized, since they exist along a spectrum of Imitation which stretches from virtual modernized translation on the one hand, to extreme freedom on the other. The paradigm poems discussed above are early variations of an influential form. Eighteenth-century poets might, and often did, choose any combination of treatment of the parent-poem: close translation, paraphrase, or extreme freedom; abbreviation or expansion; modernization or adaptation.

We will see some of the implications of these traditions when we analyze Johnson's Imitations; but since Johnson and Pope are also formal verse satirists, we must first discuss another major tradition within which their poems exist.

3

The Pattern of Formal Verse Satire in the Restoration and the Eighteenth Century

Though formal verse satire was a major genre in the Augustan age, students of satire have generally been reluctant to define its essential traits. One such trait, however, has been discussed in Mary Claire Randolph's illuminating study "The Structural Design of the Formal Verse Satire." She remarks that the satire of Lucilius, Horace, Persius, and Juvenal was "bi-partite in structure," that a particular vice or folly was attacked in "Part A," and its opposite virtue praised in "Part B." There is always more attack than praise in satire "since, paradoxically, in the very act of presenting the negative or destructive side of human behavior the satirist is establishing a positive foundation on which he can base his specific recommendation to virtue."[1] Whether introduced by direct exhortation, implication, or quotable proverb, the "admonition to virtue" is inevitably present in formal verse satire: "it must be there, spoken or unspoken, if the piece is to be more than mere virulence and fleeting invective . . . . In any case, whatever the plan, the positive rational mode of procedure advocated or unmistakenly implied in a satire will be the precise opposite of the vice or folly ridiculed."[2]

Miss Randolph's accurate remarks are based on classical Roman precedent, rather than Restoration or eighteenth-century theory or

1. *PQ*, 21 (1942) : 369, 373. Miss Randolph refers to two studies which discuss this structure in classical satire: Augustin G. C. Cartault, *Étude sur les satires d'Horace* (Paris, 1899), p. 347; and Oscar E. Nybakken, *An Analytical Study of Horace's Ideas* (Scottsdale, Pa.: The Mennonite Press, 1937), p. 12. See also the Yale diss. by Arthur H. Weston, *Latin Satirical Writing Subsequent to Juvenal* (Lancaster, Pa.: New Era Printing Co., 1915), p. 5.
2. Randolph, "Structural Design of Formal Verse Satire," pp. 374-75.

practice. Indeed, she does not believe that the structure of formal verse satire was widely discussed during the period, since Dryden was "the only critic in English literature who has come reasonably close to an apprehension of the basic structure of the genre."[3] But, she continues, Dryden's remarks could not have influenced later satirists, for, she says, his "Discourse concerning the Original and Progress of Satyr" (1693) was overlooked and unappreciated. We must therefore infer that the pattern of satire that she describes was unknown to most English satirists.

Other scholars, applying Miss Randolph's insight regarding the structure of the genre, have found that Pope's satires exhibit the pattern of praise and blame;[4] but none of them has shown that in using this pattern Pope adheres to the concept of formal verse satire described by Dryden. That is, contrary to Miss Randolph's view, Dryden's concept of the form was well-known during the Restoration and eighteenth century; it influenced the theory of commentators, the expectation of readers, and the practice of satirists. Moreover, the same concept was discussed by André Dacier in his important edition of Horace (1681–89).

Dacier's essay on Roman satire supplied both a title and much information for Dryden's "Discourse."[5] Furthermore, John Dennis often referred to him;[6] there were at least three printed English translations of his essay "Sur les satires d'Horace, où l'on explique

3. *Ibid.*, pp. 383-84.
4. See Maynard Mack, "The Muse of Satire," *Yale Review,* 41 (1951) : 80-92; John Butt, *The Augustan Age* (London: Hutchinson House, 1950), pp. 68-70; Robert W. Rogers, *The Major Satires of Pope,* Illinois Studies in Language and Literature (Urbana: University of Illinois Press, 1955), 40: 83; Rebecca Price Parkin, *The Poetic Workmanship of Alexander Pope* (Minneapolis: University of Minnesota Press, 1955), pp. 126, 166-68. See also Alvin B. Kernan, *The Cankered Muse* (New Haven: Yale University Press, 1959), pp. 11-32, and *passim*; Robert C. Elliott, *The Power of Satire* (Princeton: Princeton University Press, 1960), pp. 109-12. For an earlier study of Pope's satiric method, see Elder Olson, "Rhetoric and the Appreciation of Pope," *MP,* 37 (1939–40) : 13-35.
5. *The Essays of John Dryden,* ed. W. P. Ker (Oxford: Clarendon Press, 1926), 2: 282-83; see also Randolph, "Structural Design of Formal Verse Satire," p. 383.
6. See, for example, "To Matthew Prior, Esq.; Upon the Roman Satirists" (1721), in *The Critical Works of John Dennis,* ed. Edward Niles Hooker (Baltimore: Johns Hopkins Press, 1943), 2: 218, 220.

l'origine & le progrès de la Satire des Romains" (1687) ;[7] Jeremy Collier, Tom Brown, and Charles Gildon knew his work well; Joseph Trapp, in his *Praelectiones Poeticae* (1711), frequently drew upon him for his own discussion of satire,[8] and David Watson, in 1750, before translating several of his "Remarques" on the satires and epistles of Horace, calls them "a better Account . . . than I have any where met with."[9] Dacier's *La Poétique d'Aristote traduite en françois avec des remarques* (1692) further enhanced his reputation, and he was considered, Gildon said in 1718, along with Aristotle, Horace, and René Le Bossu, among those who had made known and fixed

7. It was included in Charles Gildon's *Miscellany Poems, Upon Several Occasions: . . . With an Essay upon Satyr by the Famous M. Dacier* (London, 1692) (Gildon comments favorably upon Dacier on sig. A7ᵛ) and as an appendix to René Le Bossu's *Treatise of the Epick Poem, to which are added an Essay Upon Satyr by Mons. D'Acier and a Treatise on the Pastoral, by Mons. Fontenelle* (London, 1695; 2d ed., 1719), and in the first volume of *The Works of Mr. Thomas Brown, Serious and Comical* (London, 1707; 9th ed., 1760). Brown is probably the translator of the essay in Gildon's *Miscellany*; see Benjamin Boyce, *Tom Brown of Facetious Memory* (Cambridge, Mass.: Harvard University Press, 1939), p. 38. In *Tom Jones* (London, 1749), Partridge tells Tom that Brown is "one of the greatest wits that ever the nation produced" (8: v).

8. See Collier's *The Great Historical, Geographical, Genealogical and Poetical Dictionary, . . . Collected from the best Historians, Chronologers, and Lexicographers . . . but more especially out of Lewis Morery [Moréri], D. D. his 8th ed. . . .* , 2d ed. (London, 1701). Collier remarks about satire: "*Satyr* amongst the *Latins*, is, in a large sence, applicable to all Discourses that recommend Vertue, and explode Vice: But the Word, as it is now commonly used with us, only signifies a stinging piece of Poetry, to lash and expose the Vices of Men." Collier closely follows Moréri's *Grand Dictionnaire historique* which may also have been the source for Dacier's similar remark. See the "Préface sur les satires d'Horace," in *Oeuvres d'Horace en Latin, traduites en françois . . . par M. Dacier* (Paris, 1691), vol. 6, **6ʳ⁻ᵛ. The same passage was translated in Brown, *Works*, 2d ed. (London, 1708), 1: 25, and in Dryden's "Discourse," *Essays*, 2: 67. Trapp also paraphrases it: see the English translation of his *Praelectiones: Lectures on Poetry Read in the School of Natural Philosophy at Oxford* (London, 1742), pp. 223-24.

9. *The Works of Horace*, 3d ed. (London, 1750), 2: li. Watson often refers to Dacier in his "Critical Dissertation on the Origin and Progress of Lyrick Poetry and Satire amongst the Ancients." See especially, 2: vii, xlvi-xlvii. Although called the "third edition," this is the first edition of the complete *Works*. The first volume, *The Odes, Epodes, and Carmen Secularae*, was printed separately in 1741 and again in 1747, and the *Works* reprinted in 1760 (4th ed.) and 1792. Note too that even Gibbon refers to Dacier as an authority on Horace (*The History of the Decline and Fall of the Roman Empire*, ed. J. B. Bury [London: Methuen & Co., 1900], 1: 350).

"the rules of criticism."[10] This broad influence justifies examination of Dacier's remarks which, we will see, support the concept of praise and blame described by Miss Randolph.

In his prefatory essay on satire, Dacier discusses Horace's attack upon vice and praise of virtue. At first view, he says, we discover nothing in Horace's satire which merits our affection. He seems more likely to amuse children than occupy men. But, Dacier, continues, "quand nous lui ôtons ce qui le cache à nos yeux, & que nous le voyons jusques au fond, nous y trouvons toutes les Divinitez ensemble, c'est-à-dire, toutes les Vertus qui doivent faire l'exercise continuel de ceux qui cherchent sérieusement à se corriger de leurs vices." Among the virtues which Horace hopes to teach in the two books of the satires are those that are able "à regler nos passions, à suivre la Nature . . . [et] à revenir de nos préjugez."[11] The most important job of the commentator on Horace is to "montrer l'usage, la raison, & la preuve de ses Preceptes; & de fair voir, que ceux qui ne tâchent pas de se corriger sur un si beau modèle, sont justement comme des Malades qui auroient un Livre tout plein de remedes pour leurs maux, & qui se contenteroient de les lire, sans le comprendre, & sans en connôitre l'utilité."[12] The commentator, therefore, aids the effect of the satire's praise of virtue by making clear the utility, reason, and proof of Horace's precepts.[13]

10. Quoted from Gildon's *The Complete Art of Poetry*, in A. F. B. Clark, *Boileau and the French Classical Critics in England* (*1660–1830*), Bibliothèque de la revue de littérature comparée, 19 (Paris: E. Champion, 1925): 287. For other English allusions to Dacier, see Clark, *Boileau*, pp. 286-88; Samuel Holt Monk's introduction to *The Preface to Aristotle's Art of Poetry*, trans. 1705 (Los Angeles: Augustan Reprint Society no. 176, 1959), pp. i-iv; Henry Fielding, *Tom Jones* (London, 1749), 11:1; Howard D. Weinbrot, "André Dacier in 'Augustan' England: Towards the Reclamation of his *Horace*," *Romance Notes*, 7 (1966): 155-60; Thomas E. Maresca, *Pope's Horatian Poems* (Columbus, Ohio: Ohio State University Press, 1966), *passim*. In *Tom Jones*, Fielding includes Dacier among "those noble critics to whose labours the learned world are so greatly indebted. Such," he says, "were Aristotle, Horace, and Longinus, among the ancients, Dacier and Bossu among the French" (11:1).
11. *Oeuvres d'Horace*, VI, sig. **8r–9r; spelling has been modernized.
12. *Ibid.*, sig. **9v. Watson translates much of this passage (*Works of Horace*, 2:xlvi-xlvii).
13. For examples of Dacier's praise of Horace's method of inculcating virtue, see his remarks on *Satires* i. 1, *Oeuvres d'Horace*, VI, 23; *Satires*, i. 9, *ibid.*, p. 558; and *Satires*, ii. 7, *ibid.*, VII, 510-11.

Dacier makes other important remarks when he discusses the *Epistles* of Horace and asks whether they are not satires. Those who deny the name of satire to the *Epistles* do not properly understand the nature of satire, he declares, for they have founded their opinion on the praise of Maecenas and Horace's other friends in the *Epistles*. Praise, they argue, does not belong in satire. But the critics are mistaken about this point; satire may include praise as well as raillery, as one can see if he reads the little treatise preceding Dacier's edition. Indeed, "Lucilius, qui passoit pour l'inventeur de cette sort de Poëme, ne faisoit pas toûjours la guerre au vice, dans ses Satires, il y loüoit aussi très-souvent la vertu. Horace lui-même n'a-t-il pas loüé Auguste & Mecenas dans les siennes? Et Perse n'a-t-il pas loüé Cornutus?"[14] Dacier concludes that it is not the mere presence of praise which differentiates the *Satires* from the *Epistles*, for some praise is essential to the satiric structure. What does differentiate them is the distinct way in which each functions in the satiric balance of praise and blame. Horace, Dacier explains, perceived that lack of order and method was the fault of the satirists preceding him. He therefore decided that his two books of *Satires* would, in general, attack vice, and that his two books of *Epistles* would praise virtue. Thus the four books fall under the rubric of satire; considered as a unit they carefully preserve the balance of praise and blame.

> Il a mis d'abord ses deux premiers Livres de Satires, parce que dans le premier il travaille à déraciner les vices; & que dans le second il s'efforce d'arracher les erreurs & les fausses opinions. Après ces deux Livres, viennent les Epîtres, qui peuvent fort bien être appellés la suite de ses Satires; & il les a mises après les Satires, parce qu'il s'attach à y donner des préceptes pour la vertu, & à allumer dans nos coeurs l'amour qu'elle merite. Ainsi ces quatre Livres sont un cours de Morale entier & [par]fait. Les deux premiers sont proprement . . . *destinez à redarguer* [to reprimand] & *à refuter*. Et les deux derniers sont . . . *destinez à insinuer* & *à enseigner*. Dans cette division Horace suivoit les maximes de Socrate, qui n'en seignoit jamais

14. *Oeuvres d'Horace*, VIII, sig. A3ʳ (original is italicized throughout).

rien, qu'il n'eût auparavant déraciné du coeur de ses disciples tout ce qui pouvoit être contraire aux sentiments qu'il leur vouloit inspirer; & cette methode est très-conforme à la nature & à la raison. Il faut arracher d'un champ toutes les épines & les méchantes herbes & le bien preparer, avant que d'y semer le bon grain. Un bon Médecin tâche de dissiper & de chasser les mauvaises humeurs de son malade, avant que de lui donner les aliments solides pour lui fair revenir la santé avec l'embonpoint. C'est, sans doute, de cette pratique des Médecins que Socrate & Platon ont pris ces purifications, ou plûtôt ces purgations dont it est tant parlé dans leurs Livres. . . . Socrate ne suit pas seulement cette methode dans chaque Dialogue, où il réfute toûjours avant que d'enseigner: il lie aussi par-là plusieurs Dialogues ensemble, comme Horace a lié ces quatre livres . . . . Cela explique admirablement le dessein d'Horace. Ses deux premiers Livres de Satires sont les purgations, . . . dont il se sert pour combattre nos passions, & pour nous délivrer des erreurs dont nous sommes remplis: & les deux derniers sont les enseignemens, . . . la doctrine pure & saine, qu'il fait succéder à ces maladies de l'ame dont il nous a guéris. C'est pourquoi ces deux derniers Livres plairont toûjours davantage à ceux qui se trouveront libres de toutes sortes de faux préjugez.[15]

This passage may have been known to Charles Gildon who, in 1692, edited *Miscellany Poems Upon Several Occasions*: . . . *With an Essay upon Satyr by the Famous M. Dacier*. In any event,

---

15. *Ibid.*, sigs. A3v–A5r (italics and Roman type inverted in text). Watson also translates this passage (*Works of Horace*, 2: li-lii). Dacier's view was a commonplace of continental Renaissance thought. See pp. 129-34 below. See also Charles Brosette's remark regarding praise and blame in Regnier's Satyre 15: "L'Auteur se plaint de la Verve poëtique, qui le contraint à faire des Vers, malgré lui, toute les fois qu'elle s'empare de son esprit; mais il ajoute que son humeur libre, & incapable du moindre déguisement, l'oblige aussi a dire la verité avec franchise; à rendre justice au merite, à blamer le vice, & à louer la vertue" (*Satyres et autres oeuvres de Regnier*, ed. Charles Brosette [London, 1733], p. 215, n. 1). Somewhat earlier Brosette also insists that "la bonté n'est point incompatible avec l'esprit de la Satire: témoin nos deux plus célèbres Satiriques, Regnier, & Boileau" (*Regnier*, p. 33, n. 22).

he made clear the requirement that satire praise the virtue opposed to the vice attacked. But for Gildon, satire is too personal and hence ineffectual. It does not do part of its proper job—making the virtue sufficiently explicit. Panegyric and epic poetry are more useful, for they deal extensively with "a Noble, and taking prospect of *Virtue.*" Thus the *Aeneid* has contributed more to the progress of virtue than Horace's *Satires,* since it forms noble images in the mind, whereas the *Satires* merely expose vice and define virtue by the uncertain path of negatives. The reader is left rambling in the dark, and so may take the opposite road. Both epic and panegyric, however, affirm positively, and paint so exact a portrait of virtue that no one can mistake it or not know it immediately. "But that which is most of all," he adds, *"Panegyric* has the effectual force *Satyr* pretends to, in chacing away *Vice* and *Folly,* by discovering the *Properties,* and *Beauties* of their contraries."[16]

One year later Dryden issued his "Discourse concerning the Original and Progress of Satyr," prefixed to his translation of Juvenal and Persius. It is the most important contemporary English discussion of formal verse satire, and contains the clearest pronouncement on the structure of the form. Dryden rejects Heinsius' definition of satire which, he says, is "wholly accommodated to the Horatian way [of low familiar speech]." He will therefore discuss his "own trivial thoughts" on the making of a modern satire, thoughts, he insists, which "will not deviate in the least from the precepts and examples of the Ancients."[17] Satire must attack only one vice and praise only one virtue. Dryden believes that Horace did not adequately follow this rule of the genre, since Persius—writing some seventy years later—was the first to point out the design of a perfect satire:

> it ought only to treat of one subject; to be confined to one particular theme; or at least, to one principally. If other vices occur in the management of the chief, they should only be

16. (London, 1692), sig. A4ᵛ–A5ʳ (italics and Roman type inverted).
17. *Essays,* 2: 100, 102. The "Discourse" and translation were anxiously awaited: see *The Gentleman's Journal: or the Monthly Miscellany. By Way of Letter to a Gentleman in the Country,* 1 (May, 1692): 25; *ibid.* (October, 1692), p. 6; *ibid.* (December, 1692), p. 27.

transiently lashed, and not be insisted on, so as to make the design double. As in a play of the English fashion, which we call a tragi-comedy, there is to be but one main design; and though there be an underplot, or second walk of comical characters and adventures, yet they are subservient to the chief fable, carried along under it, and helping to it; so that the drama may not seem a monster with two heads. (*Essays,* 2:102–3)

To better preserve variety, he urges, the vice attacked may be illustrated with several examples in "the subdivisions of it, and with as many precepts as there are members of it." Dryden then adds a rule for perfecting this unity of theme in "the design of true satire":

The poet is bound, and that *ex officio,* to give his reader some one precept of moral virtue, and to caution him against some one particular vice or folly. Other virtues, subordinate to the first, may be recommended under that chief head; and other vices or follies may be scourged, besides that which he principally intends. But he is chiefly to inculcate one virtue, and insist on that. Thus Juvenal, in every satire excepting the first, ties himself to one principal instructive point, or to the shunning of moral evil. (*Essays,* 2:104)

However, he emphasizes that the admonition to virtue may not be explicit; it may be implicit in the attack on the vice. Even in his Sixth Satire—a harsh attack upon women—Juvenal includes "a latent admonition to avoid ill women, by showing how very few, who are virtuous and good, are to be found amongst them" (*Essays,* 2:104).

Persius, the originator of this method of satire, was also the most consistent practitioner of it, since he always inculcates a profitable Stoic doctrine and exposes "the opposite vices to it": "every satire is a comment on one particular dogma of that sect [the Stoic]. . . . In general, all virtues are everywhere to be praised and recommended to practice; and all vices to be reprehended, and made either odious or ridiculous; or else there is a fundamental error in the whole design" (*Essays,* 2:104–5).

Miss Randolph has observed that Dryden emphasizes this "design" in the headnotes to each satire as well as in the essay. In the "Argument *of the first Satyr*" of Juvenal, for example, Dryden clearly notes the form of the genre when he remarks that though Juvenal here "strikes indifferently at all Men in his way: In every following Satyr he has chosen some particular Moral which he wou'd inculcate; and lashes some particular Vice or Folly."[18] Similarly, in the "Argument of the Sixth Satyr" of Juvenal, he again insists on the unity of the satiric structure. He reminds the reader that the real subject of Juvenal's attack is the lust of women, while the rest of their vices are but digressions to be skimmed over: " 'Tis one Branch of it in *Hippia*, another in *Messalina*, but Lust is the main Body of the Tree. He begins with this Text in the first line, and takes it up with Intermissions to the end of the Chapter."[19] And in the "Argument of the Eighth Satyr" (translated by Stepney), Dryden makes clear Juvenal's praise of honorable and good actions—as opposed to statues and pedigrees—as the defining traits of nobility. He thus advises his friend Ponticus to lead a virtuous life, praises the worth of noble and meanly born persons like Cicero, Marius, and Servius Tullius, and attacks the debauchery, luxury, cruelty, and other vices of the highborn Nero and Catiline.[20]

Dryden's view of the satiric pattern of praise and blame is expounded in his "Discourse" and illustrated in the Arguments prefixed to Juvenal's poems. He bases his theory on the practice of the ancients and of Boileau, on discussions of Renaissance commentators on Horace, Persius, and Juvenal,[21] and on Dacier's essay on satire. Dryden made this earlier view popular, gave it an English dress, and immense new authority. In all likelihood, his conception of satire influenced subsequent writers. Through much of the eighteenth cen-

---

18. John Dryden, et al., *The Satires of Decimus Junius Juvenalis . . . Together with the Satires of Aulus Persius Flaccus* (London, 1693), p. 2 (the original is italicized throughout).

19. *Ibid.*, pp. 87-88 (italics and Roman type inverted).

20. *Ibid.*, p. 146.

21. Dryden's indebtedness to the Renaissance commentators is mentioned in *Essays*, 2: 43-44, 282-85. However, there is no thorough study of Dryden's sources in the "Discourse." The theories of Casaubon, Heinsius, and Rigaultius are discussed in Chester Hubbard Cable, "Methods of Non-Dramatic Verse Satire 1640–1700" (unpubl. diss., University of Chicago, 1948), pp. 9-31.

tury his reputation as a poet remained high, and his merits as a translator, though not always appreciated, were often discussed. In 1785, for example, Edward Owen attacked both Dryden's Juvenal and Persius, and his essay on satire;[22] in 1791 Boswell referred to the "excellent Dedication of his Juvenal,"[23] and as late as 1802, William Gifford discussed both Dryden's translation and his remarks in the "Discourse."[24] Moreover, one finds frequent allusions to Dryden's work throughout the Restoration and eighteenth century. In his *De re poetica* (London, 1694), a collection of representative ideas on poetry, Sir Thomas Pope Blount quotes Dryden's remarks in his "Dedic. *before* Juvenal" on the origin of invective satire (p. 42). Steele alludes to the frontispiece of "the *English Juvenal*" in the *Spectator*, no. 32 (1711), while in no. 37 (1711) Addison advises Leonora to include "*Dryden's Juvenal*" in her library. In John Ozell's translation of Boileau's *Works* (1712) a bookseller's note refers to and quotes approvingly Dryden's discussion of the mock-heroic; the discussion quoted follows Dryden's description of the "design of a proper satire" (1: 138). Sir Richard Blackmore, in his "Essay on Wit" (1716), alludes to the "Dedication of *Juvenal, made English,* to the late famous Earl of *Dorset*."[25] In his letter "To Matthew Prior, Esq.; Upon the Roman Satirists" (1721), John Dennis observes that "the Generality of Readers are more delighted with *Juvenal* than they are with *Horace,* because *Dryden* is more delighted with him [in the 'Discourse']."[26] Edward Young, perhaps following Dryden's precedent, briefly compares the beauties and faults of Horace and Juvenal in the Preface to his *Love of Fame* (1725–28). Dryden also had said that Boileau was "a living Horace and a Juvenal," a remark which was later echoed in Young's "*Boileau* has joyn'd both the *Roman* Satirists."[27] In 1728 John Oldmixon paraphrases Dryden's first note

22. *A Translation of Juvenal and Persius into English Verse*, 2d ed. (London, 1786), pp. iii-iv, xiv-xvi, 195-96.
23. *Boswell's Life of Johnson*, ed. George Birkbeck Hill, and rev. L. F. Powell (Oxford: Clarendon Press, 1934–50), 4: 38.
24. *The Satires of Decimus Junius Juvenalis* (London, 1802), pp. l, lx-lxvi.
25. *Essays upon Several Subjects* (London, 1716), pp. 224-25.
26. *Critical Works of John Dennis*, Hooker, 2: 218.
27. *Essays*, 2: 26; Edward Young, *Love of Fame, The Universal Passion. In Seven Characteristical Satires*, 2d ed. (London, 1728), sig. A4ᵛ.

to Persius' First Satire thus: "DRYDEN says, the Commentators confess, that this *Labeo* is no where mention'd, but in this Satyr of *Persius*; yet *Casaubon* has found out that his Name was *Atticus Labeo*, and that he made a *foolish* Translation of *Homer*."[28] And in 1750 David Watson admits that he was "greatly obliged" to "Mr. *Dryden, in his admirable Preface before the English Translation of Juvenal*."[29]

Samuel Johnson knew the translation of Juvenal and Persius at least as early as 1728, when he took with him to Oxford "Dryden's Juvenal."[30] His admiration for Dryden was so great that in the first volume of the *Dictionary* (1755) there are about 5,600 illustrations from his works. Only Shakespeare is cited more often (8,694 times), whereas Pope provides illustrations for only 2,108 words.[31] These quotations include more than 470 citations from the "Dedication to Juvenal" and prove that Johnson knew well the exact passages in which Dryden discusses the design of formal verse satire. For example, Johnson illustrates the word *underplot* with a sentence which occurs immediately after Dryden's initial statement about the unity of the satiric structure; he borrows his illustration of the second meaning of *declamatory*, "appealing to the passions," from the passage in which Dryden notes Juvenal's adherence to satire's *ex officio* rule to give the reader "some one precept of moral virtue, and to caution him against some one particular vice or folly"; his illustration of *arraignment* is also taken from the same paragraph and immediately precedes the sentence which includes *declamatory*. In the

---

28. Père Dominique Bouhours, *The Arts of Logick and Rhetorick, Illustrated by Examples taken out of the best Authors . . . . To which are added* [*by* John Oldmixon], *Parallel Quotations Out of the Most Eminent English Authors* (London, 1728), pp. 360-61.
29. *Works of Horace*, 2: xl.
30. Allen Lyell Reade, *Johnsonian Gleanings . . . Part V: The Doctor's Life 1728–1735* (London: Privately printed for the Author by Percy Lund, Humphries & Co., 1928), 5: 225. Johnson's knowledge of Dryden's work remained with him. Late in his life he called Dryden the father of English criticism, and both praised and blamed his translation of Juvenal and Persius. See *Lives of the English Poets by Samuel Johnson*, ed. George Birkbeck Hill (Oxford: Clarendon Press, 1905), 1: 385, 446-47.
31. Lewis Freed, "The Sources of Johnson's *Dictionary*" (unpubl. Ph.D. diss., Cornell University, 1939): Dryden, p. 57; Pope, p. 73; Shakespeare, p. 76. Freed has tabulated all the illustrations in the first volume and a few—an unspecified number—from the second.

paragraph following this passage, Dryden said that Persius' "kind of philosophy is one which is the Stoic, and every satire is a comment on one particular dogma of that sect." Johnson may also have had these words in mind when he used part of the "Argument of the First Satyr" of Persius for his illustration of *dogma*. At any rate, this illustration shows that Johnson knew the headnotes in which Dryden provides historical justification for his theory of satire: "Our poet was a stoick philosopher, and all his moral sentences are drawn from the *dogmas* of that sect."[32]

Moreover, Johnson not only had "Dryden's Juvenal" with him in 1735, three years before he wrote *London*, but also referred to it frequently while preparing the *Dictionary* and writing *The Vanity of Human Wishes* in 1748.[33] Thomas Birch records that by August 1748 Johnson's amanuenses had almost finished transcribing his authorities; that by September of 1749 a small part of the *Dictionary* was "almost ready for the Press"; and that, on October 20, 1750, 120 sheets—the first three letters of the alphabet—had already been printed.[34] It is impossible to say on exactly which letter Johnson was working in the autumn of 1748, but it is likely that much or all of letter *A* had been completed. Examination of the illustrative quotations under this letter shows that Johnson cited the translations of Juvenal twenty-six times, including two citations from "*Dryd. iun.*," Persius ten times, and the "Dedication to Juvenal" eight times.[35] We also know that he gathered these and other quotations from "all such

32. See Dryden's *Juvenal and Persius*, p. 4 of "The Satires of Aulus Persius Flaccus" (new pagination and title page after p. 316 of *Juvenal*): "The Reader may observe that our Poet was a Stoick Philosopher; and that all his Moral Sentences, both here, and in all the rest of his Satyrs, are drawn from the Dogma's [sic] of that Sect" (original is italicized throughout). Note too that Joseph Nicol Scott, in his 1755 revision of Bailey's *A New Universal Etymological Dictionary* (London), borrowed Johnson's illustrations for *underpart*, *arraignment*, and *declamatory*.
33. Reade, *Johnsonian Gleanings*, 5: 115; *The Letters of Samuel Johnson*, ed. R. W. Chapman (Oxford: Clarendon Press, 1952), 1: 6, n. 2; James L. Clifford, *Young Sam Johnson* (New York: McGraw-Hill, 1955), pp. 156-57.
34. James H. Sledd and Gwin J. Kolb, *Dr. Johnson's Dictionary* (Chicago: University of Chicago Press, 1955), p. 107.
35. According to William K. Wimsatt, Jr., "there is no other part of the *Dictionary* where Johnson is so meticulous in every way as under the letter A" (*Philosophic Words* [New Haven: Yale University Press, 1948], p. 46).

English writers as were most correct in their language";[36] his immediate selection of "correct" Dryden again indicates that Johnson
knew the "Discourse" well before 1748.

Although less explicit than Johnson's, the remarks of several other
writers also suggest indebtedness to Dryden's essay; in any case,
these authors clearly show awareness of the form of a "true" satire.
In his "Letter Concerning Enthusiasm" (1708), for instance, Shaftesbury sarcastically echoes this notion of the satiric form:

> If the knowing well how to expose any Infirmity or Vice were
> but a sufficient Security for the Vertue which is contrary, how
> excellent an Age might we be presum'd to live in! Never was
> there in our Nation a time known, when Folly and Extravagance
> of every kind was more sharply inspected, or more wittily ridi-
> cul'd. And one might hope at least from this good Symptom,
> that our Age was in no declining State; since whatever our Dis-
> tempers are, we stand so well affected to our Remedys.[37]

Even minor writers and translators in the century were aware of
the demands of the satiric pattern. Thomas Sheridan briefly summarized the individual satires in his translation of Persius (1748), and
made clear the balance of praise and blame in each. The First Satire,
for example, attacks hypocrisy and superstition, and "points out a
properer Way of publick *Worship*," while the Third shows the "Folly
of *Procrastination*; and the great Necessity there is of employing our
Time to the best Purposes."[38] Shortly thereafter, Walter Harte, in his
Essay on Satire (1730), stressed that though the moral of the satire
"must be clear and understood," it is "finer still, if negatively good."
Hence Capeneus "obliquely shows / T'adore those Gods *Aeneas* fears
and knows."[39] Pope was also aware of the satiric pattern, since on
July 31, 1738, Aaron Hill wrote to him about the second part of "One
Thousand Seven Hundred, Thirty-Eight." The poem, Hill says, com-

---

36. Boswell, *Life*, 1: 188, n. 2. Powell epitomizes the remarks of Dr. Thomas
    Percy. Note too that a remark of Johnson's in Sermon 6 also suggests knowl-
    edge of Dryden's concept of satire: see p. 195 of chap. 8, below.
37. *Characteristics of Men, Manners, Opinions, Times* (London, 1711), 1: 9.
38. *The Satyrs of Persius* (London, 1748), p. xi.
39. (London, 1730), p. 10.

bines Juvenalian acrimony with Horatian ease, and "it opposes just *praise* to just *censure,* and therby doubles the *power* of either."[40] John Brown, writing his *Essay on Satire* (London, 1745), described satire's role in a similar way:

> To paint the heart, and catch internal grace;
> By turns bid vice and virtue strike our eyes,
> Now bid a WOLSEY or SEJANUS rise;
> Now with a touch more sacred and refin'd,
> Call forth a BRUTUS' or a SCIPIO's mind. (p. 23)

Perhaps the most eloquent of the minor poets' discussions of the double-nature of satire may be found in the prefatory matter to *The Tears of the Muses* (1738). The unknown author remarks that satire is "a poetical *Janus*; of whose Opposite two Faces, the fairest and best drawn you will find to be Panegyric." Hence he is justified in dedicating his poem to the distinguished "President, Officers, *and* Committie, of the Society for Encouragement *of* Learning."[41] This concept of satire seems to him "to be *New*: or not *practis'd*," for most satire is "either too *rough*, or too *gentle*," and therefore either "*corrodes*" or is merely "sportive and wanton, with what It shou'd *correct*, and discountenance." He thus proposes that the satirists copy the art of the painters, "who, by opposing their *Shades* against *Lights,* call out Darkness into open Distinction."

> So, Enormities, which *Satirists* wou'd censure, are but dimly and imperfectly mark'd, till the *Defect* admits Disgrace, from the Neighbourhood of *Perfection.*—Then Contempt stings more sharply, in *One,* by the compar'd Admiration of the *Other*: Besides, that the Censur'd are driven, at the same Time, from their last little Refuge of Vanity, and can no longer recriminate upon the Censurer his *Ill-nature,* and Malevolence of Purpose.[42]

This author to the contrary, the form—as we have seen—was long known to satirists and expected by readers. Hill, we recall, was aware

40. *The Correspondence of Alexander Pope,* ed. George Sherburn (Oxford: Clarendon Press, 1956), 4: 112.
41. Second ed. (London, 1738), p. iii.
42. *Ibid.,* pp. vii-viii (italics and Roman type inverted).

of it in one of Pope's poems, and Shaftesbury, Addison, Bishop Warburton, Edward Burnaby Greene, and Edward Owen all expressed awareness of the "bi-partite" structure of satire.[43] Warburton, for example, in his edition of Pope's *Works*, clearly points to Pope's ability to teach the virtue opposed to the vice attacked. In the *Epistle to Bathurst* (1733) the poet teaches the use of riches to others, "by the *abuse* that stands opposed to it." Thus "the *true use* of Riches [is shown] in a description of the *abuse,* and how that use is perpetually defeated by *Profusion* and *Avarice.*" Warburton notices a similar technique in Pope's *Epistle to . . . Burlington, of Taste* (1731). He glosses "*What brought Sir Visto's* ill-got wealth *to waste?*" thus: "He then illustrates the above observation by divers examples in every branch of *wrong Taste*; and to set their absurdities in the strongest light, he, in conclusion, contrasts them with several instances of the *true,* in the Nobleman to whom the Epistle is addressed."[44]

But Pope was not always praised for his use of the form. Owen Ruffhead, in his *Life of Pope* (1769), severely criticized Pope's inattention to the proper balance of praise and blame in *The Characters of Women, to a Lady* (1735). Here the satirist defeated his purpose, since he too harshly attacked the foibles of the sex, and scarcely ever interspersed moral precepts, "which may teach them to avoid or amend what is reprehensible. There is but one single line in the whole essay, in which he has offered any thing like *advice* to the fair." Young, according to Ruffhead, was not guilty of this mistake, for in the conclusion of the fifth satire in his *Love of Fame* he directed the sex not only to the "*whom*" they should charm but also "*how,* they should study to charm."[45] The *Epistle to Burlington*, however, deserves great praise because of its properly-made satiric structure. In this epistle Pope not only pleasantly ridicules false taste, but also shows the premises of true taste, first observing, for example, that

43. In addition to the remarks of Shaftesbury quoted above, see his "Essay on the Freedom of Wit and Humour" (1709), in *Characteristics*, 1: 141; see also Addison's *Spectator*, no. 209 (1711); Greene's *Satires of Juvenal Paraphrastically Imitated and Adapted to the Times* (London, 1763), pp. v, vii, xvi; and Owen, *A Translation of Juvenal and Persius*, pp. 213-14, 221-22.

44. *The Works of Alexander Pope, Esq.*, ed. William Warburton (London, 1751), 3: 229-30, 263.

45. Ruffhead, *Life of Pope* (London, 1769), p. 289.

"*good sense* is the foundation of *true taste*, whose office it is to embellish nature with suitable ornaments."[46] Ruffhead later says that it is also "observable . . . with what happy dexterity the poet, in exposing the absurdities of false taste, has negatively prescribed the rules of true taste." Furthermore, he continues, we should note the "admirable beauty in the conclusion of this poem . . . where the poet . . . gives a short summary of his precepts for true taste."[47] Indeed, Pope carried the principle of praise and blame into *The Dunciad* as well as the *Epistles*. Though his main intention was to attack bad writers and bad men, he nevertheless sincerely praised such men as Dryden, Congreve, and Addison, and even praised Cibber himself on the strength of his *Careless Husband*.[48]

Finally, Thomas Warton, in *The History of English Poetry* (1774–81), found the same pattern in Elizabethan satire. Though Hall turned the readers' eyes toward the obscene and immodest object, the effect of this "is to be counteracted by the force and propriety of [Hall's] reproof, by shewing the pernicious consequences of voluptuous excesses, by suggesting motives to an opposite conduct, and by making the picture disgustful by dashes of deformity."[49]

We have seen, then, that the concept of formal verse satire as incorporating attack upon a particular vice and praise of its opposite virtue was well-known at least from the publication of Dacier's essay on satire (1687) to the final volume of Warton's *History of English Poetry* (1781). In England, this concept was made popular through Dryden's "Discourse concerning the Original and Progress of Satyr"; several major and minor authors either referred to it or implied knowledge of it. But discussion of the form had more than theoretical interest: the judgments of Dennis, Hill, Warburton, and Ruffhead suggest that the pattern influenced the reader's expectations of satire, while the satires of Dryden,[50] and, as we will see, Young, Pope, and

46. *Ibid.*, p. 302.
47. *Ibid.*, pp. 305-6. Here, and throughout his *Life of Pope*, Ruffhead is probably indebted to Warburton. See W. L. MacDonald, *Pope and his Critics* (London: J. M. Dent & Sons, 1951), pp. 251-82.
48. Ruffhead, *Life of Pope*, p. 360.
49. W. Carew Hazlitt, ed. (London, 1871), 4: 409.
50. We know that in the headnotes to his translation of Juvenal and Persius Dryden made clear each poem's attack on vice and praise of the opposite vir-

Johnson, and the prefatory matter to *The Tears of the Muses,* suggest that it influenced the practice of satire as well. Adherence to the pattern is surely no more than a necessary rather than sufficient condition for success in formal verse satire; but contemporary awareness and use of it suggest that the terms praise and blame should be part of the modern critical vocabulary for Augustan satire.

tue. The pattern is similar in *Absalom and Achitophel* (1681), where he "taxes" the apparently extreme political innovations of the Whigs and praises the moderation of the Tories. For the contrasting sections of praise and blame, see ll. 173-79, the attack on Shaftesbury, and ll. 69-78, the praise of the Tories. The virtues of the moderate Tory and the vices of the extreme Whig are neatly set forth in the portrait of Edward Seymour (ll. 899-913). For a similar view of the poem, see C. V. Wedgwood, *Poetry and Politics under the Stuarts* (Cambridge, 1960), p. 168.

4

On the Discrimination
of Imitations and Satires

I Imitations

The context reclaimed in the preceding chapters has substantial value
for the modern critic of eighteenth-century Imitation and satire: it
offers not only some of the background necessary for a fuller understanding of specific works, but also the relevant critical tools of
analysis and judgment. Besides, it can save us from certain serious
errors, errors due in large part to the persistent lack of discrimination with which the terms Imitation and satire are used. Certain
poems of Oldham, Pope, and Johnson, for instance, have recently
been misrepresented due to ignorance of the essential role of the parent-poem in an Imitation, and of the different kinds of Imitation a
poet might write. Thus we are told that "both in literary form and
in physical appearance *London* courts comparison" with Pope's *Epilogue to the Satires,* and that "in substance and in manner it differs
sufficiently to challenge him."[1] Strictly speaking, though both poems
are political satires, neither in literary form nor in physical appearance does *London* court comparison with Pope's *Epilogue.* The former is an overt Imitation of Juvenal's Third Satire, prints the imitated lines at the foot of the page, regards the Latin author as normative and part of the beauty of the poem, and, among other things,
implies that modern London is so bad that only comparison with Do-
mitian's Rome can do justice to its degeneracy. Pope's *Epilogue,* on

---

1. John Butt, "Johnson's Practice in the Poetical Imitation," in *New Light on
Dr. Johnson,* ed. Frederick W. Hilles (New Haven: Yale University Press,
1959), p. 19.

the other hand, is an "original" poem that adapts—yet drastically alters—the Horatian dialogue, alludes to classical characters, lines, or thoughts, but does not imitate an entire earlier poem and, therefore, cannot reproduce a complete Latin original for comparison. Moreover, the specific reference to Horatian precedent is placed in the mouth of an "impertinent Censurer" and is not normative; here the modern author—an agent of God—is ethically and poetically superior to a classical figure. Johnson accepts Juvenal as a guide, but Pope rejects Horace; the former is imitative, the latter allusive. Johnson's poem, like Juvenal's, ends by showing one man helping another to write satire. The literal fact implies its own metaphor, the continuity of the small but vigorous group of those who, through the centuries, oppose vice and inculcate virtue; it is thus "communal" and draws part of its affirmation from its role as Imitation. Pope's poem ends with the rejection not only of the efficacy but the feasibility of satire.[2] The lone man, the last satirist, is reduced to a symbolic protest against worldly forces which have finally overwhelmed him; it is thus "individualistic" and draws part of its affirmation from rejection of Imitation. One poet uses the form of Imitation as an aspect of his meaning; the other avoids it because (in part) he has rejected Horace's apparent political and satiric values, and no longer can buttress his character with "*An Answer from* Horace." In *London* and the *Epilogue*, then, Johnson and Pope do differ in substance and in manner; but there can be little "challenge" since, despite similar political views and satiric tone, they are actually doing different things.

It is also an error to assume that all Imitations use the same method and that, on the basis of Imitation alone, one can make qualitative distinctions between Oldham and Johnson as Imitators of Juvenal's Third Satire. These remarks, for instance, are too monolithic regarding Imitation: "in Oldham's work we may fairly look for the inherent possibilities and limitations of this way of writing as these presented themselves to his English successors. It requires of the reader just so much familiarity with the original poem as will make him quick to recall, when adroitly prompted, some memorable passage; of the writer, a knack of analogy: the art, or trick, of awakening such recol-

2. See Pope's note at the conclusion of the second *Dialogue*, p. 162, n. 36, below.

lections."[3] Unfortunately, this ignores distinctions between the Imitator's arts. Oldham is an Imitator and modernizer whose chief allegiance is to Juvenal; if the classically-oriented reader recalls the parallel passages, that is splendid, but one is still to be primarily aware of the ancient author who, through deft modification, is made to speak "as if he were living, and writing now." It is thus unfair to attack Oldham because he "had encumbered himself with all the references (direct or oblique) to the particulars of Roman life in his original."[4] That was precisely Oldham's job; he is not encumbering himself, he is trying to translate a poem and be reasonably faithful to his author while modernizing names, places, and allusions where possible.

Similarly, it is critically unwise to praise Johnson because "*he* cuts out those [references] which refuse to be translated into English terms," and thereby "reduces Juvenal's 322 lines to 263."[5] For one thing, Johnson did not appropriately select all of his parallels;[6] for another, counting lines is a curious way of proving superiority. But, most important, Johnson's mode of Imitation is different from Oldham's. The "familiarity with the original" which is unnecessary for Oldham is vital for Johnson, and so he forces the reader into comparison by insisting upon publication of the Latin at the foot of his own page. We cannot fully understand Johnson's poem without understanding Juvenal's; but we are only interested in Juvenal in order to see how the Englishman incorporates or rejects the meaning and methods of the Roman. Our focus is thus on Johnson's poem, whereas when reading Oldham's it is on Juvenal, who happens to be wearing modern dress. "Johnson" as poet is essential in his Imitation; "Oldham" is irrelevant in his.

We should, therefore, recognize that a poem (like Pope's *Epilogue*) which employs certain classical devices and allusions is not a formal

3. Mary Lascelles, "Johnson and Juvenal," in *New Light on Dr. Johnson*, p. 38.
4. *Ibid.*, p. 45.
5. *Ibid.*
6. See Johnson's note appended to ll. 194-209: "This was by Hitch a Bookseller justly remarked to be no picture of modern manners, though it might be true at Rome" (*Samuel Johnson: Poems*, The Yale Edition of the Works of Samuel Johnson, vol. 6, ed. E. L. McAdam, Jr., with George Milne (New Haven: Yale University Press, 1964), p. 57.

Imitation, and that the Imitation itself takes many different forms. Central to all these, however, is the presence of the parent-poem, whether altered or integral. We should therefore doubt the value of a recent distinction between the Imitations of Pope and Johnson. Johnson's *London*, we are told, represents "a neoclassicism of form," and Pope's *Imitations of Horace* "a neoclassicism of matter." Pope (in *Bolingbroke*, for instance, *Epistles*, i. 1), "is not concerned with the form and tone of the Horatian epistle . . . but with its content, with the total statement of the poem . . . with [the Latin sentences'] import as they had been explained and amplified by generations of readers and commentators." Pope represents Horace as understood by "the late Renaissance," as a poet with "an ethical doctrine of eternal and unchangeable validity, whose temporal applications may vary infinitely without in the least altering the essential content of the poem." Johnson's *London*, it seems, is quite different:

> It echoes a tone, a style, a format—the famous Juvenalian *saeva indignatio* and an equally famous diatribe against city life: what it does not reproduce is the essential matter of Juvenal's poem in anything like the manner in which Pope presents Horace's. Johnson imitates primarily the surface statement, not the underlying core of the poem: thus *London* contains what one rarely finds in Pope's *Imitations*, a major passage (194–209) that is entirely inapplicable as a criticism of eighteenth-century England. Even the bare bones of the rhetorical structure that served to support Pope's poems are missing from Johnson's: all that is reproduced is a tone of voice and a bare format, the linear and topical progression of Juvenal's poem. *London* lacks the Renaissance pedigree of Pope's *Imitations*, and this seems to me to constitute an *essential* difference between the two. *London* and poems like it—much of the poetry of the later eighteenth century—form the real poetry of statement, and to lump them all together with Pope's poems or Dryden's seems a needless critical confusion.[7]

7. Thomas E. Maresca, *Pope's Horatian Poems* (Columbus, Ohio: Ohio State University Press, 1966), pp. 197-98.

Unfortunately, this distinction adds more critical confusion. What, for instance, is the "essential matter" and "underlying core" which Johnson fails to imitate? Does not Pope reject the "essential matter" of Horace's *Epistle to Augustus*? Is Johnson's fire-scene in *London* any less accurate than Pope's derivation of English satire in the *Epistle to Augustus*? Would not modern historians question Pope's estimate of Walpole's effect on eighteenth-century England? And, after all, is not literal accuracy an irrelevant criterion? Does not Johnson actually "reproduce" a tone of voice quite different from Juvenal's, and can we not say that he falters not by following Juvenal too closely but not closely enough in certain vital respects? Can one properly claim that *London* lacks a "Renaissance pedigree" without first showing Johnson's ignorance or rejection of available editions or versions of Juvenal? What, after all, does "poetry of statement" mean? Do not all poems "state" something? Does this—let us hope not—mean that Johnson is once again placed on the bad "denotative" side of poetry and that Pope (and Dryden) are on the good "connotative" side? What other poems of the later eighteenth century is *London* like? Certainly not those of Gray, Collins, Smart, Cowper, Crabbe, or Blake, and only in certain minor respects like Churchill's satires. And, finally, if Johnson's imitative neoclassicism "consists primarily in formal imitation of the ancients and observance of supposedly classical proprieties," what proprieties is he observing and how are these different from Pope's?[8] Surely this vague distinction between imitation of form and matter raises more problems than it pretends to solve and creates an artificial barrier between aspects of poetry which are intimately related.

If this will not do, in what ways can we distinguish between the imitative modes of Pope and Johnson? The attitude towards the original again serves as a sort of bench mark. Both poets have the same conception, since both announce the poem imitated and draw the reader's attention to relevant lines. But Pope is far more attentive to his job, more trusting of the peculiar value of his genre, and willing to make greater demands upon his audience. The early editions of Pope's Imitations printed the Latin and English on facing pages, with

8. *Ibid.*, p. 198.

the Latin in italics; words or phrases demanding particular attention were set in Roman type and, in some cases, in solid caps (Horace, *Satires*, ii. 1, 69–70; UNI AEQUUS VIRTUTI ATQUAE EJUS AMI-CUS; l. 121 of Pope's Imitation). Johnson, we know, insisted that the Latin be published at the foot of his *London*, since part of the beauty of the performance consisted in comparison of the poems;[9] but John-son's frequent use of "&c." instead of the complete Latin context makes us miss both Pope's meticulous awareness of the original, and the extra effort which insists all the more that the reader must know two poems before he can wholly understand one. Moreover, in *The Vanity of Human Wishes* Johnson merely included the numbers of each section imitated; the reader unfamiliar with Juvenal's Tenth Satire would either have to find his own copy or, as may be more likely, ignore it. There is always the possibility that diminution of the original's presence is due to the publisher's penury, or the com-positor's, not the poet's, art; perhaps—but if in 1738 the unknown Johnson successfully demanded the overt presence of Juvenal, in 1749 the better-known Johnson could surely have done the same. It is more likely that he did not care as much as Pope did; Johnson's later remarks reinforce this conjecture and indicate both his discom-fort with a central aspect of Imitation and, unfortunately, a limita-tion in his understanding of its great variety. For instance, in the "Life of Pope" he says of Pope's *Imitations*:

> This mode of imitation, in which the ancients are familiarised by adapting their sentiments to modern topicks, by making Horace say of Shakespeare what he originally said of Ennius, and accommodating his satires on Pantolabus and Nomentanus to the flatterers and prodigals of our own time, was first prac-tised in the reign of Charles the Second by Oldham and Roch-ester, at least I remember no instances more ancient. It is a kind of middle composition between translation and original design, which pleases when the thoughts are unexpectedly appli-

9. Aubrey L. Williams has commented on Pope's practice in reprinting the imi-tated poem (*Restoration and Eighteenth-Century Literature: Essays in Honor of Alan Dugald McKillop*, ed. Carroll Camden [Chicago: University of Chicago Press, 1963], p. 311). See also nn. 38 and 39, to chap. 1, above.

cable and the parallels lucky. It seems to have been Pope's favourite amusement, for he has carried it further than any
former poet.[10]

For Johnson it is not the modern author but "Horace" who speaks,
and the Imitation is not a respected form but an "amusement" which
pleases through the reader's awareness of lucky parallels. The modern poet has little room for freedom, since he must familiarize the
thoughts of the ancients. Moreover, by grouping the practice of Pope,
Oldham, and Rochester under one imitative mode—"a middle composition between translation and original design"—he obliterates the
large spectrum upon which these poets' relevant poems exist, a spectrum which, we have seen, extends from virtual translation to virtual
rejection of the parent-poem.

Another remark in the "Life of Pope" amplifies Johnson's later
hostility to the form.

> The *Imitations of Horace* seem to have been written as re-
> laxations of his genius. This employment became his favourite
> by its facility; the plan was ready to his hand, and nothing was
> required but to accommodate as he could the sentiments of an
> old author to recent facts or familiar images; but what is easy
> is seldom excellent: such imitations cannot give pleasure to
> common readers. The man of learning may be sometimes sur-
> prised and delighted by an unexpected parallel; but the com-
> parison requires knowledge of the original, which will likewise
> often detect strained applications. Between Roman images and
> English manners there will be an irreconcilable dissimilitude,
> and the work will be generally uncouth and party-coloured;
> neither original nor translated, neither ancient nor modern.[11]

Here Imitation seems to be the lazy poet's genre; he does not turn an
older poem into a new poetical "thing," but merely "accommodates"

---

10. *Lives of the English Poets*, ed. G. Birkbeck Hill (Oxford: Clarendon Press,
1905), 3:176. In the *Dictionary* Johnson observes that the verb amuse is
"frequently taken in a sense bordering on contempt." His illustrative quotations bear this out.
11. *Lives of the English Poets*, Hill, 3:246-47.

the old to the new. Accordingly, Johnson fears, the specialized audience for such a poem focuses upon cultural similarities or dissimilarities rather than upon the more permanent facets of a poem's value. That, I suggest, is behind Johnson's ultimate denigration of the genre of Imitation. Such compositions as West's Imitations of Spenser are pleasant in their kind, but

> are not to be reckoned among the great achievements of intellect, because their effect is local and temporary; they appeal not to reason or passion, but to memory, and presuppose an accidental or artificial state of mind. An Imitation of Spenser is nothing to a reader, however acute, by whom Spenser has never been perused. Works of this kind may deserve praise, as proofs of great industry and great nicety of observation; but the highest praise, the praise of genius, they cannot claim. The noblest beauties of art are those of which the effect is co-extended with rational nature, or at least with the whole circle of polished life; what is less than this can be only pretty, the plaything of fashion and the amusement of a day.[12]

Johnson censures the Imitation because it apparently opposes some of his fundamental concepts of poetry and life. His reasoning may have followed these lines: men experience hate and love in both Johnson's London and Juvenal's Rome. Though human nature is uniform, the "modes of life,"[13] as Johnson says in the *Adventurer*, no. 95 (1753), are mutable, and each age's expression of them must differ. Paralleling these modes not only may point the reader towards a fruitless awareness of an "irreconcilable dissimilitude," but also emphasizes the mutable modes rather than immutable nature. The author (as discussed in the *Idler*, no. 59 [1759]) who "lays out his labours upon temporary subjects, easily finds readers, and quickly loses them; for what should make the book valued when its subject is no more?"[14] Only the poet who addresses himself and his reader

12. *Ibid.*, 332-33. See p. 29 of chap. 1, for a comment on this passage.
13. *Samuel Johnson: The Idler and Adventurer*, The Yale Edition of the Works of Samuel Johnson, vol. 2, ed. W. J. Bate, John M. Bullitt, and L. F. Powell (New Haven: Yale University Press, 1963), p. 427.
14. *Ibid.*, p. 184.

to reason or passion, rather than the "accidental" states of a mind or culture, can hope to endure and win the praise of genius. The Imitation's appeal, Johnson felt, was not to "the whole circle of polished life" or even to "common readers" but to the antiquarian taste, to the mind stored with easily recalled past poetry. The comparison of one civilization's modes with another's evokes the "local and temporary. . . . the plaything of fashion and the amusement of a day." It may also be dangerous or foolish. Gray's *Bard*, for instance, unwisely revives a "mode" peculiar to Horatian Rome, a fiction present in Horace's prophecy of Nereus. "The fiction of Horace was to the Romans credible; but its revival disgusts us with apparent and unconquerable falsehood. 'Incredulus odi'."[15] Rejuvenation of similar follies in *Lycidas* helps to explain Johnson's hostility to that and other pastoral poems: we must endure our modern fictions, but the poet who willingly resuscitates the nonsense of the ancients is doing his audience and his art a grave disservice.

The Imitations of Pope and Johnson, then, both need and demand the reader's awareness of the original; but Pope—whose efforts in translating Homer forced particular attention to his text—needs and demands it more, insists on the reader's intimate knowledge of his sources and the way they function in the new poem, and brings him more actively into the poetic experience. Pope is more closely bound to the parent-poem but, paradoxically, is still wholly "original." For Johnson, however, and particularly for the "mature" Johnson, the dangers of this mode outweighed its advantages. In Pope's case and in his own *Vanity of Human Wishes* he is wrong and has misrepresented certain aspects of literary history. He has ignored the versatility and the appeal of the Imitation, underrated the possibilities of metaphor in the process of comparison and, in short, underrated both the poetic effort behind the successful Imitation and the effort the audience is willing to make to enhance its pleasure. At any rate, I hope to have shown the utility of a knowledge of certain relevant literary traditions. The different kinds of Imitation produce different poems, even though they have the same generic name; hence poems like the *Vanity* and *Fortescue* demand knowledge of the original but

15. *Lives of the English Poets*, Hill, 3: 438.

may take different attitudes towards it. Since we must be aware of the original, at appropriate places in subsequent chapters I compare and contrast *London* and the *Vanity* with Juvenal's Third and Tenth Satires respectively. However, these poems and the others discussed in the following chapters are not all formal Imitations, though all are formal verse satires.

II Satires

The term "satire" is probably vaguer than Imitation itself. In spite of the consequent problems for literary historians, this is as it should be. In the *Rambler*, no. 125 (1751), Johnson warns his readers about the difficulty of defining genres:

> imagination, a licentious and vagrant faculty, unsusceptible of limitations, and impatient of restraint, has always endeavoured to baffle the logician, to perplex the confines of distinction, and burst the inclosures of regularity. There is therefore scarcely any species of writing, of which we can tell what is its essence, and what are its constituents; every new genius produces some innovation, which, when invented and approved, subverts the rules which the practice of foregoing authors had established.[16]

Johnson is undoubtedly right both in rejecting rigid classifications and in suggesting that there are, nevertheless, "rules"—we should substitute *conventions*—"which the practice of foregoing authors had established." These remarks suggest that an analytic view of satire is more accurate and fruitful than the synoptic—than seeking, say, a "plot" or broad definition applicable to all satire. Accordingly, my remarks apply only to formal verse satire of the Restoration and eighteenth century, to that satire generally in heroic couplets, based in part upon the varied examples of Horace, Persius, and Juvenal, and including attacks upon a specific vice and praise of its opposite virtue. Much of what I say may apply to other satiric or literary modes, but much does not. In many cases, therefore, one can better

16. *The Works of Samuel Johnson* (Oxford, 1825), 3: 93.

determine the intention and tone of a satire by examining the way in which norms are used, by determining what is "praised" and how that praise functions in the work.

Mac Flecknoe, for instance, is largely punitive towards its victim and comic towards its audience;[17] it draws us away from any implicit norms by appealing to our sadistic rather than corrigible natures. Presumably, the audience enjoys seeing Dryden's easily-defeated enemy get his burlesque come-uppance. Hence Shadwell is never a threat to the author, literature, politics, society, or the organizing threads of the universe, and it is a "harmless war with words" that Panton wages (l. 84). Though one assumes that good writers are preferable to bad, Dryden focuses on abuse, not instruction.

The Dunciad also satirizes bad writers, but in a far more "tragic" context. If the norms in *Mac Flecknoe* were submerged, those in *The Dunciad* are overt but extremely tenuous, as even the light of wit, a projection from God, is put out. The poet must resort to mention of a few noble figures like Handel or Swift, whereas in his formal verse satires we see comparable figures either living and acting in Pope's home, or having some demonstrable, if limited, influence upon life. He also implicitly invokes the distant Greek, Roman, or Miltonic literary traditions through his own style and allusions and, ultimately, invokes the dying voice of the poet himself, whose final plea for light is denied in the poem and, paradoxically, granted by posterity. Nevertheless, "Universal Darkness buries All" in *The Dunciad*, and its affirmation is even more meager than that in the *Dialogues* or the generally more confident affirmation in Pope's other satiric poems.

The Dunciad, to adapt a phrase from section 1 of *A Tale of a Tub*, falls into the revelatory or apocalyptic class of satire.[18] Together with works like the *Tale* itself and *Gulliver's Travels*, it does not offer a viable modus operandi for functioning in the world; the chief aim

17. For a study of *Mac Flecknoe* as punitive and comic, see Ian Jack, *Augustan Satire* (Oxford: Clarendon Press, 1952), pp. 43-52. For similar remarks, see Edward W. Rosenheim, Jr., *Swift and the Satirist's Art* (Chicago: University of Chicago Press, 1963), pp. 13, 24, 25.
18. Swift, *A Tale of a Tub, To which is added The Battle of the Books and the Mechanical Operation of the Spirit*, ed. A. C. Guthkelch and D. Nichol Smith, 2d ed. (Oxford: Clarendon Press, 1958), p. 68. Subsequent references are cited in the text.

of such works is to force man in general and specific groups in particular to see their true state. In the *Tale*, for instance, Swift does not overtly suggest ways of ridding the world of creatures like the modern narrator; though ways may suggest themselves to the reader, that is not Swift's central task.

Similarly, *Gulliver's Travels* shows Gulliver learning to see mankind's proper state. Only then, after he has grasped the full terror of man's humanly incurable original sin, is there any hope (and a very feeble hope it is) of alleviating some of its Yahoo bestiality. Thus the foolish and massive pride of part 1 begins to lessen in part 2, where Gulliver is able to laugh at the strutting grandeur of English lords and ladies,[19] is mistaken by a monkey for "a young one of his own Species" (p. 122), and is frequently threatened by animals. Of even greater importance, however, is Gulliver's Kafka-esque dream as he is asleep on his Brobdingnagian mistress' bed. It shows him waking from false to true vision, and from dream to reality. Man is not the kingly center of his family—much less a giant among pygmies—but is a miniscule creature whose voice cannot be heard in the vast and friendless world about him; he is frustrated even in his efforts to tend to his natural functions, and is attacked by immense rats. Only his lonely heroism and good fortune can save him:

> I SLEPT about two Hours, and dreamed I was at home with my Wife and Children, which aggravated my Sorrows when I

19. *Gulliver's Travels*, The Prose Works of Jonathan Swift, vol. 11, ed. Herbert Davis (Oxford: Clarendon Press, 1959), p. 107. Subsequent references are cited in text. There are far too many articles on *Gulliver* in general and Book 4 in particular to be listed here. For a useful sample, see two recent anthologies: *Gulliver's Travels: An Annotated Text with Critical Essays*, ed. Robert A. Greenberg (New York: Norton Critical Editions, 1961); *A Case book on Gulliver Among the Houyhnhnms*, ed. Milton P. Foster (New York: Thomas Y. Crowell Co., 1961). To these should be added R. S. Crane's important essay, "The Houyhnhnms, the Yahoos, and the History of Ideas," in *Reason and the Imagination*, ed. Joseph Mazzeo (New York: Columbia University Press, 1965), pp. 231-53 (reprinted in Ronald S. Crane, *The Idea of the Humanities* [Chicago: University of Chicago Press, 1967], 2:261-82). Crane lists several of the "soft-line" essays on pp. 231-32, n. 2. For other relevant remarks, see Edward W. Rosenheim, Jr., "The Fifth Voyage of Lemuel Gulliver: A Footnote," *MP*, 60 (1962): 103-19; Ronald Paulson, *The Fictions of Satire* (Baltimore: Johns Hopkins Press, 1967), pp. 162-85; Donald J. Greene, "On Swift's 'Scatological' Poems," *Sewanee Review*, 75 (1967): 688-89.

awaked and found my self alone in a vast Room, between two
and three Hundred Foot wide, and above two Hundred high;
lying in a Bed twenty Yards wide. My Mistress was gone about
her household Affairs, and had locked me in. The Bed was eight
Yards from the Floor. Some natural Necessities required me to
get down: I durst not presume to call, and if I had, it would
have been in vain with such a Voice as mine at so great a Distance from the Room where I lay, to the Kitchen where the
Family kept. While I was under these Circumstances, two Rats
crept up the Curtains, and ran smelling backwards and forwards
on the Bed: One of them came up almost to my Face; where-
upon I rose in a Fright, and drew out my Hanger to defend my
self. These horrible Animals had the Boldness to attack me on
both Sides, and one of them held his Fore-feet to my Collar; but
I had the good Fortune to rip up his Belly before he could do
me any Mischief . . . . After this Exploit I walked gently to and
fro on the Bed, to recover my Breath and Loss of Spirits. These
Creatures were of the Size of a large Mastiff, but infinitely more
nimble and fierce; so that if I had taken off my Belt before I
went to sleep, I must have infallibly been torn to Pieces and
devoured. (pp. 92–93)

By the time he is on his third voyage, Gulliver's sorrows are aggra-
vated once more, as his pride regarding British achievements dissi-
pates. He sees the decadence "of an *English* Countenance" (p. 201)
and realizes that the present generation has replaced its ancestors'
"pure native virtues" with "every Vice and Corruption that can possibly be learned in a Court" (pp. 201–2). His meeting with the
Struldbruggs, replete with implicit self-praise and "Visions of what I
should do if I were a King, a General, or a Great Lord" (p. 209),
again corrects his faulty view of man: "I grew heartily ashamed of
the pleasing Visions I had formed; and thought no Tyrant could
invent a Death into which I would not run with Pleasure from such
a Life" (p. 214). His mistake, a "Gentleman" suggests and Gulliver
does not question, is due to "the common Imbecility of human
Nature" (p. 211).

The improper vision of human nature finally disappears during his stay with the Houyhnhnms. Gulliver confesses that the latters' virtues "had so far opened mine Eyes, and enlarged my Understanding, that I began to view the Actions and Passions of Man in a very different Light," and he sees "a thousand" new faults in himself "whereof I had not the least Perception before" (p. 258). Proper vision has thus replaced false vision, the reality the dream, and open eyes closed eyes. But Gulliver still has much to learn: "*Truth* appeared so amiable to me, that I determined upon sacrificing every thing to it" (p. 258). But truth is not "amiable"; it includes, among other things, recognition of his inescapable Yahoo situation and unfortunate expulsion from the land of the Houyhnhnms. And truth does in fact demand that he sacrifice everything to it: he is misanthropic, a willing outcast from the home and hearth he dreamed of in Brobdingnag, and is thought mad by his fellows. His brief encounter with an ideal order has rendered him incapable of living in the human world as we know it; yet he is also constitutionally incapable of living like a Houyhnhnm.[20] Though the Houyhnhnms are as normative as ever, Gulliver himself is tainted; thus his quotation from the *Aeneid*, II, 79–80, is doubly significant. Sinon is the Greek bearing the gift of the apparently harmless horse; he tells the Trojans that though Fortune has made him miserable she has not made him false and a liar (p. 292). Gulliver is not only associated with a liar, but, of more importance, with a horse and a long and costly battle to break down the walls of a great city. Open attack has failed and subterfuge is necessary; it will be the appar-

20. In "Errors Concerning the Houyhnhnms," *MP*, 56 (1958) : 97, George Sherburn cites several analogues to Gulliver's situation. He also notes that for Swift "fondness" was a derogatory term. The definitions of *fond* and related terms in Johnson's *Dictionary* verify this: virtually all agree that to be *fond* is to be "Foolish; silly, indiscreet; imprudent; injudicious." Under "To Fondle" Johnson includes these lines from Book 1 of *Gulliver*: "They are allowed to kiss the child at meeting and parting; but a professor, who always stands by, will not suffer them to use any *fondling* expressions." He cites L'Estrange as authority for *fondling*: "Partiality in a parent is commonly unlucky; for *fondlings* are in danger to be made fools, and the children that are least cockered make the best and wisest men." In addition to numerous other attacks on *fondness*, Johnson includes these lines from "*Locke on Education, sect. 4*" to illustrate *cocker*, a synonym for *fondle*: "Most children's constitutions are spoiled by *cockering* and tenderness."

ently innocent *Gulliver's Travels,* merely another travel-book, that we will invite into our "city" and that will (Swift hopes) destroy our pride. The *Travels'* central purposes are to evoke a savage truth, open humanity's gates to the horse "enemy"[21] and break down the walls of our pride before even thinking about subsequent improvement. Without this the purity of the Houyhnhnms "love thy neighbor like thyself" is impossible. The norms—or, instead, the ideals—in *Gulliver* demand total revision of corrupt human nature if they are to be operative.

Revelatory satire, then, is primarily concerned with depicting a terrible situation within or around us, rather than holding out hope for man's change or portraying the presence of a clearly workable norm for this world. The latter is the case in Augustan formal verse satire. Perhaps this important difference between the two satiric modes may be seen by contrasting *Gulliver's Travels* and *The Vanity of Human Wishes.* In both the Christian must recognize and accept his original sin before he can hope to ameliorate it. But the methods of the satirists are different. Johnson overtly rasises these questions: "Where then shall hope and fear their objects find?/Must dull suspence corrupt the stagnant mind?" And he just as overtly answers them: "Enquirer, cease, petitions yet remain/ Which heav'n may hear, nor deem religion vain." The norm is clear; so is the vividly portrayed result of adherence to it: "Celestial wisdom calms the mind, /And makes the happiness she does not find." But this wisdom evokes unhappiness in Gulliver; he does not know that he cannot live up to it; it separates him from the communion of man and—for some modern readers—even makes that wisdom suspect.[22] In his letter to

21. Earl R. Wasserman has recently mentioned this passage: "Surely the reader is expected to recall that Sinon was, in fact, the most heroic of liars and that through his deceitful protestation of truthfulness he persuaded the Trojans to admit another kind of fictitious horse—to the destruction of their city" ("The Limits of Allusion in *The Rape of the Lock*," *JEGP,* 65 [1966]: 444).

22. "To this Hour," Gulliver says of his wife and children, "they dare not presume to touch my Bread, or drink out of the same Cup" (pp. 289-90). Herbert Davis observes that an Anglican priest could not "use such words unconsciously, and such a one as Swift must have been willing to allow these overtones to remain—the bread and the cup; and even the word *presume,* from the opening of the prayer before the act of communion; even

Cousin Sympson Gulliver argues that the numerous reformations he hoped to effect "were plainly deducible from the Precepts delivered in my Book" (p. 7). The formal verse satirist would probably not have left these for an uncertain deduction.

Similarly, Young's *Love of Fame,* Pope's *Imitations of Horace* and his *Ethic Epistles,* and Johnson's *London,* all offer norms whose presence and varying degrees of hope and efficacy are demanded by the form itself. These poems attack abuses in the national or human situation, and insist that, in some way, one may either correct, punish, or escape from them. Of course here too they work in different ways. The *Love of Fame* offers so many facile norms that its credibility as a satire is threatened, and Pope's *Epilogue to the Satires* offers so little hope for the practicability of its norms that it exists at the furthest end of the spectrum of formal verse satire. But it is one nevertheless: Pope balances the portrait of the perverted court Heaven with a vision of the true Heaven. One sees protest plus achievable (if neglected) norms in the *Epilogue,* but protest plus darkness in *The Dunciad.* The poet is still alive, if ultimately silent, in the former, but asleep and a victim of Dullness in the latter. One poem ends in Britain's spiritual defeat, the other in universal darkness; one shows the inability of the good man to affect the vicious about him and, consequently, falling back on a protective Heaven; the other shows all communication cut off as God's creating word is nullified. Even *London* which (heretically) portrays an ineffectual God in that city, also portrays a viable norm for man in this world, and shows his refusal to be defeated, since the poem ends in the vigorous propagation of satire. In formal verse satire achievement of the norm is difficult—sometimes incredibly so—but possible; there is generally a living example and often a benevolent,

---

the phrase *suffer them,* of the children's eating in the same room; even the tone ringing so clearly in the phrase *to this hour.* There is here . . . evidence enough of Swift's intention to emphasize Gulliver's complete estrangement from the human race, his inability to live any longer in communion with his own kind" ("Swift's use of Irony," in Maximillian E. Novak and Herbert J. Davis, *The Uses of Irony: Papers on Defoe and Swift Read at a Clark Library Seminar,* April 2, 1966 [Los Angeles: William Andrews Clark Memorial Library, 1966], pp. 55-56).

actively engaged God. He may reject the depraved world, but—like God in the Biblical tale—He preserves order as long as there is one good man. In the revelatory *Dunciad* the last good man dies with the final word of the poem; and in comic satire like *Mac Flecknoe* normative benevolence is submerged under comic hostility.

The essential pattern of formal verse satire, we have seen, is attack on one vice and praise of its opposite virtue. This scheme offers tremendous scope for use of norms. Neither in Roman nor in English satire was the use of the satiric pattern limited to one rigid form. The praise might be implicit in the vice attacked, as in Juvenal's Sixth Satire, on women; or it might emerge as one major and one or more minor normative statements, as in *London;* perhaps, as in several of Pope's satires, the speaker and a small group of friends might embody an example of the good life; there might also be a long series of attacks followed by a shorter section recommending the opposite virtue, as in *The Vanity of Human Wishes;* or, as in Young's first six satires in the *Love of Fame,* the poet might use interlocking sections of praise and blame and, as in the Seventh, overt panegryic of Walpole and George I. In his *Two Epistles to Mr. Pope Concerning the Authors of the Age* (1730) Young places most of the "blame" part of his satire in the first epistle, written from London, while he reserves the second, from Oxford, for most of the "praise." Epistolary satire, indeed, adds even more possible variation to the satiric pattern. As I will show later, satiric poems called *epistles* were likely to include more praise and to be more moderate in tone and diction than the harsher non-epistolary satire. Thus Pope's *Epistle to Dr. Arbuthnot* is amply stored with satiric attacks, but it has large sections of overt praise and a "happy" ending, since the poet and his values triumph. The *Epilogue to the Satires,* on the other hand, includes far less praise, and ends with the defeat of the poet's values in this world (though not, of course, in the better, divine, world, which is untainted). In short, the pattern of formal verse satire, like the Imitation, is capable of immense variation, and affords the poet an appropriate and fluid guide to his art.

Accordingly, in the following chapters I will focus on problems specifically relevant to Imitation and satire: since historical evidence suggests that these are proper criteria, in what ways can the presence of the original and/or the pattern of formal verse satire illuminate several satires of Young, Pope, and Johnson?

5

Edward Young's
Love of Fame, The Universal Passion.
In Seven Characteristical Satires

Both individually and collectively, the seven satires in Young's *Love of Fame* were the most important formal verse satires between the death of Dryden (1700) and the publication of Pope's *Epistle to Burlington* (1731). Each gained immediate popularity and the "complete" poem had at least six different reprintings between 1728, the first collected edition with the Preface, and 1752.[1] In its unified form the poem was read throughout much of the eighteenth and nineteenth centuries, and relevant sections were often, sometimes favorably, compared to Pope's *Epistle to a Lady*.[2] An anonymous author

1. *Love of Fame* was issued in seven separate numbers: One through Four in 1725; "Satire the Last," now Seven, in 1726; and the satires on women, Five and Six, in 1727 and 1728 respectively. The London 1728 "second edition"—which I use as my text—is thus the first collected edition and the first to include the important Preface. Though there were changes in the 1757 edition of his *Works*, and the sixth (1763) edition of *Love and Fame*, they are not relevant for our purposes. For some of these, see Charles Edward Frank, "Edward Young's Satires: Materials for an Edition of *Love of Fame, The Universal Passion*" (unpubl. Ph.D. diss., 1939, Princeton University) pp. 42-58. In addition to the several remarks quoted below regarding the *Love of Fame*, see Swift's letter to Pope, May 1, 1773, in Pope's *Correspondence*, ed. George Sherburn (Oxford: Clarendon Press, 1956), 5: 11-12, and Pope's reply, *ibid.*, 3: 372; William Hazlitt, *Lectures on the English Poets* (London, 1818), p. 229; W. Thomas, *Le Poète Edward Young (1683-1765)* (Paris: Hachette, 1901); Charlotte Elizabeth Crawford, "The Satires of Edward Young" (unpubl. Ph.D. diss., Yale University, 1937); Crawford, "What was Pope's Debt to Edward Young?" *ELH*, 12 (1946): 157-67. In the *DNB* Leslie Stephen appends several references to his life of Young, and Francesco Cordasco includes other modern works in *Edward Young: A Handlist of Critical Notices and Studies* (New York: Published for the Long Island University Press by Burt Franklin, 1950).
2. See Lady Irwin's letter to Lord Carlisle (1733), in *Historical Manuscripts Commission. XVth Report* (1897), appendix, part 6, p. 97 (as quoted in

called Young "the finest Satirist that this or any other Age has produced";[3] Aaron Hill regarded him as a genius;[4] "W. H. S. P. C. O."
believed that "the rough, but nervous *Young* presides o'er" the few
satirists with "art";[5] Joseph Warton praised the "wit, observation
on life, pleasantry, delicacy, urbanity, and the most well-bred
raillery" of the work;[6] in the *Gray's Inn Journal*, no. 86 (1754),
Young filled the seat of satire in "An Election in Parnassus" because
Pope decided "to take his seat for ethics";[7] and Samuel Johnson
insisted that *"The Universal Passion* is indeed a very great performance."[8] In spite of the enthusiasm of these judgments, Young's
early and later contemporaries had misgivings about his poem, and
so, in 1766 the *Biographia Britannica* reported that "these satires,
once in great favour and esteem, are wearing out of fashion";[9] and
in 1767 Goldsmith observed that "Young's Satires were in higher
reputation when published, than they stand in at present."[10] Today

Miss Crawford's dissertation, p. 187); Owen Ruffhead, *Life of Alexander
Pope* (London, 1769), p. 289; *Works of Alexander Pope*, ed. Joseph Warton
(London, 1797), 3: 212, 218, 226-27; Percival Stockdale, *Lectures on the
Truly Eminent English Poets* (London, 1807), 1: 552, 556 (his comparisons
are general, and not to the *Epistle to a Lady*); George Eliot, "Worldliness
and Other-Worldliness: The Poet Young" (1857), in *Essays of George Eliot*,
ed. Thomas Pinney (New York: Columbia University Press, 1963), p. 363.
3. *An Essay upon the Taste and Writings of the Present Times* (London,
1728), p. 4; as quoted in Miss Crawford's "Satires of Edward Young,"
p. 198.
4. See Hill's *Plain Dealer*, nos. 92, 110 (1725). For information regarding
Young and Hill, see Dorothy Brewster, *Aaron Hill: Poet, Dramatist, Pro-
jector* (New York: Columbia University Press, 1913), pp. 161-64, and 164,
nn. 22, 23.
5. "The Satirists Satirized," in *Gentleman's Magazine*, 11 (October, 1741):
550. Donald J. Greene conjectures that "W. H. S. P. C. O." is "William
Hawkins, Student [or Scholar] of Pembroke College, Oxford" ("Some
Notes on Johnson and the *Gentleman's Magazine*," PMLA, 74 [1959]:
78). Hawkins was Professor of Poetry at Oxford, 1751–56.
6. *Works of Alexander Pope*, Warton, 3: 218.
7. As quoted in *The Gleaner: A Series of Periodical Essays* . . . , ed. Nathan
Drake (London, 1811), 1: 402.
8. *Lives of the English Poets*, ed. G. Birkbeck Hill (Oxford: Clarendon Press,
1905), 3: 394.
9. *Biographia Britannica: or the Lives of the Most eminent Persons Who
have flourished in Great Britain and Ireland* . . . (London, 1766), 6: 260,
note G. The remark is borrowed from *"The Universal Museum and Complete Magazine for May, 1765."* See also David Erskine Baker's *Companion
to the Playhouse* (London, 1764), 2: sig. Ii^r.
10. *The Beauties of English Poesy* (London, 1767), 2: 135.

they are largely in the specialists' realm and read, perhaps unfortunately, not for the limited pleasure they offer, but as an influence on Pope's satire. There are several reasons both for the popularity and relative failure of *Love of Fame,* and at least one of the latter relates to its treatment of the pattern of praise and blame.

I *Temperament, Circumstances, and Talent*

Young hoped to offend no one and to please the powers-that-be. This unlikely and, Young to the contrary, un-Horatian, role for a satirist may have been a function of his temperamental and psychological needs, and allows us to make certain conjectures regarding the relationship of psychological or biographical causes to literary effects. If our conjectures are correct, we may be able to say *why* a poem fails, and perhaps isolate certain traits of mind and spirit, and matters of finances, that made the poet unfit for his task. It should be clear, however, that in order to avoid a mere "old-fashioned" biographical approach these aspects of Young's character must be shown to have influenced the writing of the poem itself. If this is so, then the psychological reason for *why* the poem fails may offer a significant clue to *how* it fails though, of course, it cannot substitute for that *how*. Biographical criticism is peripheral to the central task of literary analysis; but, in this instance at least, it helps to clarify our critical focus and, moreover, is supported by numerous comments of Young's contemporaries and Young himself.

For instance, many of his extant letters to Thomas Tickell plead for aid in getting preferment in Ireland. Young admitted that his "prudential Motive for taking Orders" was his expectation that Carteret, Lord Lieutenant of Ireland, would make him his Chaplain.[11] When his requests and gift of a sermon were ignored, he complained of Carteret's coldness and, a few months later, lamented that "some Church Preferment has been lately disposed of" in violation of Carteret's (apparent) promise to him.[12] He thus begged

11. Richard Eustace Tickell, *Thomas Tickell and the Eighteenth Century Poets (1685–1740)* (London: Constable, 1931), p. 106.
12. *Ibid.,* p. 142.

Tickell "to get my Lord to make me his own Chaplain, . . . that I may be entitled to his Favour as Occasion offers on this Side of ye Water."[13]

Young did not depend solely upon Tickell's unsuccessful efforts. The first satire of *Love of Fame* was dedicated to the Duke of Dorset, whom Tickell knew and later served, and who subsequently succeeded Carteret as Lord Lieutenant of Ireland.[14] On May 3, 1726, probably through Bubb Dodington's intercession with Walpole, Young received a royal pension of £200,[15] and in gratitude wrote *The Instalment,* celebrating Walpole's installation as Knight of the Garter. His second satire includes an offering to Philip Dormer Stanhope, an early companion of Young's and soon to become the Earl of Chesterfield; he dedicated his third satire to Dodington; the fourth to the powerful Whig Sir Spencer Compton (later the Earl of Wilmington, to whom the second *Night* of *Night Thoughts* was addressed) ; he inscribed the sixth to the wealthy widow Lady Elizabeth Germain, without her knowledge or permission; while in the seventh he again responded gratefully to Walpole's earlier help. In 1728 he dedicated *A Vindication of Providence* to Queen Caroline; in the same year wrote *Ocean, with an Ode to the King;* and in late 1729 or early 1730, after having been a Chaplain to the King since 1726, begged Mrs. Howard, the King's mistress and later Countess of Suffolk, to help obtain the proper reward for his sufferings and dedicatory zeal to the royal family: "As for Zeal, I have written nothing without showing my duty to their Majesties, and some pieces are dedicated to them."[16]

In short, during the period surrounding the *Love of Fame* Young was virtually obsessed with preferment and patronage, and sought to show his affection to rich or powerful figures in the state. He is a

13. *Ibid.,* pp. 145-46. See also pp. 103-6, 122-23, 130, for further examples of Young's efforts to gain preferment.

14. Dorset served from 1730–37 (*ibid.,* p. 123).

15. Henry C. Shelley, *The Life and Letters of Edward Young* (Boston: Little, Brown & Co., 1914), p. 90: "From their earliest days at Oxford to the close of his long life, Dodington entertained a sincere regard for Young, and there can be no question that it was he and he alone who persuaded Walpole to award the poet a pension."

16. *Ibid.,* p. 101.

satirist who hopes not only to please, but to please the Establishment, and his compliments and flattery are not merely a conventional and, ultimately, irrelevant fawning nod to wealth and power; they are an integral part of the conception and structure of the entire work: the central models for emulation are Queen Caroline, King George, and Walpole. We will soon see how these figures finally torture the integrity of the separate and collected works; but we should first stress that there is nothing inherently wrong about flattery in satire. Indeed, it is one possible way for the "praise" layer of a formal verse satire to emerge. Pope, for instance, frequently employs the device. Pope's flattered figures may be "Chiefs, out of War, and Statesmen, out of Place"; they are his friends because they are virtuous men who lack power. The distinguished Arbuthnot and Fortescue finally embrace Pope's point of view; he, not the person to whom it is written, controls the values of the work. When Walpole appears in a normative way, it is in his more amiable private role, in which he too laughs at those foolish men who court his public hours. Pope always preserves his speaker's dignity: the noble Bathurst, Burlington, and Bolingbroke listen to him with respect. While reading, one is always aware that as a "democratic" satirist Pope will attack anyone—scribbler, peer, or king, who offends against the proper order of the literary, political, social, intellectual, or divine state. The entire Timon-Chandos controversy, after all, is a tribute to Pope's satiric independence. That is not the case with Young. Where Pope is not afraid to offend, Young is afraid not to make friends, since, as he states in his Preface, Poetry was too often blind and was likely to "mistake her way to preferments and honours." The Preface, in fact, is a fairly accurate gloss of Young's genteel and amiable intention in the *Love of Fame*.

He is "not conscious of the least malevolence to any particular person thro' all the Characters" (sig. A2^r). As a "reasonable and virtuous man" he is naturally moved not by individual attacks, but "the general conduct of mankind" (sig. A3^r); but he thinks it wisest "to smile at it, and turn it into ridicule" because this is least destructive to one's own peace, and "gives vice, and folly the greatest offence" (sigs. A3^{r-v}). "*Laughing Satire*," he explains, is better for

99

oneself because the agreeable passion of laughter drives out any disagreeable passions; it is also more effective against vice, since society laughs at a satirist in a disagreeable or serious passion. Horace
exemplifies the delicacy of the former, Juvenal of the latter:

> He appears in good humour while he censures; and therefore
> his censure has the more weight, as supposed to proceed from
> Judgment, not from Passion. *Juvenal* is ever in a Passion; he
> has little valuable but his Eloquence, and Morality: The last
> of which I have had in my eye, but rather for emulation, than
> imitation, thro' my whole work. (sig. A4^r)

"Delicacy" is important for Young; he insists that wit "can never,
or should never succeed, without" it, and that with wit alone an
author "betrays too great a contempt for mankind, and opinion of
himself" (sig. A4^v). Hence we admire Cervantes more than Rabelais;
the latter is ungentlemanly, indecent, and in need of pardon for his
errors as well as praise for his learning (sig. a1^r). Wit not only must
include delicacy; it must avoid ambiguities and indiscriminate laughter. The satirist who forgets this shows "a poverty of wit . . . and . . .
a want of virtue," both of which will turn his satire and the world
against him (sig. a1^v). Poetry, he concludes, adapting Plato, is the
son of the unpleasant goddess Poverty and the pleasant god Riches;
in the present age, particularly with Wisdom as governess, we "might
have much more of the father, than the mother" (sig. a3^r).

The values of the Preface suggest one reason why the *Love of
Fame* was popular: in theory it threatened no one's ease, served more
to soothe than to upset its readers, assumed a universal benevolence
and overtly rejected those authors who suggest that witty contempt is
a viable attitude towards man's aspirations and achievements. When
put into practice it insists that "The man who *pardons, disappoints*
his foe" (2: 31), and makes clear that "The Sex we honour, tho'
their faults we blame" (5: 83). Thus the anonymous author of an
Imitation of Horace, *Satires* i. 9, refers to *Love of Fame* in this comforting way:

> Good-natur'd YOUNG, well-learned and well-bred,
> Studies to lay prevailing folly dead.

How gently he the well-turn'd Satire deals,
Smiles while he strikes, and while he wounds he heals![17]

And Joseph Warton, seconded by Nathan Drake some years later,[18] was pleased to find that the work was "without a single mark of spleen and ill nature."[19]

Though several of Young's critics praised his good nature, several others found that he had rather too much of that trait for a satirist, and suggest that the seeking of preferment in his life and letters has carried over into his art. Swift observes that Young "must torture his Invention,/ To flatter *Knaves* or lose his *Pension*,"[20] and most other contemporary—and later—commentators make similar remarks regarding Young's "extravagent strain of praise."[21] These are epitomized by Sir John Hawkins:

> One of the earliest of lord Melcombe's clients was Dr. Edward Young, the author of the Satires, of the Night-thoughts, and of the Revenge, a tragedy; a man who, by a strange fatality, could never attain to any of those distinctions in his profession, which are generally understood to be the rewards of learning and piety, and must be supposed to have failed by the ardour with which he solicited, and the servile adulation which he practiced to come at them, of which latter disposition he has given such instances in the dedications to his Satires to the several persons of high rank, to whom they are addressed, as also in the exordium to each of the Night-thoughts at their first coming abroad, for in the later editions they are omitted, as . . . a dis-

17. *Gentleman's Magazine*, 1 (November, 1731) : 493.
18. *Essays, Biographical, Critical, and Historical, Illustrative of the Tatler, Spectator, and Guardian* (London, 1805), 3: 252.
19. *Works of Alexander Pope*, Warton, 3: 218.
20. "On Poetry: A Rapsody," in *The Poems of Jonathan Swift*, ed. Harold Williams, 2d ed. (Oxford: Clarendon Press, 1958), 2: 650. Swift also attacks Young, on poetic grounds, in "A Copy of Verses Upon Two Celebrated Modern Poets" (2: 393). The lines, probably written in 1726, were published in 1734. Some of Swift's disapproval must be attributed to disagreement with Young's politics; but his literary judgment is nevertheless accurate.
21. Sir Herbert Crofts, "Life of Young," in Johnson's *Lives of the English Poets*, Hill, 3: 367.

grace to manhood, and must have put the vainest of his patrons to the blush.[22]

Since Young's personal "servile adulation" clearly extends to his literary works, we would be well-advised to pay particular attention to the way in which the "praise" functions in his satires. But there are clear virtues and flaws in *Love of Fame* which are a function of Young's talent and which, so far as I can tell, biographical detail can not adequately explain.

Young's fine poetic skills emerge throughout. He can stratch the genteel polish of his verse with an attack on those who seek the praise even of blockheads: it is "as if a Fool should mean/ By spitting on your face to make it clean" (1: 9). His epigrammatic quality catches the masked anguish of the fashionable world: "aching bosoms wear a visage gay,/And stifled Groans frequent the Ball, and Play" (1:

22. *The Life of Samuel Johnson, LL.D.*, 2d ed., rev. (London, 1787), pp. 329-30. For similar observations, see the anonymous *Of the Depravity of Human Nature: [An Epistle] to Dr. Edward Young* (London, n.d.), p. 14; Boswell, *Life of Johnson*, Hill-Powell, 3: 251; *Olla Podrida*, no. 21 (1787), in Drake's *Gleaner*, 3: 317-18; Drake, *Essays Biographical, Critical, and Historical*, 3: 259; *Biographia Dramatica*, compiled by David Erskine Baker, Isaac Reed, and Stephen Jones (London, 1812), 1: 766 (the relevant remark was selected by Baker. The line he referred to was originally the conclusion to the second of the *Night-Thoughts*. Young omitted it and the final thirty-eight lines from the second and subsequent editions. See Henry Petit, "A Bibliography of Young's *Night-Thoughts*," in *University of Colorado Studies*, Series in Language and Literature, no. 5 [Boulder, Colo.: University of Colorado Press, 1954], p. 21); George Eliot, "Worldliness and Other-Worldliness," in *Essays*, Pinney, p. 344.

Much of the criticism of Young's excessive flattery is perceptive; but one must examine the individual remark to determine whether the writer is actually expressing a prejudice and quarreling with Young for not sharing it. George Eliot, for instance, berates Young because his apparent conception of God is not sufficiently exalted ("Worldliness and Other-Worldliness," *passim*). Note especially p. 370—"we remember no mind in poetic literature that seems to have absorbed less of the beauty and the healthy breath of the common land-scape"—and p. 371—"we never find him dwelling on virtue or religion as it really exists—in the emotions of a man dressed in an ordinary coat, and seated by his fire side of an evening, with his hand resting on the head of his little daughter." Though she sometimes hits the mark squarely, her essay is vitiated by preconceptions regarding poetry and theology; these also seem to have blinded her to chronology, since (on p. 363) she claims that Young's theory of the universal passion (1725-28) imitated Pope's "ruling passion." The latter appeared in the *Epistle to Bathurst* (1732) and *Essay on Man* (1733-34).

16). His mockery of the rich man who buys culture is also expressed in a terse epigram: "Thy books are *furniture*. Methinks 'tis hard/ That Science should be purchas'd by the yard" (2: 27). One splendid couplet portrays the lumbering, dull, absurd quality of a grave pseudo-scholar: "*Crassus* a *grateful* sage, our awe, and sport!/ Supports grave forms, for forms the sage support" (2: 33). One chilling couplet's implications are brilliantly implied through a scientific and nearly "metaphysical" conceit: "*Like Cats in air-pumps*, to subsist we strive/ On joys too thin to keep the Soul alive" (5: 94). Young is an intelligent enough poet to know that theory sometimes collapses in the face of practice; hence the following lines attacking lust for money are grimly passionate rather than wittily delicate:

> That *fame* is *wealth*, fantastick poets cry;
> That *wealth* is *fame*, another Clan reply,
> Who know no guilt, no scandal but in *rags*;
> And *swell*, in just proportion to their *bags*.
> .   .   .   .
> [The beardless miser] glories to late times to be convey'd,
> Not for the poor he has *reliev'd*, but *made*.
> Not such ambition his great fathers fir'd,
> When *Harry* conquer'd, and half *France* expir'd.
> He'd be a slave, a pimp, a dog for gain,
> Nay a *dull sheriff* for his *golden chain*. (4: 76–77)

The satires on women include acute psychological observations. We hear, for instance, that "For want—but not of health, are Ladies ill,/ And *tickets* cure beyond the *doctor's bill*" (5: 95). The rapid collapse of a marriage between a witty man and woman of too similar personalities (5: 100), and the description of a newly-wed in tears because her husband impertinently fell asleep after consummation of their bliss (5: 102) are equally perceptive. In the same satire Young evokes the sadness of the human situation through the foolish old lady who denies her age. We note that Johnson, in line 36 of *The Vanity of Human Wishes*, profited from the third line below.

> O how your beating breast a Mistress warms
> Who looks thro' spectacles to see your charms!

> While rival *undertakers* hover round,
> And with his spade the *sexton* marks the ground,
> Intent not on her own, but others doom,
> She plans new conquests, and *defrauds* the tomb.
> In vain the cock has summon'd *sprights* away,
> She walks at noon, and blasts the bloom of day.
> Gay rainbow silks her mellow charms infold,
> And nought of *Lyce* but *herself* is old.
> Her grizzled locks assume a *smirking* grace,
> And art has *levell'd* her deep-furrow'd face.
> Her strange demand no mortal can approve,
> We'll ask her *blessing*, but can't ask her *love*. (5: 114)

Though he attacked ambiguity, the multiple meanings of *spark*, below, make this portrait one of Young's richest:

> Some Ladies are too beauteous to be wed,
> For where's the man that's worthy of their bed?
> If no disease reduce her pride before,
> *Lavinia* will be ravisht at threescore.
> Then she submits to venture in the dark;
> And nothing, now, is wanting—but her spark. (6: 126)

Satire Six, against women, seems to me the best of the poem, partly because it includes so many individual couplets of extraordinary wit. The innuendo of these lines, for one:

> Ladies there are who think *one* crime is *all*;
> Can women, then, no way but *backward* fall? (6: 136)

But Satire Six is most impressive in its satiric vision of what Young ultimately flees from—a portrait of the apocalypse:

> What swarms of amorous *grandmothers* I see?
> And Misses, *antient* in iniquity?
> What blasting whispers, and what loud declaiming?
> What lying, drinking, bawding, swearing, gaming?
> Friendship so cold, such warm incontinence,
> Such griping avarice, such profuse expence,

Such dead devotion, such a zeal for crimes,
Such licens'd ill, such masquerading times,
Such venal faith, such misapply'd applause,
Such flatter'd guilt, and such inverted laws,
Such dissolution thro' the whole I find,
'Tis not a world, but Chaos of mankind. (6: 145)

Young is at his best in passages like this; and he is almost as good in the sections—like those from 5: 114 and 6: 126, above—depicting the human condition.

We have moved from discussion of some of Young's personal problems to their possible influence on certain aspects of his satire, and on to a few of his more impressive poetic qualities. Our focus is thus becoming more sharply literary; readers of the *Love of Fame*, after all, have not only criticized its flattery, but its excessive use of epigrams and antitheses, its simple-minded attitude toward *the* universal passion, and its superficial and ineffective satire. Though Johnson defended the epigrammatic quality,[23] *The Universal Museum and Complete Magazine*, among others, insisted that the satires "consist of a string of epigrams written upon one subject, and tire the reader before he gets near the end." The same author notes the work's "simplicity of subject,"[24] a simplicity which Swift treated ironically several years earlier when he observed: "*Young*'s universal Passion, *Pride*,/ Was never Known to spread so wide."[25] And Johnson, who regarded Young as "a man of genius and a poet" nevertheless felt that "he plays . . . only on the surface of life; he never penetrates the recesses of the mind."[26] Part of the superficiality stems from Young's theory of causation: what men aim at through their vices "is, generally, publick opinion, and esteem. Which truth is the subject of the following Satires; and joins them together, as several

23. Johnson, *Lives of the English Poets*, Hill, 3: 394.
24. *Biographia Britannica*, 6: 260, note G, followed *The Universal Museum*, as did *The Annual Register . . . For the Year 1765*, 4th ed. (London, 1784), p. 33 (new pagination after p. 272); and Drake, *Essays, Biographical, Critical, and Historical*, 3: 252. See also George Eliot, "Worldliness and Other-Worldliness," *Essays*, Pinney, p. 362.
25. "On Poetry: A Rapsody," in *Poems*, Williams, 2: 640.
26. *Lives of the English Poets*, Hill, 3: 399, 394.

branches from the same root" (sig. A3ᵛ). But it is hard to believe
that everything from a man's desire for gold to a woman's desire to
read philosophy can be explained by love of fame; the trunk cannot
support the weight of all these branches, and the tree falls.

There are other times when Young's theory forces him into difficult situations. He usually uses generic or ideal types in order to avoid
naming individual culprits; hence in the middle of his justification
for his own satire, after listing Pope, Donne, Dorset, Dryden, Rochester, and Addison as either dead or not writing, he remarks:

> *Congreve,* who crown'd with lawrels fairly won,
> Sits smiling at the Goal while Others run,
> He will not write; and (more provoking still!)
> Ye Gods! he will not write, and *Maevius* will. (1: 5)

The reader is not likely to share Young's provocation or the fervor of
his prayer to the gods if a generic Maevius is the villian; one feels
that in a genuinely dreadful situation Maevius' identity would be
narrowed or, as Pope will do with Atticus, Bufo, Sporus, and several
dunces, placed in a context which will show us—not merely tell—how
dangerous the character really is. In its present form the onus is
partially placed on successful Congreve who merely smiles while seeing a bad author write. Moreover, the clarity of "Congreve" set
against the obscurity of "Maevius" limits the satiric force of the lines.
This flaw in the rhetorical texture is seen even in some of the poem's
panegyric. After criticizing those who solemnly hide their essential
vapidity, Young remarks that the screen actually reveals the fool. He
then gives an instance of the fool's opposite, "For 'tis the wise man's
interest to be *seen*" (2: 35). Alas, Young is so general at this point
that his praise falls upon a dash, we cannot possibly see the wise
man before us, and the entire paragraph is silly:

> Hence, ——, that openness of heart,
> And just disdain for that poor *mimic,* Art;
> Hence (manly praise!) that manner nobly free,
> Which all admire, and I commend in thee. (2: 35)[27]

27. According to "A Key to the Universal Passion," the dash (to which the

He repeats this unhappy device when, after announcing that he will "blame" the faults of the sex, he ringingly declares that it is

> A theme, fair——! doubly kind to me,
> Since satyrizing *those,* is praising *thee.* (5: 84)[28]

There is another important literary aspect of *The Universal Passion*: it is written, Young tells us, "In Seven Characteristical Satires." Though Warton overstates when he calls them "the first characteristical satires in our language" (witness Zimri and Achitophel), he nevertheless suggests some of the appeal for the reader in the early eighteenth century.[29] As I hope to show, Young's use of the "character" offers certain reasons for the work's comparative failure; but it also raises an interesting problem of structure. On the one hand the *Love of Fame* is composed of seven satires organized around varying groups who share the same basic trait; accordingly there could be any reasonable number of individual satires. On the other hand, after having written Satires One, Two, Three, Four, and "Satire the Last," what is now Seven, Young added Five and Six, on women, thus making his praise and blame more comprehensive. Moreover, only Satires Three and Four do not offer overt, stated (rather than implicit) evidence for being part of an over-all design. Near the end of the First Satire we hear: "Here breathe, my Muse! and then thy task renew/ Ten thousand Fools unsung are still in view" (1: 19). The Second Satire begins with: "My Muse, proceed, and reach thy destin'd end." Satires Three and Four may be viewed as amplification upon the "Ten thousand Fools"; Satire Five clearly seeks to parallel man's ambitions with woman's "nicer" follies, since "Nor reigns *Ambition* in bold *man* alone" (5: 83); the final portrait of Satire Four (155–56) shows the salutary effect of Queen Caroline on vicious English women, and is therefore intended as a female, royal norm to

---

"Key" adds an unwarranted "D—") applies to Dodington, but this is unlikely since shortly before and after these lines Young had praised Stanhope. See *The Poetical Works of the Reverend Edward Young* (London, 1741), 1: unsigned, unnumbered, p. 2., following p. 304 of the text.

28. The "Key," in *The Poetical Works of . . . Young,* p. 3, records this passage but offers no name for the dash.

29. *Works of Alexander Pope,* Warton, 3: 218.

balance that of George I in the final satire. At the outset that satire tells us that *"Brunswick's* glory crowns the whole design . . ./ That glory [Walpole], which thy counsels make so bright" (7: 161) ; and at the conclusion of the "attack" section of this satire (and hence of *all* the satires), Young says: "Here cease, my muse! the *Catalogue* is writ" (7: 166), even though there are "disappointed thousands" not yet satirized. Throughout, then, Young seems to have aimed at broadening the scope of his satire and working towards his final characters and models for emulation: Caroline among the women, and George and Walpole among the men. Furthermore, in the Preface he states that the "truth" of men striving for "publick opinion and esteem . . . is the subject of the following Satires; and joins them together, as several branches from the same root" (sig. A3ᵛ). The "characteristical" structure of the individual satires—the branches— requires examination; but the "unity of design"—the roots—demand even more. *Love of Fame* must stand, lean, or fall in the collected form that Young chose, a form in which the "character" plays an important but nevertheless subservient role to the unifying concept of the *universal* passion.

Young's characters generally include only one aspect of the love of fame; they are simple rather than complex, flat rather than round, and, after seven satires, often uninteresting and repetitive. Young's women suffer particularly from the charge of repetition. Tullia, for example, is "For ever most *divinely* in the *wrong*" (6: 127), while Syrena, "Because she's right, she's ever in the wrong" (6: 133). Zantippe's *"last word* is her eternal right" (5: 88) ; Stella's *"Eyes* shine as bright,/As if her tongue was never in the right" (5: 92) ; one unnamed astronomer-woman "never took the height/Of *Saturn*, yet is ever in the right" (5: 194) ; and Tullia "thinks it *vulgar* to defend the *right*" (6: 127). It is sometimes difficult to distinguish between Young's women, particularly since they often share an essential trait. Zantippe's apparent superiority to her husband prompts Young to cry: "must our wives be *wise?*" (5: 88) ; Julia "knows her *wiser* husband is a *fool*" (6: 132) ; and *"Brunetta's* wise in actions great, and rare" (6: 133). Similarly, among others, Sempronia—*"Of pride,* and *av'rice* who can cure the Fair?" (5: 93)—and Cleora, whose eyes

"The height of *avarice,* and *pride* confess" (6: 138) sound too similar in certain ways.

Benjamin Boyce has remarked that Young's Alicea is a slattern, whereas Pope's Artimisa is not only that: "she is also the mannish sort (Young's Thalestris [Satire five]) and the reader of Locke and Malebranch." Furthermore, "it takes more than three of Young's women to constitute [Pope's] Atossa," in his *Epistle to a Lady*; Atossa possesses "inner conflicts"[30] which one misses in Young's characters. Boyce's judgment is correct, as the complexity of this couplet shows: Atossa "Shines in exposing Knaves, and painting Fools,/ Yet is, what-e'er she hates and ridicules" (ll. 119–20). This combines sadism and masochism, wisdom and ignorance, screening of character and exposure of it, exaltation and inferiority, whereas Young's less anguished Aspasia is solidly committed to one folly: she "reaps no fruit from her superior sense,/ But to be *teaz'd* by her own excellence" (6: 131). We thus agree with Boyce that "Pope notices the complications and unresolved tensions in human nature that Young usually ignores, and he consequently creates the impression of possessing greater depth and insight."[31]

There is another important aspect of Young's characters that makes them immediately attractive but ultimately not durable. The portrait of Florio's tulipomania is one of Young's best:

> But *Florio*'s Fame, the product of a shower,
> Grows in his garden, an illustrious flower!
> Why teems the Earth? why melt the vernal Skies?
> Why shines the Sun? to make *Paul Diack* [the tulip] rise.[32]
> From morn to night has *Florio* gazing stood,
> And wonder'd how the Gods could be so good.

30. Benjamin Boyce, *The Character-Sketches in Pope's Poems* (Durham, N.C.: Duke University Press, 1962), pp. 124-25. For a discussion of satiric portraits, see William F. Cunningham, Jr., "Charles Churchill and the Satiric Portrait," *Essays and Studies in Language and Literature,* ed. Herbert H. Petit, Duquesne Studies Philological Series, vol. 5 (Pittsburgh: Duquesne University Press, 1964), pp. 110-32.
31. Boyce, *Character-Sketches,* p. 129.
32. The "Key" merely notes: "*Paul Diack,* who gave Name to a *Tulip,* was an honest, toping [*sic*], old Citizen of *London,* and a great Stock-Jobber" (*The Poetical Works of . . . Young,* p. 2, at end of text).

What shape? what hue? was ever nymph so fair?
He doats! he dies! he too is *rooted* there.
O solid bliss! which nothing can destroy
Except a cat, bird, snail, or idle boy.
In Fame's full bloom lies *Florio* down at night,
And wakes next day a most inglorious Wight;
The Tulip's dead! see thy fair Sister's fate,
O C— —! and be kind ere 'tis too late. (2: 24–25)

The character effectively communicates the degradation, vanity, and folly of the "florist." He is completely passive, does nothing to foster the growth of his tulip (it is "the product of a shower"), regards the seasons and the natural movement of the sun as subservient to his flower's needs, demeans God (or the "Gods") in assuming that they share his passion, immobilizes and unmans himself by stationary courtship of "Paul Diack" who is lovelier than any woman, fixes his bliss upon the most transient of pleasures and, briefly, has his fame, which he did nothing to foster, blasted. All this is effectively and comically executed; but it has several blemishes. In spite of its use of the gods, seasons, inversion of roles, and our knowledge that tulipomania is but one example of the frighteningly prevalent love of fame, the portrait is nevertheless oriented towards one foolish man's folly, a folly which is not of long continuance, and hence not really dangerous to the florist or the world. In a brief portrait immediately following Florio's, we see a Quaker servant, Adam, destroy his doting master's prized tulip. Adam, "Serene," tells his amazed master: "lo! 'twas crusht by me;/ Fall'n is the *Baal* to which thou bow'dst thy knee" (2: 25). The return to order is easy, without conflict, and without pain to anyone but the florist who, we hear, is "A Friend" of the satirist himself. One feels that such a folly is not dangerous, and the satirist admits as much:

> "But all men want *amusement*, and what crime
> In such a Paradise to fool their time?"
> None: but why proud of this? to Fame they soar;
> We grant *they're Idle*, if they'll ask no more. (2: 26)

So far as Young's vision extends, they do ask no more and they commit no crimes. But he is short-sighted, and in the greater portrait of tulipomania in *The Dunciad,* we see why. Dullness must arbitrate between a florist and a naturalist, since the latter has killed a cherished tulip while pursuing a butterfly:

> "Hear thy suppliant's call,
> Great Queen, and common Mother of us all!
> Fair from its humble bed I rear'd this Flow'r,
> Suckled, and chear'd, with air, and sun, and show'r,
> Soft on the paper ruff its leaves I spread,
> Bright with the gilded button tipt its head,
> Then thron'd in glass, and nam'd it CAROLINE:
> Each Maid cry'd, charming! and each Youth, divine!
> Did Nature's pencil ever blend such rays,
> Such vary'd light in one promiscuous blaze?
> Now prostrate! dead! behold that Caroline:
> No Maid cries, charming! and no Youth, divine!
> And lo the wretch! whose vile, whose insect lust
> Lay'd this gay daughter of the Spring in dust.
> Oh punish him, or to th' Elysian shades
> Dismiss my soul, where no Carnation fades." (4: 403–18) [33]

We realize, first of all, that the florist is speaking to Dullness, who knows that she will soon reacquire the few remaining light acres of the world. Moreover, Young's passive character who courted a tulip, has now become an active mother-figure who "suckled" the flower, controlled the elements, and improved upon nature's own efforts. A man has turned a flower into an apparently "divine" thing; when its death disproves its divinity the man seeks redress or, failing this, reaffirmation of that divinity through his own death. For the florist life is meaningful only when it is not life, when, that is, death is no longer a threat. Thus his hatred for change, for attack upon his flower, is manifest in the double-entendre of lines 415–16: in addition to the

---

33. *Alexander Pope: The Dunciad,* The Twickenham Edition of the Poems of Alexander Pope, vol. 5, ed. James Sutherland, 3d ed. (London, 1963), pp. 381-82.

primary meaning of the naturalist's passion for a butterfly knocking the flower into dust and death, the lines also evoke a grotesque image of the naturalist's sexual intercourse with a tulip and, therefore, desecration of apparently changeless divinity.

Young followed his mild character with consolation; Pope follows his grim one with denial of consolation, since the Queen reconciles the two men, assures them that both have done their parts in propagating Dullness, recommends that they attend to the other, sleeping, dunces, and concludes:

> "O! would the Sons of Men once think their Eyes
> And Reason giv'n them but to study *Flies*!
> See Nature in some partial narrow shape,
> And let the Author of the Whole escape:
> Learn but to trifle; or, who most observe,
> To wonder at their Maker, not to serve!" (4: 453–58).

Though I am not suggesting indebtedness, one can see that Pope has denied some of Young's basic assumptions, and taken his satire on tulipomania out of the merely personal sphere and elevated it to a danger to the universe. The florists do ask more than being idle, since they have moved from passive to active perversion of the masculine role and God's ordering of nature and the seasons. Pope's florist actively addresses himself to the rejection of God and the evocation of dullness in man, to confusion of the part for the whole and, ultimately, denial of service to God, since man "studies" the flower (or fly, or any other trifle) to the exclusion of service to Him. Many of Young's characters, then, not only are too simple and, in the long run, repetitive (and therefore tiresome), but also lack a dimension of seriousness and urgency. Hence, as I have said, one sometimes wonders just how necessary his satiric tools really are. But there are other times when Young is as startlingly apocalyptic as Pope himself and, in fact, anticipates the return to chaos in book 4 of *The Dunciad*. The uncongenial juxtaposition of these two qualities needs analysis.

In this discussion I have considered matters of biography, temperament, and talent, and moved progressively closer into analysis of the *Love of Fame* itself. At this point, I should like to apply Dryden's notion of praise and blame, since, I believe, that can best account for the uneasy amalgam of apocalypse and nirvana that the seven satires finally contain. Application of this criterion has other advantages as well: it uses a standard familiar to Young and his audience and appropriate to a satiric work which attacks destructive love of fame and invites some form of constructive moderation of that "love"; it points us directly toward one central weakness in the poem and indirectly towards another; and it suggests how the problems of Young's temperament and circumstances regarding his need to flatter, can be translated into more immediately relevant literary terms.

II The Perils of the Satiric Pattern; the Genteel Mask and the Apocalyptic Vision

Part of Young's satiric method in the first six satires is to use interlocking sections of praise and blame for lesser examples of the love of fame and their antidotes; in the Seventh he includes a long panegyric of Walpole and George I. Indeed, the pattern of blame and praise is present with such a vengeance that it not only explains one aspect of the structure of the poem, but ultimately lessens its merit as well. For instance, we soon see that each branch of the love of fame attacked has its opposite virtue praised. After Young criticizes nobles who spend and build unwisely, he says:

> By your Revenue measure your expence,
> And to your *funds* and *acres* join your *sense*. (1:14)

After censuring the foppery, false gaiety, ostentation, and guilty intrigues of nobles at court, he offers the virtues of the happy country, which, it seems, had some influence on a similar scene in Johnson's *London*:

> Give me, indulgent Gods! with mind serene,
> And guiltless heart to range the sylvan scene.

113

No splendid Poverty, no smiling Care,
No well-bred Hate, or servile Grandeur *there*;
There pleasing objects useful thoughts suggest,
The *sense* is ravisht, and the *soul* is blest;
On every Thorn delightful Wisdom grows,
In every Rill a sweet Instruction flows. (1: 18)

If he discusses nasty wits, he will quickly add "draw your *wit* as seldom as your *sword*" (2: 30) ; when social customs, like the masquer-
ade, come before service to the nation, he reminds us that "*Worth*
of *politeness* is the needful ground" (3: 56) ; the soldier is warned
to be more afraid of boasting than a bomb, since "A *soldier* should
be modest, as a *maid*" (4: 78). The satires on women were added, in
part, to show that love of fame is indeed a universal passion; and so
Young also uses the blame-praise pattern in his Fifth and Sixth Satires.
A talkative woman must "learn—*to hear*" (5: 87) ; a woman who
unwisely marries for money will be told that "Man's rich with little,
were his judgment true" (5: 93). Praise of solitude after satire of
passion for the town (5: 98–99), exhortation to "wed not acres, but
a noble mind" (5: 108), the knowledge that "Good-breeding is the
blossom of good sense" (5: 112), and the exemplary "prudent *Por-
tia*" (5: 114–15) are among the subjects of praise which oppose
follies attacked in Satire Five. Similarly, in Satire Six we see immodest women reminded that "Those charms are greatest which
decline the sight" (6: 123) ; a woman should "veil her very *wit* with
modesty" (6: 128) ; and she who ignores small things for the "great"
commits a fundamental error regarding life. We then hear this
couplet, the second line of which Johnson knew (and misquoted) :[34]

Think nought a *trifle*, tho' it small appear;
Small sands the mountain, moments make the year. (6: 133)

The individual satires have been working towards the expansion and
resolution offered in Satire Seven, and here too, as we would expect,
the satiric pattern is essential. The expansion is seen in the movement
from the private to the public sphere:

34. *The Letters of Samuel Johnson*, ed. R. W. Chapman (Oxford: Clarendon
 Press, 1952), 1: 255, and 255, n. 2.

The Follies past are of a private kind,
Their sphere is small, their mischief is confin'd;
But daring men there are (awake, my muse,
And raise thy verse) who bolder frenzy chuse;
Who stung by glory, rave, and bound away;
The *world* their Field, and *human-kind* their Prey. (7: 163)

Young treats the martial figure and the corrupt courtier at length and, in some of the best couplets of the poem, sketches the abuses to be dealt with in "Some future strain" (7: 167).

Having surveyed its effects, Young now turns to the cause of the universal passion. Though Ambition was sent "by heaven's indulgence . . ./ To warm, to raise, to deify mankind" (7: 168), it has different effects upon different minds: "Ambition in the *truly-noble mind*" is always joined with virtue to perform noble deeds. "In *meaner minds* Ambition works alone," but puts on the aspect of virtue in order to deceive and conquer. In the *"basest minds"* Ambition wears no mask: "All I have sung are instances of *this* [base ambition]" (7: 170–71), he says, and then adds generalized counsel imploring his victims to "desist from your erroneous strife" (7: 172). Virtuous Ambition can be found only where reside the several traits of wisdom, inward dignity, outward state, good purpose, great achievement, public blessings, and desire for deserved glory. Since Satire Seven concerns the public sphere, Young focuses primarily upon George I—who "publick blessings thro' half *Europe* pours" (7: 174)—and secondarily on Walpole, to whom the satire is dedicated and who is able "At will, to raise, or hush the *civil* storm" (7: 175). The King is the particular exemplar of the traits of true Ambition and the noblest model for our emulation. But the Minister is the more immediate source of power—hence "Smile, *Walpole*, or the *nine* inspire in vain," and though *"Brunswick's* glory crowns the whole design," it is a glory which Walpole's "counsels make so bright" and "which on thee reflects a light" (7: 161). Thus the final portrait of the poem is not of the godlike Brunswick, but of the earthly Walpole, an alert Palinurus at the helm, attentive to his King's dangerous passage across the seas. This, we see, is the conduct of the true minister who is a foil to treacherous courtiers:

> Such *courtiers* were, and such again may be,
> *Walpole*, when men forget to copy thee. (7: 166)

The poem ends with a vision of sweetness and light, of Walpole's immense power used in a beneficent way; there is a clear and named character before us, the reader is consoled with the possibility of easy emulation if not of a quasi-divine King, then certainly of his Prime Minister. Both men differ from the reader in degree only, since we all have received the love of fame from Heaven itself, and since—Young's rejoinder to the contrary—it is unlikely that his audience would conceive of itself as being of either the *"meaner"* or *"basest"* minds. Even these, however, seem able to change under Young's gentle well-turned satire, for they can all "desist from . . . erroneous strife;/ Be wise, and quit the false *sublime* of life" (7: 172). The final satire shows the true sublime and true public virtue counteracting public vice; it thus shows the final workings of the satiric pattern. By the time the reader arrives at this point, however, he has been wearied by its repetition—my selection above is a small sample—and he is likely to be unhappy with the implications of the fawning encomium of Walpole, unconvinced by the splendor of his King, and, as I hope to show, perplexed and disturbed by ethical and satiric contradictions at the core of the poem, many of which are related to Young's inappropriate selection of subjects of praise to balance those of blame.

The follies I have just discussed are modest and call for modest rebuttals; but the best (and, paradoxically, the worst) parts of the *Love of Fame* come when Young raises his voice. The second paragraph of Satire Three, for instance, portrays England in decay, and gently chastises Dodington who conceals his voice, for

> When wanted *Britain* bright examples more?
> Her *learning*, and her *Genius* too decays,
> And *dark*, and *cold* are her declining days;
> As if men now were of another cast,
> They meanly live *on alms* of ages past. (3: 44)

Nevertheless, the voice of the satirist will prevail, since "they who boldly dare,/ Shall triumph o'er the sons of cold Despair." If they do

116

not prevail over those who despair, there are two consolations: at least they—Young among them—will have used original or "new cast" older material, and not merely the borrowed and badly improved "mold" of most present writers. Moreover, "Late times the verse may read, if these refuse,/And from sour Critics vindicate the muse" (3: 44). In sixteen lines Young has moved from decay to triumph, from lack of appreciation in a declining culture, to future respect by—one must assume—a more enlightened culture of "late times." But the ease of the triumph over "cold Despair" makes us feel that the entire battle is trumped up, and that Young hardly believes that his generation is declining, particularly since the stature of Dodington, who knows "the basis of a solid fame" (3: 43) is so clear. Young also admits that though Dodington can "give protection," all he himself can give is "a worthless strain" (3: 43). He is, therefore, caught in a curious bind by the need to praise his patron and lower his own camparative abilities. His worthless strain will, on the one hand, triumph over the decadent poets of today; on the other hand, if his present readers reject him, the same worthless strain will "vindicate the muse" hereafter. In short, a wiser, later age will properly appreciate the worthless lines which contemporary, declining, England refuses to read. In his desire to establish his patron as a norm—a subject of praise—Young has ignored the demands of logic.

One may make a similar objection at the end of this satire. Here the harsh focus turns towards political decay, when "The *Legislature* joyn'd with *Drury-lane!*" (3: 56) and when Heidigger's festive games contribute to the degradation of government:

> See Commons, Peers, and Ministers of State,
> In solemn council met, and deep debate!
> What godlike enterprize is taking birth?
> What wonder opens on th' expecting earth?
> 'Tis done! with loud applause the council rings!
> Fixt is the fate of *whores*, and *fiddlestrings*! (3: 58)

This is followed, first, by a Juvenalian passage on the ease of the knave's and the difficulty of the good man's gaining his proper "price." He then rounds out his satire with more praise of Dodington who has had the wisdom to regard Young: the opening couplet proclaimed, "Long, *Dodington,* in debt, I long have sought/ To ease the burthen of my grateful thought" (3: 43). Young's "presaging thoughts" see his patron

> By *Walpole*'s Conduct fir'd, and friendship grac'd,
> Still higher in your Prince's favour plac'd;
> And lending, *here,* those awful Councils aid,
> Which you, *abroad,* with such success obey'd. (3: 60)

The glorious triumvirate of George, Walpole, and Dodington is intended as the opposite of the corrupt "Commons, Peers, and Ministers of State." Again, Young's need to praise his powerful patrons eats away at the logic of his poem, since it is surely incongruous that so noble a King and Prime Minister preside over Parliament's applause regarding whores and fiddlestrings. Similarly, Lady Elizabeth Germain is among those "great souls" who "Give *gold* a *price,* and teach its *beams* to *shine,*" foster the public happiness "Thro' *secret* streams," and "*Relieve* our *wants,* and *spare* our *blushes* too" (6: 140); yet how convincing a norm can she be when Young begins Satire Six by admitting that "I know her not"? (6: 121)

There is, then, a problem concerning the appropriateness of some of Young's satiric norms, and this problem may be an outgrowth of Young's need to praise his past, present, and intended patrons and to adapt them to the satiric pattern. The dubious relevance of this praise and its relationship to the work's generally schizophrenic nature was noted in Swift's poem written in 1726 and published in 1734, "On Reading Dr. Young's Satires, Called the Universal Passion." The first part of his remarks is based largely upon what is now Satire Seven.

> If there be Truth in what you sing,
> Such Godlike Virtues in the *King,*
> A *Minister* so filled with Zeal,
> And Wisdom for the Common-Weal.
> If *he,* who in the Chair presides,
> So steadily the *Senate* guides:

If Others, whom you make your Theme,
Are Seconds in this glorious Scheme;
If ev'ry *Peer* whom you commend,
To Worth and Learning is a Friend.
If this be Truth, as you attest,
What *Land* was ever *half* so *blest*?
The *Traders* now no longer cheat;
No Falsehood now among the *Great*,
Now, on the Bench fair *Justice* shines,
Her scale to neither Side inclines;
Now *Pride* and *Cruelty* are flown,
And *Mercy* here exalts her Throne;
For, such is good Example's Pow'r,
It does its Office ev'ry Hour,
Where *Governors* are good and wise;
Or else the truest Maxim lyes:
For this we know, all antient Sages
Decree, that *ad exemplum Regis*,
Thro' all the Realm his *Virtues* run,
Rip'ning, and kindling like the Sun.
If this be true, then how much more,
When you have nam'd at least a *Score*
Of *Courtiers*, each in their Degree
If possible, as good as He.[35]

Young's satires do indeed offer extensive justification for this euphoric vision of England, and it begins in the Preface, where we see his concern with not hurting himself or his audience, and his corresponding praise of his own age. The opening lines of the first satire remind us that the exemplary Dorset will "*patronize*" a Muse [of Satire] You cannot *fear*" (1: 3); when man is bad and requires correction, much of the fault is really not his, since "So weak are human kind by nature made" (2: 24); one of his unnamed characters—recognized as Stanhope—is so distinguished that Young wonders whether his "Satire can agree/ With so consummate an *human-*

---

35. *Poems of Jonathan Swift*, Williams, 2: 391-92.

ity" (4: 29) ; Young himself certainly does not wish to lash his victims, since "The man who *pardons, disappoints* his foe" (2: 31). Dodington, the patron of Satire Three, not only protects the poet, but also knows "the basis of a solid fame" (3: 43) ; indeed, Dodington's fame was "By *Walpole's* Conduct fir'd," and so he succeeds in counsel both abroad and, Young prophesies, in England (3: 60). The Fourth Satire, to Sir Spencer Compton, also includes an ample share of a positive view of its world. Compton himself is so extraordinary that he is both "The *crown's* Asserter, and the *people's* Friend," and can "Kingdoms' fates, without ambition, weigh" (4: 63) ; he need not fear Young's satire which, like woodbine on a tree, breathes its "sweets on the supporting boughs" of Compton (4: 63). Moreover, the satirist is not so rigid a friend of right that he cannot see that being in the wrong may be comforting, not to mention fashionable: "Tho' wrong the mode, comply; more sense is shewn/ In wearing *others'* follies, than your *own*" (4: 69). When Young satirizes women he first reassures them and even thanks them for their apparently gentle folly. He affirms that "The Sex we honour, tho' their faults we blame;/ Nay thank their faults for such a *fruit-ful* theme" (5: 83). Woman, it seems, is man's sole "reward for all this grief, and toil" of life (5: 89) : "A tender smile, our sorrow's only balm,/ And, in life's tempest, the sad Sailor's calm" (5: 90). Woman need only learn to modify her less pleasing eccentricities, be like the numerous characters he praises, and then, once "kind and virtuous, you'll be blest and wise" (5: 117). Satire Six continues much but, as we will see, not all, of the tone of the preceding satire on women. Hence he praises his subjects of satire: "Ye Fair! to draw your excellence at length,/ Exceeds the narrow bounds of human strength" (6: 122) ; and so he will draw their pictures in miniature. But, as throughout the seven satires, virtually each character blamed has its opposite praised; since Young is "drawing" from life, the reader is consoled not only by the gentle satire, but by the abundance of normative figures in his society. This is truly a blest society and, as Swift noted, stems from the happy example of the King whose virtues run throughout the realm and whose image can be found in at least a score of other characters. Here indeed is satire which emphasizes the good not the bad; shows mankind in follies which cannot only be gently and easily cured, but can lead, as well, to imitation of the noble pattern of the King and his Prime Minister. Young appears to be an amiable satirist, and if his poem both preserved and amplified its dominantly genteel tone, he would be regarded as the fortunate spokesman of a modern and normative Augustan age.

But there are several disturbances on the apparently quiet surface of *Love of Fame*, and the most distinguished verse—verse often worthy of Pope—stunningly portrays a vision not of the happy world of Augustus but of the apocalypse. I cannot find any evidence to suggest that Young is using the superficial texture of his satire to suggest the terrors of a grossly corrupt age; he is not ambiguous but confused, and though capable of looking into the heart of darkness is incapable of seeing it as it is. In spite of major differences between these works, Lear, Gulliver, the speaker of Pope's *Dunciad*, Benito Cereno, and Kurtz are a few of those who have had a vision similar to Young's: they see "the thing itself," man's bestial nature, the return of night, "the Negro" and the "horror" of the heart of darkness; all respond with unflinching gaze, and all pay for their insight. Madness or death is not for Young's speaker; he briefly sees what they do, but backs off, more like a morally miniscule Marlowe than a Kurtz. The difference between their response and Young's marks one difference between their greatness and his mediocrity. The second part of Swift's poem aptly describes both the incipient terrors and the contradictory outlook of *Love of Fame*:

> Or take it in a diff'rent View;
> I ask, if what you say be *true*,
> If you allow, the present Age
> Deserves your *Satire's* keenest Rage;
> If that same *Universal Passion*
> With ev'ry *Vice* hath fill'd the Nation;
> If *Virtue* dares not venture down,
> But just a *Step* below the *Crown*:
> If *Clergymen*, to shew their Wit,

> Prize *Classicks* more than *Sacred Writ*:
> If Bankrupts, when they are undone,
> Into the *Senate-House* can run,
> And sell their Votes at such a Rate,
> As will retrieve a lost Estate:
> If *Law* be such a partial *Whore*,
> To spare the Rich, and plague the Poor;
> If these be of all Crimes the worst,
> What *Land* was ever *half* so *curst*?[36]

The curst quality of England emerges at once; we are troubled by the contrast between the ecstatic praise of Dorset and the impassioned apology that opens the first satire. This is a "licentious age" that demands "our rage," an age

> When *purchas'd follies* from each distant land,
> Like Arts improve in *Britain*'s skilful hand;
> When the *Law* shews her teeth, but dares not bite,
> And *South-Sea* treasures are not brought to light;
> When *Churchmen* Scripture for the Classics quit,
> Polite Apostates from God's *grace* to *wit*;
> When men grow *great* from their *revenue spent*,
> And fly from Bayliffs into Parliament;
> When dying Sinners, to blot out their score,
> Bequeath the *church* the leavings of a *whore*;
> To chafe our spleen when Themes like these increase,
> Shall *panegyrick* reign, and *censure* cease? (1:4)

At the end of Satire One Young asks his Muse to rest, but will soon return to his task, since "Ten Thousand Fools unsung are still in view," and the land is running mad (1:19). True to his word, the satirist proceeds, "Tho' *toil*, and *danger* the bold task attend," for "'Tis most Ill-nature to *repress* thy rage" (2:23). We soon hear that Britain's intellectual glory is declining (2:44); just as he is about to rest from his "fury [and] . . . throw down my pen,/ In comes a Coxcomb, and I write agen" (3:50). He does, indeed, give ample

36. *Ibid.*, 392.

cause for writing, as we see the blurring of standards at the masquer-
ade, where "The *Legislature* joyn'd with *Drury-lane*!" (3: 56) ; in
this "converted land" we "see the *fifty churches* at a stand" (3: 57),
and in Parliament "Commons, Peers, and Ministers of State" fix "the
fate of *whores*, and *fiddlestrings*!" (3: 58). We would thus certainly
agree with the defense of his rage when he asks:

> How terrible it were to common sense,
> To write a *satire* which gives none *offence*? (3: 58)

Now all of this contradicts the dominant tone and intention of *The
Universal Passion*; it is not clear how one can both disappoint his
foes by pardoning them and cure them by offending them. Nor do
we see the danger in writing satire aimed at offending no one. If the
land is so full of brilliant models of praise, it is hard not to feel the
inappropriateness of the Juvenalian view of an entire nation mad
with folly; and, as we have seen, if George, Walpole, and Compton
are as noble as portrayed, the portrait of Parliament, in Satire Three
must be false. The poem's internal contradictions are serious.

More serious still is the poet's apparent inability to evaluate what
he sees. He frequently hints at or portrays overt disaster and then
backs off from its implications. Thus after explaining that it is ill-
natured to repress his rage, he proclaims:

> And if these strains some nobler Muse excite,
> I'll glory in the verse I did *not* write. (2: 23)

After concluding that his satire in such an age must "make *foes*" (3:
59), he proceeds to make friends by praising Dodington; after describing the female declining beauty (see p. 104, above), he tries to
ameliorate the character's sadness by inserting an apparently Horatian turn of ridicule:

> She grants indeed a Lady *may* decline,
> (All Ladies *but* herself) at *ninety nine*. (5: 114)

But the most startlingly apocalyptic poetry appears in his second
satire on women and in "Satire the Last" on public vice. Analysis of
central aspects of these satires will show weaknesses in the entire
poem.

Since women are inclined to "every bolder vice of bold mankind" (6:143), Young invokes Juvenal to help him lash follies so rank that it is no longer possible to smile at them, or, in fact, to regard them as folly; he must attack Vice. Women of this age are unrestrained, abandon their decency, show their naked ugliness in stalking over the law, the Bible, the demands of marital fidelity, or even kindness to one's husband; they are governed by passion and will betray their husband's lives and secrets; they pervert the order not only of young and old, but of friendship, charity, and zeal as well (6: 143–44). Young's final couplet is an accurate summation of his essential point:

> Such dissolution thro' the whole I find,
> 'Tis not a world, but Chaos of mankind. (4: 145)

Delicate women, he continues, are "A match for nothing—but the *Deity*" (6: 146); they defy Heaven while becoming enslaved to earth. This emphasizes the need for Young's satire because (in a line Pope was later to improve), "They dread a Satire, who defie the skies" (6: 147).

The repetition of terms and images of dissolution and rebellion is important in understanding Young's plan. Most women are not avowed atheists, they merely God's *"attributes* dethrone" (6:147)—all, that is, except those which promise mercy to sinners like themselves. They create God in their own image: "He's like themselves; or how cou'd he be good?" Thus they depose the pure and just Jehovah, and "set up in his stead/ A Deity, that's perfectly *well bred*" (6: 148). Women are virtuous in show only, spiritually akin to Satan, and blasphemers of the clergy (6: 148–49). As the enemies of God's plan and the allies of Satan's, women's "worst of ills" show their most destructive qualities. Gaming women endanger the peace of themselves, their husbands, their country, their fellow human beings, and—even—God Himself. Thus gaming spoils the lady's physical and spiritual looks (6: 150), gives her a headache (6: 151), and threatens her life (6: 152); the country's best families pass their fortunes to a "set of thieves that live on spoil,/ The *scandal*, and the *ruin* of our isle!" (6: 151); the children of these families cannot marry because their portions have been gambled away (6: 152), and, moreover,

> Why must strong youths *unmarry'd* pine away?
> They find no woman disengag'd—*from play*. (6: 154)

Just as a husband can be "cuckol'd by *Spadil*" (6: 152), so maidens are engaged to cards. The catalogue of unnatural events builds up so that gaming women attempt to take on the attributes of their own kind of godhead and blaspheme the true God (6: 150–51). Young is forced to cry:

> Ye Gods! with *new* delights inspire the fair;
> Or give us sons, and save us from despair. (6: 154)

Without new delights for women the men will also be lost to a deadly sin; and with sons only, the propagation of the race is threatened. Thus Young, the genteel satirist, has pictured a world so terrifying that no earthly solution is possible; only an appeal to God is left, and if this is not answered Britain and its inhabitants are ruined.

In spite of this vision of impending disaster Young—unlike Lear or Kurtz in comparable situations—reverses his field and focuses on "yonder flood of light/ That bursts o'er gloomy *Britain*" (6: 155). Queen Caroline's character immediately dispels our natural fear of a crumbling society, and reminds us that Young intends these "private" follies to be seen in a small sphere—"their mischief is confin'd" (7: 163). Young thus states that her "Excess of goodness" is an adequate balance for the faults hitherto portrayed:

> When in my page, to ballance numerous faults,
> Or godlike deeds were shown, or generous thoughts,
> She smil'd, *industrious* to be pleas'd, nor knew
> From whom my pen the *borrow'd* lustre drew. (6: 155)

Caroline, he says, is like an unfallen Eve giving feminine beauty to the world (6: 156). It seems that Young is incapable of grasping either the presence of tragedy in his own poem, or the destructive power of the facile portrait of Caroline's goodness. The title page motto of this satire is *Ars poetica*, 93: "*Interdum tamen & tollit*

Comoedia vocem": "Yet at times even Comedy raises her voice."[37]
This might suggest a tribute to man's refusal to be subdued without
a protest, a suggestion of laughter in the face of the absurd; instead
it suggests Young's limited range of emotional response. He can consider his portrait of malicious women destroying the nation as one
aspect of limited folly, and hence continues to regard the poem as
comic.

The speaker's inadequacy of response is clearer still in the final
satire, the expansion of his attack to public vice or folly. Other persons satirized, he says, will "furnish laughter for another year" (7:
166), but in the meanwhile they will patiently have to await some
future strain:

> Some future strain, in which the Muse shall tell
> How *science* dwindles, and how *volumes* swell.
>
> How commentators each *dark* passage shun,
> And hold their farthing candle to the *sun*.
>
> How tortur'd texts to speak our sense are made,
> And every vice is to the scripture laid.
>
> How misers squeeze a young, voluptuous peer,
> His sins to *Lucifer* not half so dear.
>
> How *Verres* is less qualify'd to steal
> With sword and pistol, than with wax and seal.
>
> How lawyers' fees to such excess are run,
> That clients are redrest, 'till they're undone.
>
> How one man's anguish is another's sport,
> And even denials cost us dear at court.
>
> How man eternally false judgments makes,
> And all his joys and sorrows are *mistakes*. (7: 167)

The quality of the verse and the method of placing each couplet in
a new paragraph demand and hold our attention, and here, as else-
where in the *Love of Fame*, we see subjects which Pope treated in the
two *Epilogues to the Satires* and *The Dunciad*. What is to Pope the

---

37. *Horace: Satires, Epistles and Ars poetica*, Loeb Classical Library, trans.
H. Rushton Fairclough (Cambridge, Mass.: Harvard University Press, 1926),
p. 459.

symbol of imminent decay is to Young the symbol of a subject too frightening to contemplate, a subject the implications of which demand either an immediate denial (as in the treatment of women), or a flight back to the solid world of secure concerns, as exemplified in Young's reaction to the lines above:

> This swarm of themes that settles on my pen,
> Which I, like summer-flies, shake off again,
> Let others sing; to whom my weak essay
> But sounds a prelude, and points out their prey.
> That duty done, I hasten to compleat
> My own design; for *Tonson*'s at the gate. (7:168)[38]

In many cases Young's genteel follies have modest and sensible opposites recommended; but there is too often a terrible contrast between his apocalyptic vision and his genteel mask, between the objects he attacks and the norms which he sets against them. It sometimes appears that Young is placing a finger in a dyke with massive cracks, and is blithely confident that, after all, his efforts will save us from the flood.

Young's *Love of Fame*, then, includes thoughts, lines, and complete sections which are worthy of Pope's greatness and his greatest subjects. Paradoxically, these qualitatively superior sections offer a central reason for history's ultimate lack of interest in the complete poem—they suggest that he could not expand his moments of deepest vision, that he did not really understand his subject. In Swift's terms, he did not know that the land he calls blest he describes as curst and that the patrons whose help he so badly needed, whom he holds up as models for all of us and opposites to several of the vices attacked, are inadequate to their task. There is a marshmallow at the moral center of his poem. Add to this contradiction of vision and reaction

38. It is likely that this and the preceding, indented, passage show Young's reading of Boileau as he appeared in Ozell's translation. Canto 6 of *Le Lutrin*, for instance, includes eight paragraph-couplets portraying the grim vision of "Dangerous Heresies," while Satire Nine includes these lines:
> *Parnassus* thus with Wit is over-run,
> Like Swarms of Insects in a Summer's Sun.
See *The Works of Monsieur Boileau* . . . (London, 1712), 1:77, and 237, respectively.

the occasional absurdities his theory forces him into, the excessive use of the satiric pattern of blame and praise, and the general lack of probing insight in his characters, and we can see why though "of too great eminence to be passed over without notice,"[39] Young's satires are brilliant in part and failures on the whole. To a certain extent they fit a suggestive remark of Percival Stockdale: "I am grieved to think that Young is sometimes, in poetry, what a dancing-master is in manners."[40]

39. Hugh Blair, *Lectures on Rhetoric and Belles Lettres* (Dublin, 1783), 3: 171.
40. *Lectures on the Truly Eminent English Poets*, 1: 552.

6

Satire and Epistle:
The Traditional Distinction
and the Practice of Pope

I The Traditional Distinction

We recall that in his "Remarques sur le titre des epîtres" André
Dacier views both Horace's *Satires* and *Epistles* as generically satiric;
but it is the *Satires* which attack vice and the *Epistles* which praise
virtue; satires reprimand and refute, and epistles gently penetrate
the spirit (*insinuer*) and instruct. Dacier was one of the best-known
proponents of a distinction which was, in fact, a critical commonplace
with continental forbears at least as early as 1559. In that year
Lodovico Dolce remarks that in "the satires it was Horace's intention
to remove the vices from the breast of men, and in the epistles to
plant there the virtues."[1] Vauquelin de la Fresnaye and three of the
major scholar-critics of the sixteenth and seventeenth centuries prop-
agate a similar theory. In his *Poetics* (1561), for example, Julius
Caesar Scaliger observes of Horace's epistles: "just as medicine
either preserves from illness or carries illness off, these epistles pro-
pose those things with which we may abstain from vice, satire fights
with those by which vices are driven out."[2] Isaac Casaubon's famous

---

1. See the second *Discorso sopra le epistole* appended to his translation of
   Horace's *Epistles*, in Bernard Weinberg, *A History of Literary Criticism in
   the Italian Renaissance* (Chicago: University of Chicago Press, 1961),
   1: 143.
2. I am indebted to Professor John Oates for this and subsequent translations
   in the present chapter. *Poetices libri septem*, 5th ed. (Heidelberg, 1617):
   "Nam quemadmodum medicina aut preservat à morbis, aut eos tollit: ita
   Epistolae proponunt ea, quib à vitio abstineamus, Satyra illis pugnat, quibus
   vitia extirpentur" (p. 808). "Scaliger's Poetice" was in Johnson's own
   undergraduate library at Oxford: Allen Lyell Reade, *Johnsonian Gleanings*

129

De Satyrica Graecorum poesi, & Romanorum satira (Paris, 1605), includes a long discussion of Horace's two different kinds of satire. Some satires, he says, are critical, and written "for marking, laughing at and sharply criticizing men filled with vice"; others, however, are didactic and hope chiefly "to teach virtue and to inspire love of it." All of those poems called satires belong to the first category, for it is impossible to find one of them "which is free at every place from satiric sharpness. The epistles," however, "belong to the second category. . . ; there precepts of virtue are gathered for the most part stripped bare, but sometimes they are inserted in friendly conversation"; thus Horace's arguments about poetry are "more for the sake of teaching than for criticizing." Those who exclude the epistles from the genre of satire, he continues, "are not to be borne." After all, "did not even Lucilius write satires in the form of epistles?" Did not Persius write letters to Cornutus, among others? Does not Horace praise "Augustus and other friends," and is it not clear "from Trebatius in Horace" that Lucilius "did not always in his satires lash out at evil men?"[3]

(London: Privately Printed for the Author by Percy Lund, Humphries & Co., Ltd., 1928), 5:229. Johnson's translation of Pope's *Messiah* (1731) appeared with a motto from the *Poetics* (*ibid.*).

3. "Flacci Satiras duorum generum esse inter se diversorum. ná aliae sunt [critical], & ad notandos, ridendos, interdum & acrius increpandos vitiosos compositae: aliae ad praecipiendum de virtute, & eius amorem insinuandum, [didactic], non auté [critical]. Libri duo quos vulgo hodie Satirarú, veteres Sermonum titulo semper inscribunt, prioris generis sunt: in quibus nullam temere eclogam . . . invenias, Satirici aceti ab omni parte expertem. Epistolae, ad posteriorem quá diximus speciem pertinent, ibi praecepta virtutis plerumque nuda cógeruntur: interdum amicis sermonibus inseruntur. multa etiam in illis de poetices studiis erudite Flaccus disputat, magis docendi, quàm reprehendendi cuiusquam gratia" (pp. 290-91). . . . Ferendi non sunt, qui Epistolarum libros Satirarum appellatione ac numero consent excludendas. quid? nonne & Lucilius epistolarum forma Satiras quasdam scripserat? . . . . epistolae etiam sunt, quas maximus ille Horatii imitator Persius ad Plotium Macrinum, Annaeum Cornutum, & Caesium Bassum misit. at laudat Augustum & alios amicos in Epistolis Horatius: quod argumétum Satirae non conuenit. imo verò quam optimè convenit, & appellationi Satirae: ut postea evincemus: & formae eius carminis, quam illi primus auctor & inventor dederat. Lucilium enim in suis Satiris non semper malos lacerasse, verùm & bonos interdum laudasse, credamus Trebatio apud Horatium sic dicenti:
Attamen & iustum poteras & scribere fortem
Scipiadam ut sapiens Lucilius.

Daniel Heinsius also distinguishes between satires and epistles, though for him the satires have a philosophical quality not discussed in Casaubon's comparable section. The plan of Horace, he says, was to join "truth which is the soul of philosophy, and freedom which is the chief virtue of satire. Therefore he may teach virtue with different approaches, in the first books, those truly satires . . . by criticizing, in the later books which we now call epistles" by hortatory or doctrinal means, "by precept and teaching." Thus:

> In the first books he attacks not only the morals of men, but also the opinions of the philosophers, with the greatest urbanity, wit, charm, cleverness and humor; in the latter he preserves truth which he teaches, stripped of any authority. This he states in the beginning not without reason. You have both schemes and order in Plato. Thus Socrates nearly always argues before he teaches, as in the *Great Alcibiades* and elsewhere.[4]

As we might expect, this view was shared by numerous other commentators. Torrentius, for one, insists that the epistles fall under the generic term satire, but that the poems called satires show the "vices of men criticized in a variety of ways with Roman liberty and verbal license," whereas the subject of the epistles—"about morals or about poetry"—distinguishes them from the satires.[5] Rappolti also argues

ubi Horatius se quoque Augusti laudes Sermonibus suis intexturum recipit. atque ita fecit, maximè epistola prima libri secundi" (pp. 292-93).

4. *Quintus Horatius Flaccus. Accedunt nunc Danielis Heinsii de satyra Horatiana libri duo.* . . (Leiden, 1629): "Simul enim veritatem, quae est anima philosophiae; & libertatem, quae praecipua Satyrici est virtus, conjunxit. Quare cum diversa ratione doceat virtutem; in prioribus, ipsis nimirum Satyrarum libris, [critically], sive reprehendendo; in posterioribus, quas Epistolas nunc dicimus, quod magis erat usitatum, [hortorary] nonnunquam, nec non alibi [doctrinally], seu praecipiendo ac docendo; in prioribus fidenter, non in mores tantum hominum, sed philosophorum quoque opiniones, plurima urbanitate, sale, lepore, dicacitate & risu incurrit; sicut in Posterioribus, nudam sine auctoritate veritatem sequitur, quam docet. quod & in principio nó sine causa prositetur. Utramque autem rationem in Platone habes, ut & ordinem. Ita Socrates perpetuo fere arguit, priusquam docet. Ut in magno Alcibiade, & alibi" (p. 226).

5. *Q. Horatius Flaccus, cum erudito Laevini Torrentii commentario.* . . . (Antwerp, 1608): "*Sermones* autem cùm dicimus, Epistolas etiam, atque adeò illam quoque quae ad Pisones inscribitur, comprehendimus. Quamquam enim hae maiore cura ac diligentia conscriptae sunt, hoc ad rem potiùs

that in the epistles the poet "teaches virtue as much as possible . . . in a hortatory manner, but in the [satires] he attacks vice . . . [by disparaging] in a reviling manner."[6] Desprez, whose Horace *In usum Sereniss. DELPHINI*" was well-known, similarly thought that the epistles include matters "concerning the formation of habits with true virtue,"[7] while other writers throughout Europe and throughout the sixteenth to eighteenth centuries continued to say that Horatian satires and epistles were both generically "satiric," but that the former was critical and sharper, the latter overtly instructive and gentler.[8]

quam tractat referendum est. . . . Accedat quod quae absentibus scribuntur meritò *Epistolae* nominantur, ad quarum differentiam appellatae sunt *Satyrae*, quibus hominum vitia variè ac promiscuè, Romana libertate, verborumque licentia, reprehenduntur" (p. 414). "Hoc Horatii opus [Epistles], pars altera Sermonum eius est. Sed . . . meritò vel ob id tantùm Epistolarum titulo publicata, quòd ea, quae partim de moribus, partim de poësi dicere instituerat, per literas ad absentes amicos, & quidem diversis temporibus atque occasionibus datas, tractat" (p. 620).

6. *D. Frid. Rappolti, commentarius in Q. Horatii Flacci, satyras & epistolas* . . . (Leipzig, 1675): "Quanquam enim hoc intersit inter libros Sermonum & qui Epistolarú nomine inscribuntur, quòd istis . . . exhortatoriè potissimum virtutem doceat Poëta, illis . . . conviciatoriè vitia & delicta insectetur: ita tamen connexos semper utrosque consuerunt eruditiores . . ." (p. 452).

7. *Quinti Horatii Flacci opera. Interpretatione, notis & indice illustravit Ludovicus Desprez* (Amsterdam, 1695): "Haec pars Horatii sermonum altera dici potest, continens Epistolas, in quibus eleganter & ornatè quidem ad amicos scribit non tam de rebus domesticis & futilibus, quàm de gravissimis quibusque, puta de moribus verâ virtute informandis" (p. 723).

8. For other contemporary discussions of the satire and epistle, see *L'Arte poetica del signor Antonio Minturno* (Naples, 1725), pp. 273-74 (this is a reprint of his 1563 Venice edition); *Q. Horatii Flacci operum pars prima. . . . Quibus notas addidit Eduardus a Zurck* (Haarlem, 1696), p. 451; Charles Brosette, ed., *Satyres et autres oeuvres de Regnier* (London, 1733), pp. 10-11, n. 38, and p. 246, n. 2; *Q. Horatii Flacci eclogae . . . restivit Willielmus Baxter . . . et varietate lectionis . . . auxit Io. Matthias Gesnerus* (Leipzig, 1752), pp. 313-14; *Q. Horatii Flacci carmina, cum annotationibus Joannis Bond. Ad usum scholarum* (Paris, 1765), p. xi (this "Oratio Praevia" is not Bond's). There are also English and French discussions of interest. See Ambrose Philips, *Spectator*, no. 618 (1714); Jean Marmièr, *Horace en France, aux dix-septième siècle*, Université de Rennes, Faculté de lettres et de sciences humaines publications (Paris: Presses Universitaire, 1962), pp. 199-211, 227-33, 273, 309; Eduard Fraenkel, *Horace* (Oxford: Clarendon Press, 1957), pp. 308-63 (Fraenkel refers to two studies regarding "the novelty of Horace's *Epistles*," [see p. 309, n. 1]); and see Eugene R. Purpose, "The 'Plain, Easy, and Familiar Way': The Dialogue in English Literature, 1660–1725," *ELH*, 17 (1950): 47-58; Jay Arnold Levine, "The Status of the Verse Epistle before Pope," *SP*, 59 (1962): 658-84. There are also useful remarks scattered throughout C. O.

Dacier's observations on this distinction offer an interesting chron-
ological and geographical fulcrum, for they are both a repository for
the continental tradition and one of the springboards by which the
tradition was fostered in contemporary Europe and England. For instance, Dacier states that in his first book of *Satires* Horace "travaille
à déraciner les vices; & que dans le second il s'efforce d'arracher les
erreurs & les fausses opinions"; in the *Epistles*, "il s'attach à y donner
des preceptes pour la vertu, & à allumer dans nos coeurs l'amour
qu'elle merite." Similarly, "il faut arracher d'un champ toutes les
épines & les méchantes herbes . . . avant que d'y semer le bon grain."
The sources of much of Dacier's expression are Vauquelin de la
Fresnaye's "Discours" on satire (1604) and book 3 of his *Art poétique* (1605). Since Boileau's *Art poétique* was silent regarding the
epistle, Saint-Marc's, and other, editions of Boileau reprint this section of Vauquelin's poem:

> Si puis après on veut la toile ourdir & tistre,
> Du Vers sententieux de l'enseignante Epistre,
> Le Vray fil de la trame Horace baillera,
> Libre, grave, joyeux, à qui travaillera;
> Et tu verras chez luy qu'aux Satyres il tâche
> Arracher de nos coeurs les vices qu'il *attache: *attaque.
> Et que tout au contraire aux Epistres il veut
> Mettre & planter en nous toutes vertus s'il peut.
> Une Epistre s'éscrit aux personnes absentes,
> La Satyre se dit aux personnes présentes
> Sans grande difference: & pourroient proprement
> Sous le nom de Sermons se ranger aisément. (3: 275–86)[9]

Brink, *Horace on Poetry* (Cambridge, 1963), and Niall Rudd, *The Satires
of Horace* (Cambridge, 1966).

9. As quoted from *Oeuvres de M. Boileau Despréaux*, ed. M. de Saint-Marc
(Paris, 1747), 2:59; original is italicized throughout; some accents have
been added. Saint-Marc's edition was reprinted in (among other times and
places) Amsterdam, 1772; see 2:291 of that edition for the relevant passage.
For a complete study and edition of Vauquelin's work, see Georges Pellisier,
L'Art poétique de Vauquelin de la Fresnaye (Paris, 1885). Pellisier notes
similar lines in Vauquelin's own "Discours" on satire: "il semble qu'en ses
Satyres son intention ait esté d'arracher le vice du coeur des hommes, d'en
desfricher et deraciner les mauvaises herbes; pour en ses Epistres y planter
au lieu les vertus et y enter et greffer des fruits d'un bon ordre" (p. 141).

Dacier also adapts Scaliger's image of satire and epistle as medicine, Casaubon's discussion of epistolary praise by Lucilius, Horace, and Persius, and Heinsius' example of Socrates arguing before teaching. Shortly thereafter, in 1696, Eduardus a Zurck's Haarlem edition of Horace borrows liberally from Dacier's "Remarques"; moreover, as its many editions suggest, Dacier's *Horace* was popular throughout much of eighteenth-century France.

It is likely that serious English students of Horace and Roman satire knew several of the major and minor sixteenth-century Latin texts; but it is demonstrably true that even the intelligent common reader would have been aware of the works of Scaliger, Casaubon, Heinsius, Dacier, and Desprez. In his "Discourse on the Original and Progress of Satire," for example, Dryden often refers to and adapts the first four writers, and says of Dacier in particular:

> I am now almost gotten into my depth [concerning the origin of satire]; at least, by the help of Dacier, I am swimming towards it. Not that I will promise always to follow him, any

For the complete context, see Vauquelin's Préface to his *Satyres françoises* (1604), "Discours pour servir de préface sur le sujet de la Satyre," in *Les Diverses poésies de Jean Vauquelin*, ed. Julièn Travers (Caen, 1869), 1: 131-32; and for a study of the mutations in medieval and Renaissance French satiric theory (among other verse forms), see Warner Forest Patterson, *Three Centuries of French Poetic Theory: A Critical History of the Chief Arts of Poetry in France, 1328–1630* (New York: Russell & Russell, 1966).

It is probable that Boileau knew Vauquelin's work; Saint-Marc notes several analogues and verbal parallels between the two *Arts*. It is also probable that he knew Dacier's remarks on the Horatian epistle. The Préface (1698) to his Épître 10 echoes Dacier (see p. 64, above): "j'ai lu plusieurs fois cette épître à un fort grand nombre de docteurs de Sorbonne, de pères de l'Oratoire et de jésuites très-célèbres, qui tous y ont applaudi, et en ont trouvé la doctrine très-saine et très-pure": *Oeuvres de Boileau*, ed. A. Charles Gidel [Paris: Garnier Frères, 1928], pp. 144-45). He also remarks: "que ces deux épîtres, quoique dans le style enjoué, étoient pourtant des épîtres morales, où il n'étoit rien enseigné que de vertueux" (p. 144). Dacier and Boileau were friends and, on at least one occasion, entertained Matthew Prior: "The last few months that Prior spent in Paris [in 1699] were notable for his acquaintance with the French literary men, and we find him going to dine one evening with Boileau, Fontenelle, Abbé Régnier, and Monsieur Dacier at some fine home in Charonne, and perhaps the next 'with Boileau and the *beaux Esprits* at Auteuil'" (Charles Kenneth Eves, *Matthew Prior: Poet and Diplomatist* [New York: Columbia University Press, 1939], p. 137).

more than he follows Casaubon but to keep him in my eye, as my best and truest guide, and where I think he may possibly mislead me, there to have recourse to my own lights, as I expect that others should do by me.[10]

At about the same time a writer for the *Gentleman's Journal* heard "that there is a new *Horace, in usum Delphini* printed at *Paris* . . . . It is," he says, "a bold undertaking after Mr. *Dacier.*"[11] In his letter to Matthew Prior "Upon the Roman Satirists" (1721), John Dennis includes all but Desprez—who had little to say about qualitative distinctions between the satirists—among the major writers on his subject.[12] In the same year Alexander Cunningham[13] often refers to these and other commentators while, as I have noted earlier, David Watson later translated Dacier's remarks on the epistles and called them "a better Account . . . than I have anywhere met with."[14]

The work of these Continental critics was familiar to a practicing poet like Pope as well as to English editors, theoreticians, and readers

10. See *Essays of John Dryden*, ed. W. P. Ker (Oxford: Clarendon Press, 1926), 2:53.
11. *The Gentleman's Journal: or the Monthly Miscellany. By Way of Letter to a Gentleman in the Country*, 1 (October, 1692): 20. For other favorable mention of Dacier's *Horace*, see *ibid.*, 2 (June, 1693):195; *ibid.*, 3: (June, 1694):173.
12. *The Critical Works of John Dennis*, ed. E. N. Hooker (Baltimore: Johns Hopkins Press, 1943), 2:218, 220. Hooker notes that Prior "associated with Dacier in Paris during the period of his friendship with Boileau" (2:490); hence Dennis refers to him as "Your Friend, *Monsieur Dacier*" (2:220).
13. *Q. Horatii Flacci poemata* (The Hague, 1721), *passim.* Note, too, that Philip Francis' popular translation of Horace (London, 1746), includes "Critical Notes collected from the best Latin and French Commentators"; Dacier is by far the most frequently cited authority. Furthermore, many educated readers were likely to own an edition of Dacier as well as other texts, commentaries, or translations. One finds a combination of seven such works in Gibbon's library: see *The Library of Edward Gibbon: A Catalogue of His Books*, intro. Geoffrey Keynes (London: Jonathan Cape, 1940), pp. 153-54. The sale catalogue of Johnson's library includes five editions of Horace (Torrentius and Bentley among them), "Juvenalis & Persius, Casaubon . . . 1695," and one other edition of Juvenal (*A Catalogue of the Valuable Library of Books of the Late Learned Samuel Johnson* [London, 1785], pp. 11, 20, 25-26).
14. *The Works of Horace*, 3rd ed. (London, 1750), 2:li. Bentley also offers high praise to Scaliger, Casaubon, and Heinsius (*Q. Horatius Flaccus, ex Recensione & cum Notes atque Emendationibus Richardi Bentleii*, 3rd ed. [Amsterdam, 1728], pp. 549, 610, 564).

of literature. Ruffhead, on Warburton's authority, reports that between Pope's fifteenth and twentieth years "he devoted himself entirely to the reading of the most considerable poets and critics in the Greek, Latin, French, Italian and English languages," and that at twenty he reviewed much of his earlier studies in a more rigorous manner.[15] He probably read Scaliger during this period, and he later told Spence that his *"Poetics* is an exceeding useful book in its kind, and extremely well collected";[16] and, of course, Dryden's essay on satire, which Pope knew,[17] alluded to most of the sources necessary for a study of Roman satire. Perhaps of even greater importance, is the fact that he owned or used copies of Heinsius, Desprez, Bentley, and Cunningham,[18] and that at one point he explicitly acknowledges Dacier's authority, and at another even adapts one of his notes. In a letter to the Duke of Buckingham, September 1, 1718, Pope declares that the Frenchman's critical "remarks on Horace shew more good Sense, Penetration, and a better Taste of his author, . . . than any of Madame Dacier's on any author whatever."[19] And Warburton reports that in Pope's *First Epistle of The First Book of Horace Imitated* (1738), the "poet has happily served himself of this impertinence [recorded by Dacier regarding a critic's note on *Hic Murus aheneus esto*] to convey a very fine stroke of satire."[20]

We are, therefore, justified in assuming that the widely held notion of Horatian satire as including poems both largely acerbic

15. Owen Ruffhead, *The Life of Alexander Pope, Esq.* (London, 1769), pp. 17-19.
16. *Anecdotes . . . of Books and Men. By Joseph Spence*, ed. James M. Osborne (Oxford: Clarendon Press, 1966), 1: 20. Osborne notes that "Pope refers to [Scaliger's *Poetics*] in the *Narrative of Dr. Norris* (1713) and in the Preface to the *Iliad* (1715)" *(ibid.)*.
17. *The Correspondence of Alexander Pope*, ed. George Sherburn (Oxford: Clarendon Press, 1956), 1: 99.
18. For discussion of Pope's texts, see Bonamy Dobrée, "Pope's Horace," *Times Literary Supplement* (August 12, 1939), p. 479; Lillian D. Bloom, "Pope as Textual Critic: A Bibliographical Study of his Horatian Text," *JEGP*, 47 (1948) : 150-55; Robert W. Rogers' corrective review of Mrs. Bloom, above, *PQ*, 28 (1949) : 397-98; *Alexander Pope: Imitations of Horace*, The Twickenham Edition of the Poems of Alexander Pope, vol. 4, ed. John Butt, 2d ed. (London: Methuen & Co., 1953), p. xliii.
19. *Correspondence*, Sherburn, 1: 492.
20. *The Works of Alexander Pope, Esq.* ed. William Warburton (London, 1751), 4: 112.

(satire) and largely gentle and instructive (epistle) would have been known to Pope through several possible sources, and that it might have influenced his practice in poems of these kinds. An examination of the tone of Pope's satires and epistles will reveal that this is, in fact, the case. This does not mean that one of Pope's satires will inevitably be harsher than an epistle; nor does it mean that the distinction between the two similar forms will always be clear or reliable.[21] To state this would, on the one hand, be artificially to twist the poet's practice to meet the historian's theory, since even some poets aware of the common distinction may have chosen to ignore it; on the other, it would be unfaithful to the Renaissance view of Horatian satire which Dacier discusses. Both forms are "satiric," both attack, and both praise; the differences are in degree, not essence. Accordingly, we must recall, with Dacier, that the contrast between them need not be rigorous and consistent; specific poems may be slightly, partially, or primarily satiric or epistolary, and may include generous portions of the opposite voice. At times, indeed, we should say no more than that a poem *tends* toward one genre or the other; thus the *Epistle to Bathurst* (1733) includes sections which suggest parts of *The Dunciad* (1743), and the *Epistle to Dr. Arbuthnot* (1735) punitive sections which pillory their victims. Perhaps a "satiric spectrum" ranging from moderate attack and substantial praise, to harsh attack and little praise, would be helpful in isolating and discussing certain central aspects of the particular satire at hand. *Bathurst*, for instance, clearly lacks *The Dunciad*'s gloom, and even *Arbuthnot*'s attack on Sporus has certain modifying qualities, for he is reduced to such a contemptuous position that we can

---

21. A remark by Joseph Spence, in *Polymetis* (London, 1747), shows the danger of insisting on too hard (or too universal) a distinction between the forms: "I do not remember that any one of the antients says any thing of [Horace's] epistles: and this has made me sometimes imagine, that his epistles and satires might originally have passed under one and the same name; perhaps that of Sermones. They are generally written in a style approaching to that of conversation; and are so much alike, that several of the satires might just as well be called epistles, as several of his epistles have the spirit of satire in them. This latter part of his works, by whatever name you please to call them (whether satires and epistles, or discourses in verse on moral and familiar subjects,) is what I must own, I love much better even than the lyric part of his works" (p. 22).

no longer regard him as a threat to anyone. In this epistle the satiric adversary is demolished and Pope is triumphant; in the *Dialogues* (1738) the adversary is triumphant and England is demolished.

We can see the distinction between the forms in several ways: the conception of the value and efficacy of the particular poetic mode; the reason for writing; the *ethos* of the speaker; the different treatment of similar subjects; and, overlapping with several of these topics, the conception of Horatian satire itself.

II The Practice of Pope

The satirist is generally concerned with broadly social, public, or political matters, and so the implications of his remarks should be considered by the administrators of the state and by the public at large. Thus the final *coup* of the speaker of Pope's *First Satire of the Second Book of Horace Imitated* (*Fortescue* [1733]), is to make clear that his "grave *Epistles,* bringing Vice to light"[22] will be applauded by the King and could be written by a Bishop; most important of all, they are "Such as Sir *Robert* would approve." With the public coercive powers of the Throne, Church, and Administration behind Pope, "the Case is alter'd" and "the Plaintiff will be hiss'd,/ My Lords the Judges laugh, and you're dismiss'd" (ll. 151–56). Indeed, the central metaphor of the poem is that of a trial, and the central irony that of seeing the plainiff in a public courtroom, with all the machinery of the law behind him, nevertheless hoist with his own petard.

Even so superficially moderate a satire as *The Second Satire of the Second Book of Horace, Paraphrased* (*Bethel* [1734]) not only demands an audience that is extensive, but also portrays a vision of mankind too brutal to be found in the epistles. In this poem the main

---

22. John Butt's gloss of this line suggests Pope's conscious awareness of the satire-epistle distinction. (The line itself, of course, suggests that Pope thought this particular satire highly epistolary; there is no precedent for it in Horace.) "'You call your satires, libels: I would rather call my satires, epistles. They will consist more of morality than of wit, and grow graver, which you will call duller.' Pope to Swift, Apr. 2, 1733" (*Imitations of Horace,* p. 21).

object of attack is Man, who is "all . . . one intestine war" (1. 72) because of his gluttony; this deadly sin is not limited to one segment of society, for the glutton will rise pale "from a Clergy, or a City, feast!" (1. 76) The ill-treated body attacks even man's soul:

> What life in all that ample Body, say,
> What heav'nly Particle inspires the clay?
> The Soul subsides; and wickedly inclines
> To seem but mortal, ev'n in sound Divines. (ll. 77–80)

The glutton's soul will "subside" in more senses than one—the "Luxury" inherent in his sin leads to social ostracism and personal despair. Lord Fanny will thus be "To friends, to fortune, to mankind a shame," and so will commit the ultimate crime of suicide (ll. 105–10). Pope again reinforces the public nature of his satire when he insists that he "Who thinks that Fortune cannot change her mind,/ Prepares a dreadful Jest for all mankind" (ll. 123–24); and he portrays an excrutiatingly wicked and foolish world in his brief characters of the "ungracious Son," the "booby Lord," the "Scriv'ner or a City Knight" (ll. 173–78), and, worst of all, the penurious couple who considered it a "lucky day . . . when they found/ A lost Bank-bill, or heard their Son was drown'd" (ll. 55–56).

The public and political quality of the satires are most intense in the two *Dialogues*, "Something," though not very much, "like Horace." In the first *Dialogue* we hear references to Jenkins' ear, the Patriot opposition to Walpole, old Whigs, the Lord Chamberlain and stage-licensing, Lyttleton and the Prince of Wales, Fleury, Queen Caroline, and *The Gazeteer*. Much of the poem attacks the hierarchy of evil that has reversed the accepted order of "old England." Instead of turning to the ruling classes as models of piety and virtue, the people now see Vice glorified in "*Greatness*": "Her Birth, her Beauty, Crowds and Courts confess,/ Chaste Matrons praise her, and grave Bishops bless" (ll. 145–46). The "World" is drawn behind the triumphant chariot of Vice, who "Mounts the Tribunal" to see England betrayed, battered, seduced. Anything or anyone—"Country, Parent, Wife, or Son!" (1. 158)—will be offered for gold, and anyone— "Soldier, Churchman, Patriot, Man in Pow'r" (1. 161)—will do the offering. The nation is the satirist's object of attack, and the leaders of Church and state are the most culpable.

The second *Dialogue* is even more political in nature, as Pope ironically laments because "my Country's Ruin makes me grave" (l. 207), and he futilely attempts "To rowze the Watchmen of the Publick Weal" (l. 217). The satirist is thus not a man writing to one other man, but is "a Friend to ev'ry worthy mind"; he reacts not like the gentle gadfly but "as Man, who feel[s] for all mankind" (ll. 203–4).

The demands of the epistle—here confined to *Arbuthnot* and the *Imitations of Horace*—produced a very different kind of poem. In this form the poet is writing to an absent and esteemed friend. He talks about himself, or a situation relevant to him and his correspondent, or the follies indigenous to them; by implication the folly is extensive; in practice—the poem before us—it is limited to a smaller circle. The solution is thus not to replace Walpole, purge the Church, declare war on Spain, or return to the good old days of British valor; instead, it is in the private realm, for, ultimately, this sort of epistle is "about" the writer himself. Pope must "learn to smooth and harmonize my Mind," to "keep the equal Measure of the Soul" (*Cobham*, ll. 203, 205);[23] he speaks of "That God of Nature, who, within us still,/ Inclines our Action, not constrains our Will" (*ibid.*, ll. 280–81); he will try to correct "Th' unbalanc'd Mind," hopes to cure "the Mind's disease," and insists: "The Man that loves and laughs, must sure do well" (*Murray*, ll. 24, 58, 129). Thus in his epistles he says that all his care is "What right, what true, what fit, we justly call" (*Bolingbroke*, l. 19); but these consist not in broad public concerns but in the individual's relationship with himself. Hence he asks certain "sober questions of my Heart" (*Cobham*, l. 211), dislikes things "That keep me from Myself" (*Bolingbroke*, l. 41), observes that "He's arm'd without that's innocent within" (*ibid.*, l. 94), and

23. The following shortened references have been used in the text: *Cobham* for *The Second Epistle of the Second Book of Horace, Imitated* (1734); *Murray* for *The Sixth Epistle of the First Book of Horace, Imitated* (1738); *Bolingbroke* for *The First Epistle of the First Book of Horace, Imitated; Fortescue* for *The First Satire of the Second Book of Horace, Imitated.* Quotations from these poems, *Sober Advice from Horace*, the *Epistle to Dr. Arbuthnot*, and the two *Dialogues* (*Epilogue to the Satires*) are from *Imitations of Horace*, Butt.

berates Bolingbroke not because he has betrayed the Opposition's cause, but because he is "Careless how ill I with myself agree" (*ibid.*, l. 175). Similarly, the satirist is a good man because of his antipathy of good to bad; in the epistle he is good because of his good parents. One might say that the satirist is filled with rage because the world's paradise without has been destroyed by highly placed villains, whereas the epistolary writer is annoyed because he has not yet achieved a vaguely achievable paradise within.

Such different views will also structure both the writer's ostensible reason for writing and his apparent conception of the importance of what he writes. In the *Epistle to Dr. Arbuthnot*, for instance, Pope insists that he "Can sleep without a Poem in my head" (l. 269), and complains: "Heav'ns! was I born for nothing but to write?" (l. 272) The Advertisement to *Arbuthnot* proclaims that Pope wrote this *"Bill of Complaint"* only because his "Person, Morals, *and* Family" (*Imitations*, p. 95) were scurrilously attacked; he does not *want* to be a satirist, insists that his poems have no effect anyway (ll. 83–100), and, in general, wishes only to be left alone with his few good friends. In the *Second Epistle of the Second Book* he again complains—"D'ye think me good for nothing but to rhime?" (l. 32), and then insists, "Sure I should want the Care of ten *Monroes*,/ If I would scribble, rather than repose" (ll. 70–71). Indeed, there is little point in his writing at all, since "out of twenty I can please not two" (l. 81). In the epistles, then, satiric poetry offers little efficacy or pleasure to either poet or audience.

The case is altered in the satires. Pope tells Fortescue, for example, that "Fools rush into my Head, and so I write" (l. 14); instead of not being able to please two of twenty, Pope is there able to please Kings, Bishops, Ministers, and Judges; the satirist is not nearly so reluctant here as in *Arbuthnot*, for instead of family, person, and morals being attacked, now he merely says: "But touch me, and no Minister so sore" (l. 76). Satire is his peculiar weapon and "Pow'r to hurt," and "What-e'er my Fate" (l. 92), even if death, he will be "arm'd for *Virtue*," and "Brand the bold Front of shameless, guilty Men" (ll. 85, 92, 105–6). Far from being useless his satire can make vicious men tremble. He emphasizes the relative public strength of his satire—and by implication its difference from an epistle—even more in the *Dialogues*. In *Arbuthnot*, we recall, the young Pope published because his distinguished friends urged him to (ll. 135–46); in the second *Dialogue* he must "print to day" (l. 3) because "Vice with such Giant-strides comes on amain" (l. 6). Pope is not concerned with revenging himself and his parents upon his attackers—his urgent satire is based upon "The strong Antipathy of Good to Bad" (l. 198), and the Bad are not enemies of Pope, but of God, who ordains and directs his poem:

> O sacred Weapon! left for Truth's defence,
> Sole Dread of Folly, Vice, and Insolence!
> To all but Heav'n-directed hands deny'd,
> The Muse may give thee, but the Gods must guide. (ll. 212–15)

Pope's satire is thus "diadem'd with Rays divine," is "Touch'd with the Flame that breaks from Virtue's Shrine" and "ope's the Temple of Eternity" (ll. 232–35) for the Good. This is not merely "satire" but sanctified lines of immortal verse (l. 247). As a satirist Pope is God's agent; he punishes offenders at this moment rather than at the end of their lives:

> Yes, I am proud; I must be proud to see
> Men not afraid of God, afraid of me:
> Safe from the Bar, the Pulpit, and the Throne,
> Yet touch'd and sham'd by *Ridicule alone*. (ll. 208–11)

In spite of Divine guidance and his own passionate defense of virtue, the satiric pose places Pope alone in a world of decaying British values (*Dialogue* 1: 171–72), and so the satires take on a tragic quality, a quality of inexorable nobility in the face of defeat. Compared to the white heat of the *Dialogues* the portrait of Sporus is a springtime romp: *Arbuthnot* and its epistolary form is closer to comedy; the satires closer to tragedy.

As agent of an angry God Pope's satiric pose is also angry; he is willing to die in virtue's cause, and knows that his may be "the last Pen for Freedom" (*Dialogue* 2: 248). Throughout the satires Pope is convinced that he is right in his cause, that the virtuous are his friends, that God has inspired him, and that a positive eternity is waiting. In the epistles the speaker's pose is gentler, more mundane, less certain, and more aware of the human situation. Accordingly, in *Cobham* the fearless satirist is no more; he worries because in the city "a nodding Beam, or Pig of Lead,/ God knows, may hurt the very ablest Head" (ll. 102–3). He even admits that he may have a whim "To court applause by printing what I write" (ll. 150–51); in *Bolingbroke* he admits that he must "put my self to school" (l. 47), and later observes that his noble self-image as "demi-god" may be dissipated by "A Fit of Vapours" (l. 188).

The more tolerant *ethos* of the epistles helps to account for the vast difference between the satiric and epistolary treatment of similar themes. In both *Fortescue* and *Sober Advice from Horace* (1734), Pope treats Lady Mary with, let us say, little respect: even "P–x'd by her Love, or libell'd by her Hate" (l. 84) is moderate compared with the scurrility of the latter poem. In *Arbuthnot*, however, Pope merely alludes to her provocation of him (l. 369), and in *Bolingbroke* (l. 164) says that his own untidy linen is sometimes as bad as hers. In *Arbuthnot* flattery is an amusing, if distressing, form of madness ll. 104–24); in the second *Dialogue* it turns Pope's stomach and "is Excrement" (ll. 181–84). In the epistle to Bolingbroke Pope attacks gold as another example of what not to admire (ll. 77ff.); in the first *Dialogue* this foolish passion has been turned into "golden Chains," the path to slavery, corruption, and the loss of "Old *England*'s Genius" (ll. 147 ff.). Perhaps of greatest interest, however, is Pope's treatment of the degradation of the stage and of farces in particular. In *The Dunciad* they are signs of uncreation, of the debasement of western culture, the final triumph of the *translatio stultitiae*, and, accordingly, the end of Britain as the last bastion against darkness. In the *Epistle to Augustus* (1737), to be sure, Pope criticizes farce as unworthy of the Lords who compose much of its audience, but the criticism both lacks the apocalyptic quality of *The Dunciad* and includes an overt comment on its laughable—if sad—aspect:

> With laughter sure Democritus had dy'd,
> Had he beheld an Audience gape so wide.

Let Bear or Elephant be e'er so white,

The people, sure, the people are the sight. (ll. 320–23)

These several differences in tone, content, and method, imply that Pope's practice was influenced by the theoretical distinction between satire and epistle. The distinction may have been reinforced in Pope's mind by what he considered Horace's own practice; in the poems I have cited he is, after all, an imitator, and thus has placed certain limits upon his freedom. But the satiric form as Pope finally used it is overtly un-Horatian; in being most satiric (that is, most acerbic) Pope explicitly denounces the Horatian way of genteel urbanity. In the first *Dialogue* he ironically puts the Horatian apologia into the mouth of an "impertinent Censurer" attempting to dissuade Pope from writing his harsh satire:

But *Horace*, Sir, was delicate, was nice;

Bubo observes, he lash'd no sort of *Vice*:

Horace would say, *Sir* Billy *serv'd the Crown,*

Blunt *could do Bus'ness,* H--ggins *knew the Town,*

In *Sappho* touch the *Failing of the Sex,*

In rev'rend Bishops note some *small Neglects,*

And own, the *Spaniard* did a *waggish thing,*

Who cropt our Ears, and sent them to the King.

His sly, polite, insinuating stile

Could please at Court, and make Augustus smile:

An artful Manager, that crept between

His Friend and Shame, and was a kind of *Screen.* (ll. 11–22) [24]

Horace, leagued with Pope's satiric victims, becomes a victim himself; England no longer had room for the epistle or for moderate

24. These lines have been discused in John M. Aden's excellent article, "Pope and the Satiric Adversary," *SEL,* 2 (1962) : 282, and by Lilian Feder, "Sermo or Satire: Pope's Definition of his Art," in *Studies in Aesthetics and Criticism, 1660–1800: Essays in Honor of Samuel Holt Monk,* ed. Howard Anderson and John Shea (Minneapolis: University of Minnesota Press, 1967), pp. 152-54. G. K. Hunter and Rachel Trickett both observe that these lines echo Dryden's translation of Persius, *Satires,* 1: 231-36 ("The 'Romanticism' of Pope's Horace," *Essays in Criticism,* 10 [1960]: 390, and *The Honest Muse* [Oxford: Clarendon Press, 1967], p. 95, respectively). One should also see Hunter's essay for a reading of *Bathurst* rather different from my own.

satire. It is part of Pope's greatness as a poet that he knew when literary precedent was and was not suited for his aims; accordingly, we should not conclude that the distinction between satire and epistle is Horace's alone and not Pope's, and that it appears only in his overt Imitations: Pope's use of the distinction appears in his "independent" poems as well.

The *Ethic Epistles*, for instance, are not epistolary in the same way as the *Imitations of Horace*, but they do include many of the same traits that we have found there. They often "attack," but with moderation, and generally aim at illicit individual rather than political success; they are placed in the country rather than the city or else usually avoid specifically urban scenes; they are moderate in diction (there is nothing there like *Sober Advice from Horace*) and show the poet not as an agent of God, but as a man talking to men. Many of the "characters" in these epistles also share the dominant traits of the Atticus portrait in *Arbuthnot*, whose final couplet reads:

> Who but must laugh, if such a man there be?
> Who would not weep, if *Atticus* were he! (ll. 213–14)

The same sense of sadness motivates the portrait of Wharton in the first epistle, *Of the Knowledge and Characters of Men* (1733). This man of extraordinary abilities can make Senates wonder, is generous, and has an angel's tongue, but his ruling passion makes him "the scorn and wonder of our days."[25] This self-destructive desire for praise makes him battle against himself, so that he tyrannizes the wife and rebels against the king he loves. The character is permeated by the sense of a great man who could not conquer his own worst tendencies, and so "He dies, sad out-cast of each church and state" (l. 204).

The term "weep" appeared for Atticus, and "sad" for Wharton. Pope uses "Sad" again when describing the dual character of Narcissa in the second epistle, *Of the Characters of Women, To a Lady* (1735). She too is a creature made unhappy by her own irresolute nature: "Now Conscience chills her, and now Passion burns" (l. 65) ; she is

---

25. *Alexander Pope: Epistles to Several Persons*, The Twickenham Edition of the Poems of Alexander Pope, vol. 3, pt. 2, ed. F. W. Bateson, 2d ed. (London: Methuen & Co., 1961), pp. 30-33, ll. 179-207. Subsequent references to this work are cited in the text.

"A very Heathen in the carnal part,/ Yet still a sad, good Christian at her heart" (ll. 67–68).[26] Indeed, much of the second epistle (and the *Ethic Epistles* in general), use images or scenes of death, sickness, friendlessness, transiency, childlessness, and lovelessness. By and large, Pope concerns himself with the individual's rather than society's malfunctioning psychology, and he tempers his analysis with a desire to correct a sad situation rather than punish an evil one. The old distinction between attacks on vice or folly is also useful in setting the satire apart from the epistle: in the former Pope will "Brand the bold Front of shameless, guilty Men" (*Fortescue*, l. 106); in the latter he says: "If Folly grows romantic, I must paint it" (*Characters of Women*, l. 16).

The Addison couplet has another important aspect: "Who but must laugh, if such a man there be?" he asks. In the fourth ethic epistle, to Burlington (1731), Pope echoes this line, and again suggests that misuse of one's native endowments is absurd. Thus Timon's extensive grounds—"his building is a Town,/ His pond an Ocean, his parterre a Down" (ll. 105–6)—merely set off his own meagre figure before God:

> Who but must laugh, the Master when he sees,
> A puny insect, shiv'ring at a breeze! (ll. 107–8)

In the epistles man is often sad, often silly, and generally not a danger to anyone but himself. Hence Timon's lavish waste of money and lack of "Sense" have positive results, since his several laborers are thus clothed and fed: "What his hard Heart denies,/ His charitable Vanity supplies" (ll. 169–72). Moreover, Timon's depredations of taste are temporary—the land and its people will soon restore sanity, "And laughing Ceres re-assumes the land" (ll. 173–76).

In the *Epistle to Bathurst*, however, it would seem that the poet is not only attacking in a harsh way, but also attacking the misuse of gold in a political, public fashion; after all, he laments that gold "bribes a Senate, and the Land's betray'd" (l. 34). But Pope's reaction to this bribery is not to become the inspired and passionate

---

26. "Sad" here primarily means "grave" or "sober"; but the connotation of unhappiness is nevertheless present. As a sober good Christian she would necessarily be made unhappy by her heathen behavior.

enemy of gilded Vice; nor does he even show this vice triumph. Instead, he adapts a *reductio ad absurdum* and, on the one hand, throws us backwards in time into a barter system, and on the other predicts future political decay. By the former method he attempts to laugh present bribery out of court; by the latter he avoids the satirist's obligation—witness the *Dialogues*— to attack present vice. Thus he begs that "bulky Bribes" be reinstated, so that gifts of a thousand jars of Spanish oil, bales of British cloth, or a hundred roaring oxen—not to mention whores, pigs, bulls, and sundry other forms of wealth—be delivered directly to one's door. The sight, we fancy, would be both comic and effective in reducing the problem of bribery. As for the second point, we hear that gold "*Can* pocket States, *can* fetch or carry Kings," and that "A single leaf *shall* waft an Army o'er" (ll. 72–73; ital. added). Some of the most powerful and political lines in the poem are recited by "A wizard" as a prophecy. The words "*At length*" adequately protect Pope from being forced into the *ethos* of the satirist's hatred for the vice which is all about him, and his auditor's reaction—" 'All this is madness,' cries a sober sage" (l. 153) —forces us to place the onus equally on the briber, "Much injur'd Blunt" (l. 135), and on the audience who refuses to be warned, as well as on the bribed Senate. The allusion to "watchful Ministers" also suggests a normative quality absent in the *Dialogues*.

> Much injur'd Blunt! why bears he Britain's hate?
> A wizard told him in these words our fate:
> "At length Corruption, like a gen'ral flood,
> "(So long by watchful Ministers withstood)
> "Shall deluge all; and Av'rice creeping on,
> "Spread like a low-born mist, and blot the Sun;
> "Statesman and Patriot ply alike the stocks,
> "Peeress and Butler share alike the Box,
> "And Judges job, and Bishops bite the town,
> "And mighty Dukes pack cards for half a crown.
> "See Britain sunk in lucre's sordid charms,
> "And France reveng'd of ANNE's and EDWARD's arms!"
>
> (ll. 135–46)

This foretelling wizard becomes a current reality in *The Dunciad*, where "a WIZARD OLD" extends the cup of destructive self-love (4: 517). But in these lines from *Bathurst*, and those immediately following, Pope nevertheless surely rises a key above his usual epistolary voice; but he never lapses into the satirist's, particularly since even Blunt's scandalous manipulation of the South Sea stocks is softened by the presence of God's benevolent, if mysterious, method:

> Hear then the truth: " 'Tis Heav'n each Passion sends,
> "And diff'rent men directs to diff'rent ends.
> "Extremes in Nature equal good produce,
> "Extremes in Man concur to gen'ral use."
> Ask we what makes one keep, and one bestow?
> That POW'R who bids the Ocean ebb and flow . . . . (ll. 161–66)

One cannot seriously attack misuse of riches without also attacking Him who "Builds Life on Death, on Change Duration founds" (l. 169). We are reminded that the *Essay on Man* is written in four epistles, and that it is the satires, especially the *Dialogues* and *The Dunciad* that deny that whatever is is right.

Finally, we might observe that the central normative character of *Bathurst*, in fact, of all the *Ethic Epistles*, is the Man of Ross. One of his praises is that he helps to settle disputes out of court—"Balk'd are the Courts" (l. 272)—that is, his is the private sphere. He is obscure of fame, birth, and fortune; he is loved by children, the poor, the aged, and the sick, and hated by quacks and attorneys; he represents simplicity, retirement, and a direct approach to human beings, as opposed to the complications and often dishonest indirection of medicine or law. His portrait contrasts with the public involvements and ultimate decay of Sir Balaam; and he is an epistolary norm, just as the Bolingbroke of the *First Satire of the Second Book* (*Fortescue*) is a satiric norm.[27]

I believe it now clear that Pope's satires are harsher in tone, more apocalyptic in scope, more biting in attack, and less affirmative in vi-

27. Pope's epistolary intention also appears in his letter to Oxford, November 7, 1731, where he observes: "I have . . . taken the Liberty to call at Your Door, in my way to Moral Virtue; as you will see when we meet" (*Correspondence*, 3: 241).

sion. The painted ceilings of Timon's villa (ll. 141–48) would symbol-
ize moral collapse in *The Dunciad*,[28] and laughing Ceres' reassump-
tion of the land would be several millennia away, while the wizard's
prophecy in *Bathurst* would be an achieved disaster in the *Dialogues*.
The satires include their pertinent sections of affirmation, but they
are shorter, less encouraging, and less central than those in the epistles. The "Friend" of the first *Dialogue* urges Pope to surrender his
satiric attacks and join the main stream of gilded English slavery.
After his long and terrifying speech Pope concludes the poem with
this couplet:

> Yet may this Verse (if such a Verse remain)
> Show there was one who held it in disdain. (ll. 171–72)

In spite of its forceful tone, the couplet's very existence is precarious;
the poet cannot be sure that his opposition verse will "remain," particularly since he is the only "one" who scorns the world of the adversary. The role of the adversary, indeed, is a good guide to the
poem's epistolary or satiric qualities and, therefore, the poem's place
on the satiric spectrum.

III   The Satiric Spectrum

The third ethic epistle begins with the disagreement of Pope and
Bathurst regarding the role of gold and the conception of God. Bathurst's is a pagan god toying with foolish man,[29] while Pope thinks
"more highly of our kind" and sees "careful Heav'n" benevolently

---

28. My use of *The Dunciad* in this essay does not mean that I regard it as a
formal verse satire; whatever its genre, however, it does include enough
satiric traits of tone, target, and vision, to make a useful contrast with
the epistles.
29. For a long and important discussion of this poem, see Earl R. Wasserman,
*Pope's Epistle to Bathurst: A Critical Reading with An Edition of the
Manuscripts* (Baltimore: Johns Hopkins Press, 1960), pp. 11-57; and for a
very different use of the concept of a "satiric spectrum," see Edward W.
Rosenheim, Jr., *Swift and the Satirist's Art* (Chicago: University of Chicago
Press, 1963), pp. 1-34. There are interesting discussions of the role of the
satiric speaker in Henry W. Sams, "Swift's Satire of the Second Person,"
ELH, 26 (1959): 36-44, and in Ronald Paulson, *The Fictions of Satire*
(Baltimore: Johns Hopkins Press, 1967), pp. 75-79.

adapting itself to man's folly. Hence when, in spite of "Nature's care," man discovered gold, God supplied both spendthrift and miser to insure a balance (ll. 13–14). But Pope refuses to be distressed by differences between the two men and, instead, seeks common ground:

> Like Doctors thus, when much dispute has past,
> We find our tenets just the same at last. (ll. 15–16)

Throughout the poem Pope subtly manipulates Bathurst, convinces him of his point of view and, since Pope and Heaven "are of a mind" (l. 8), turns a modern pagan into a good Christian. Thus at the outset the rakish Lord believes "the word, from Jove to Momus giv'n/ That Man was made the standing jest of Heav'n" (ll. 3-4). Halfway through the poem he has reversed his earlier position and is an orthodox Christian whose understanding of a benevolent God is now quite like Pope's: he will "teach us" to move between the extremes of prodigality and avarice. Accordingly, he must agree with the amiable description below:

> To Worth or Want well weigh'd, be Bounty giv'n,
> And ease, or emulate, the care of Heav'n.
> Whose measure full o'erflows on human race,
> Mend Fortune's fault, and justify her grace.
> Wealth in the gross is death, but life diffus'd;
> As Poison heals, in just proportion us'd:
> In heaps, like Ambergrise, a stink it lies,
> But well-dispers'd, is Incense to the Skies. (ll. 229–36) [30]

He encourages Pope to speak further about the Man of Ross, and listens patiently to the tale of Sir Balaam which, since the devil is so active an agent, is meant to show that there "are other worlds prepar'd" for those who misuse wealth and regard it and virtue as merely a name (l. 334). Bathurst's silence at the end of the poem can only signal his acceptance of Pope's world, one in which the use of gold may either ally or alienate one from God. Hence the final word Bathurst speaks is "Agreed" (l. 338), whereas the first line of the poem

---

30. Warburton attributes this paragraph to Bathurst (*Works of Alexander Pope*, 3:243). The mistake is understandable.

associates him with "Doctors [who] disagree." The epistolary structure of the poem moves from pagan to Christian, a misanthropic to
a benevolent God, and disagreement to agreement. Furthermore, the
tale of Sir Balaam contains several grim items which, nevertheless,
are held in comic suspension.[31] The tale includes a malicious devil,
two disastrous shipwrecks and ill-gotten wealth, dishonest acquisition
of a stolen diamond, a lost soul, a violation of the sabbath, rejection
of the Church and the Christian life, a death ordained by the devil,
a cuckolded husband, a foolish, lascivious son who is killed in a duel,
a noble daughter who is poxed, a wife's loss of her estate through
gambling, Sir Balaam's acceptance of a French bribe, the Commons'
impeachment of him, and his death by hanging:

> Wife, son, and daughter, Satan, are thy own,
> His wealth, yet dearer, forfeit to the Crown:
> The Devil and the King divide the prize,
> And sad Sir Balaam curses God and dies. (ll. 399–402)

Surely here is the devil's plenty; but the spirited quality of the verse,
the frequent jokes, and virtual gaiety of tone protect us from many
of the lines' terrifying implications. We see a vastly diminished devil
tempting an equally diminished "Job"; we see the devil in familiar
places like the 'Change and Parliament; we see him foolishly go to
a great deal of bother for a person like Balaam and, as well, do a
petty think like give his lady a cold. This epistle to a Lord does not
wish to rouse theological fervor, but modestly to coerce a rational
man back to orthodoxy. Pope does this in so amusing, persuasive,
and gentle a way, that not even a long passage regarding one of
Satan's successes can disturb the poem's quality of reconciliation.
Bathurst's implied consent to the point of the tale is more important
—in this context—than the tale's potentially frightening aspects.

Bathurst, then, is near the epistolary end of the satiric spectrum.

---

31. This and my subsequent remarks disagree with Wasserman's. He finds that
"the satiric venom of the poem will be drained into the ultimate object of
the satire, Sir Balaam" (*Pope's Epistle to Bathurst,* p. 43), that the tale
"is a bitterly satiric parable" (*ibid.,* p. 45), and that "Pope has wrung
from his final line ['and sad Sir Balaam curses God and dies'] every possible horror" (*ibid.,* p. 53).

Arbuthnot is both clearly an epistle and harsher in tone than *Bathurst*. Here Pope must defend not only his *"Person, Morals,* and *Family,"* but his role and integrity as a satirist. Arbuthnot is apt choice of "adversary" in many ways, and his title of Doctor is particularly appropriate. The first lines image Pope as a tired, beleaguered poet who tells his servant to "Tye up the knocker, say I'm sick, I'm dead" (l. 2). Shortly thereafter he again introduces a "medical" image when he calls Arbuthnot a "Friend to my Life," and credits him with prolonging his life and, thereby, propagating his poetry (ll. 27–28). This irony—Arbuthnot urged him not to write—introduces another irony and the beginning of a major reversal in the poem:

> What *Drop* or *Nostrum* can this Plague remove?
> Or which must end me, a Fool's Wrath or Love?
> A dire Dilemma! either way I'm sped,
> If Foes, they write, if Friends, they read me dead. (ll. 29–32)

However good a doctor he may be, Arbuthnot cannot cure the plague of bad poets who threaten to kill Pope. Accordingly, it is Pope himself who must become the doctor; it is he who must cure society—and thereby his own person, morals, and family—of the beasts who bite and kick (l. 78), the mad creatures with poisoned saliva (ll. 105–6), "the Itch of Verse and Praise" (l. 224), the Fop who "wounds an Author's honest fame," (l. 292) and, among others, the venomous Sporus who "stinks and stings" (l. 310). Since Arbuthnot's remedies are ineffectual, Pope uses his own, the satiric lash (l. 303), and uses it most harshly in the portrait of Sporus. This portrait is vital for several reasons: for one, it is preceded by Arbuthnot's rejection of his genteel animosity towards satire, and his use of some of Pope's own terminology. Earlier Pope had insisted: "take it for a rule,/ No creature smarts so little as a Fool" (ll. 83–84); and now Arbuthnot, in his own satiric lines, calls Sporus:

> ". . . that Thing of silk,
> *"Sporus,* that mere white Curd of Ass's milk?
> "Satire or Sense alas! can *Sporus* feel?
> "Who breaks a Butterfly upon a Wheel?" (ll. 305–8)

When Pope turns the butterfly into an obscene and dangerous bug, and then a toad, Arbuthnot has been irrevocably drawn into the satiric process, and the only objection he thereafter raises is the feeble: "why insult the Poor, affront the Great?" (l. 360)

The Sporus portrait is the height of Pope's invective, an invective which, at first, does not seem consistent with the earlier characterization of this as a springtime romp. Sporus, after all, is venomous, satanic, a grotesque parody of the *concordia discors*, a fawning puppet, an unreliable friend, and a dangerous enemy. But what clearly emerges from this portrait is Pope's triumph and Sporus' defeat; Arbuthnot's strength has been added to the application of the severely medicinal lash;[32] Sporus has trembled, been broken on a wheel, controlled by the satirist, called a blockhead, a toothless dog, a man of dubious sexual powers, and bi-sexual. From this point the poem's tone becomes progressively calmer, there is more and more "praise," and Pope finally introduces and portrays the warm family life which Sporus had threatened. For all his danger, Sporus is demolished by the angry satirist; for all his prudence Arbuthnot comes to see the true value of satiric medicine which saves rather than endangers lives. Hence the defeat of Sporus epitomizes the defeat of corruption generally, and the danger of unnatural death by mad poets or mad enemies is gone. Pope can pray for a natural death like his father's:

> His Life, tho' long, to sickness past unknown,
> His Death was instant, and without a groan.
> Oh grant me thus to live, and thus to die!
> Who sprung from Kings shall know less joy than I. (ll. 402–5)

And at this point he can give his attention to easing the burdens of the normal physical sickness and decay of the human situation. Pope now becomes a sort of spiritual doctor who prays for aid to his mother and his friend; hence Arbuthnot, once the preserver of Pope, sees Pope the (hoped for) preserver of Arbuthnot:

> O Friend! may each Domestic Bliss be thine!

. . . .

32. For a useful essay regarding satire as medicine, see Mary Claire Randolph, "The Medical Concept in English Renaissance Satiric Theory: Its Possible Relationships and Implications," *SP*, 38 (1941) : 125-57.

May Heav'n, to bless those days, preserve my Friend,
Preserve him social, cheerful, and serene,
And just as rich as when he serv'd a QUEEN! (ll. 406, 415–17)

The final lines—which are probably spoken by Arbuthnot—image Arbuthnot in complete agreement with the person he formerly urged not to write.[33] Like those of the preceding paragraph, they also obliquely suggest harmony with Heaven:

Whether that Blessing be deny'd or giv'n,
Thus far was right, the rest belongs to Heav'n. (ll. 418–19)

The poem ends, then, with the sick and venomous enemy defeated, the adversary convinced of his friend's proper point of view, a beautiful scene of filial piety, and a suggestion of the cooperation of the Heavens: it began with fears of a strange death, adversary and friend in disagreement, an attack upon the family, and the dog-star raging (l. 3). This is consistent with an epistolary poem. *Arbuthnot* is harsher than *Bathurst*; but its "happy" ending and demolition of the enemy dissociate it from more satiric poems.

If *Arbuthnot* is a satiric epistle, *The First Satire of the Second Book of Horace . . . To Mr. Fortescue*, introduces us to a more epistolary satire. The relationship between the satirist and the adversary helps us to place the poem on, but not too deeply in, the satiric side of the spectrum. For instance, Pope, who fears that some think his satire too rough, comes to Fortescue for advice:

Tim'rous by Nature, of the Rich in awe,
I come to Council learned in the Law. (ll. 7–8)

His advice is simply "I'd write no more" (l. 11). Pope preserves his timorous character and agrees that he will

Publish the present Age; but where my Text
Is Vice too high, reserve it for the next. (ll. 59–60)

The sole condition for his silence is that he be left alone; since society does not do this—"But touch me, and no Minister so sore" (l.

33. Thomas A. Maresca has recently made a convincing case for attributing these lines to Arbuthnot (*Pope's Horatian Poems* [Columbus, Ohio: Ohio State University Press, 1966], pp. 108-10, and p. 116, n. 36).

76)—and, instead, chooses to threaten his life (ll. 101–4), Pope
arms himself with his satiric weapons, casts off his earlier withdrawn
role, and actively engages himself against evil.

Martial imagery is the vehicle which characterizes both Pope and
his opponents. "Plums, and Directors, *Shylock* and his Wife,/ Will
club their Testers, now, to take your Life!" (ll. 103–4) The "Tester"
here is not, as Johnson and others have thought, merely a coin, but
an armored head-piece; wealthy and powerful figures are banding
together to attack the poor and weak poet.[34] Pope now arms himself
to combat the "shameless guilty men" who vastly outnumber him.
He buttresses his character not only by using martial images at appropriate times, but also by making clear that this is a role he has
been forced into, since one of his main attributes is an ability to
turn the destructive arts of war into constructive arts of gardening.
His friends include "Chiefs, out of War" (l. 126), one of whom is
Peterborough, "whose Lightning pierc'd th' *Iberian* Lines" (l. 129).
In Pope's company the master of ranks in the military square

> Now, forms my Quincunx, and now ranks my Vines,
> Or tames the Genius of the stubborn Plain,
> Almost as quickly, as he conquer'd *Spain*. (ll. 130–32)

Pope, then, has justified his out-of-character indignant response, and
has shown that he is not merely an angry middle-aged man; his own
good character, the nature of his friends, and his willingness to
attack either high or low—"Scriblers or Peers" (l. 140)—if they
unjustly defame him, raise him in our esteem. At this point Pope
virtually repeats his earlier remark as he again asks for advice:

> This is my Plea, on this I rest my Cause—
> What saith my Council learned in the Laws? (ll. 141–42)

34. See Johnson's *Dictionary* (1755), and Thomas R. Edwards, Jr., *This Dark
Estate: A Reading of Pope* (Berkeley and Los Angeles: University of California Press, 1963), p. 81: " 'testers' are either very old coins or relatively
valueless ones." But the *OED* adds: "A piece of armour for the head, a
head-piece, a casque; also a piece of armour for the head of a horse; a
kind of mask or visor with holes for the eyes, aperture for the ears, etc."
Nathan Bailey offers these definitions: "the value of Six-pence in Money. . . .
the Tester or upper Part of a Bed; also a Head-piece" (*An Universal Etymological English Dictionary*, 3rd ed. [London, 1726]).

Pope's change of character alters the entire tone of the poem. In the first sentence a frightened poet came for advice on how best to defend himself; in the second a fearless poet willing to die for virtue argues his case. He has moved from timorous to fearless, passive to active, ignorant advice seeker regarding the law to both trial lawyer (ll. 109–10) and judge of society. Fortescue's reaction changes as well. His "I'd write no more" is now "Your Plea is good" (l. 143). In his legal jargon he still urges caution, since "Laws are explain'd by Men," and "in *Richard's* Times/A Man was hang'd for very honest Rhymes" (ll. 144–46). Having been urged to "See *Libels, Satires*" (l. 149) in the legal codes, Pope replies:

> *Libels* and *Satires*! lawless Things indeed!
> But grave *Epistles,* bringing Vice to light,
> Such as a *King* might read, a *Bishop* write,
> Such as Sir *Robert* would approve—. (ll. 150–53)

While explaining the differences between "lawless" satires and "grave *Epistles*" Pope himself has become a lawyer. The learned counsel is properly instructed and insists that "The case is alter'd —you may then proceed" (l. 154). The movement from "I'd write no more" to "you may . . . proceed" would be heartening if it were not built upon so cynical and flimsy a foundation. On the basis of Pope's moral position Fortescue merely agrees that the case is good, and cautions against writing; it is not justice but legality that matters, since "Laws are explained by Men." Hence in his reply Pope goes directly to the seats of temporal, spiritual, and political power. With King, Bishop, and Prime Minister on his side it is absurd to bring suit against Pope.[35] Fortescue is therefore not concerned with the virtue of "bringing Vice to light" but with the "explanation" of law by men of matchless power.

> In such a Cause the Plaintiff will be hiss'd,
> My Lords the Judges laugh, and you're dismiss'd. (ll. 155–56)

The Judges do not evaluate right and wrong, but the power of men who—Pope fantasizes—will approve his satire. Fortescue, then, is

35. Edwards, *This Dark Estate*, p. 83, has made a similar point.

an amiable, witty, and prudent lawyer who nevertheless learns something from his once timorous and legally naive friend. He recognizes the goodness of Pope's case, but wholly sides with him only when Pope appears to please the establishment. This cyncial recognition of the realities of jurisprudence—a reality which strangely associates Pope and virtue with Walpole and George II—is a modest but significant move into a more satiric voice. *Arbuthnot* shows us the enemy demolished and the victor in close harmony with truth, goodness, and virtue; *Fortescue,* for all its wit, shows us the enemy merely laughed at, very much alive, and the "victor" in a dangerous and unreliable alliance with forces that Pope will soon bitterly attack: in the first twenty-seven lines of *Dialogue I* of the *Epilogue to the Satires,* Pope berates Bishops, the King, and Sir Robert, and we there see that none of these figures cares to read "grave *Epistles,* bringing Vice to light." In *Fortescue* high morality has been tainted by expediency, and the adversary cannot be wholly won over to Pope's arguments based on virtue.

The adversary in the two final *Dialogues* points these poems towards the extremely harsh end of the satiric spectrum. Here Pope no longer communicates with a man of similar values, but with an "impertinent Censurer" who represents the manners and morals of the Court and time-serving, "delicate," satire which pleases the King and Prime Minister. The adversary thus urges that Pope attack Scripture, honesty, and his own friends, while encouraging him to "charitably comfort Knave and Fool" (ll. 37–62). Fortescue's advice that Pope may "proceed" to write satire thus changes to Pope's own lament: "Adieu Distinction, Satire, Warmth, and Truth!" (l. 64) Shortly thereafter he cries:

> So—Satire is no more—I feel it die—
> No *Gazeteer* more innocent than I!
> And let, a God's-name, ev'ry Fool and Knave
> Be grac'd thro' Life, and flatter'd in his Grave. (ll. 83–86)

Of course Pope is obviously and temporarily putting on the mask of one who agrees with the Friend, thereby showing some of the implications of his view. But it is nevertheless appalling when we recall that in the more epistolary poems Pope could move the adversary into his moral view of the world. And it is doubly appalling to hear that adversary deliver a long panegyric upon Court figures to whom Pope should dispense charity and grace. The perversion of these theological terms results in the Friend's perversion of a beatific vision:

> But let all Satire in all Changes spare
> Immortal *S—k*, and grave *De—re*!
> Silent and soft, as Saints remove to Heav'n,
> All Tyes dissolv'd, and ev'ry Sin forgiv'n,
> These, may some gentle, ministerial Wing
> Receive, and place for ever near a King!
> There, where no Passion, Pride, or Shame transport,
> Lull'd with the sweet *Nepenthe* of a Court;
> There, where no Father's, Brother's, Friend's Disgrace
> Once break their Rest, or stir them from their Place;
> But past the Sense of human Miseries,
> All Tears are wip'd for ever from all Eyes;
> No Cheek is known to blush, no Heart to throb,
> Save when they lose a Question, or a Job. (ll. 91–104)

Pope replies: "Good Heav'n forbid, that I shou'd blast their Glory" (1. 105), insists upon "the Dignity of *Vice*" (1. 114), and draws a picture which almost matches *The Dunciad* at its grimmest. Vice is triumphant and controls the Gospel, while Virtue is carted like a whore; old England is dragged through the dust in disgrace; young England has become a servant to foreign gold. Every segment of society is corrupt, and every one hears that "Not to be corrupted is the Shame" (1. 160) and that—following the pattern of perverted grace and charity—"Nothing is Sacred now but Villany" (1. 170). Even in order to communicate with the adversary, Pope must meet him on his own ground, ground that makes Fortescue's expediency a minor blemish. The portrait of political corruption in *Bathurst*, we recall, was put off to the future, placed in a comic context, and appreciably softened by the presence of a benevolent God. The satiric vision sees present corruption and a God who has removed Himself from significant functioning in the political world and, as I have said earlier, includes a final affirmation that is consciously aware of its flimsy existence.

The second *Dialogue* takes us even further down the satiric road, for here in spite of ridiculing the adversary, effectively attacking his values, and letting him show his own folly, Pope cannot convince him of his errors, realizes that hope for sanity on earth is virtually gone, and that God no longer actively engages in benevolent work but, instead, in punitive action through Pope's pen. Satire and the satirist will soon be dead, and Pope must find his reward in Heaven, the proper picture of which contrasts with the parody drawn earlier by the impertinent censurer. In the "Temple of Eternity"

> . . . other *Trophies* deck the truly Brave,
> Than such as *Anstis* casts into the Grave;
> Far other *Stars* than * and ** wear,
> And may descend to *Mordington* from *Stair*:
> Such as on HOUGH'S unsully'd Mitre shine,
> Or beam, good DIGBY! from a Heart like thine.
> Let Envy howl, while Heav'n's whole Chorus sings,
> And bark at Honour not confer'd by Kings;
> Let Flatt'ry sickening see the Incense rise,
> Sweet to the World, and grateful to the Skies:
> Truth guards the Poet, sanctifies the line,
> And makes Immortal, Verse as mean as mine. (ll. 236–47)

Pope's association of himself with Heaven paradoxically signals the moral decadence of the earthly world. Satire was traditionally associated with the topical, with perversions of the particular day and country; it was an humble genre, far below the dignity of the epic, often prosy and, in Pope's term, "mean." But Pope alters this conception by associating himself with all of humanity and with God's agent of retribution. For instance, the Friend's most typical objection is that vice not of immediate concern to Pope is none of his business. "Where's th' Affront to you?" (l. 157) he asks, and later "What's that to you?" (l. 163) and "How hurt he you?" (l. 165) Pope's answer makes clear that personal pique does not inspire his personal satire, that he is the real "Friend," and that the other "Friend's" moral isolationism is a form of spiritual myopia:

> Ask you what Provocation I have had?
> The strong Antipathy of Good to Bad.
> When Truth or Virtue an Affront endures,
> Th' Affront is mine, my Friend, and should be yours.
> Mine, as a Foe profess'd to false Pretence,
> Who think a Coxcomb's Honour like his Sense;
> Mine, as a Friend to ev'ry worthy mind;
> And mine as Man, who feel for all mankind. (ll. 197–204)

Expansion of the term *muse* coincides with Pope's expansion of his powers of sympathy. "No Pow'r the Muse's Friendship can command;/ No Pow'r, when Virtue claims it, can withstand" (ll. 118–19), he tells the Friend. But it is not the pagan muse that Pope here refers to, since we soon hear that satiric ridicule is a "sacred Weapon! left for Truth's defence," and that it is "To all but Heav'n-directed hands deny'd." That weapon is one which "The Muse may give thee, but the Gods must guide." Thus guided, "The Muse's wing shall brush . . . away" the cobwebs which the "tinsel Insects" of the Court spin "o'er the Eye of Day!" (ll. 212–23) The once humble Muse of Satire is elevated to the role of a "Priestess Muse" who is "diadem'd with Rays divine" (ll. 234, 232). But we recall that Pope the satirist must have divine protection because there is no human protection, and that he may be forced into immortality all the sooner because of mortal dangers. Thus even though truth is the only thing that does not drop "dead-born from the Press" (l. 226), though it "guards the Poet," and "sanctifies the line" (l. 246), it is still subject to its earthly trials:

> Yes, the last Pen for Freedom let me draw,
> When Truth stands trembling on the edge of Law:
> Here, Last of *Britons*! let your Names be read;
> Are none, none living? let me praise the Dead,
> And for that Cause which made your Fathers shine,
> Fall, by the Votes of their degen'rate Line. (ll. 248–53)

All this, in short, shows the immensity of the world's degradation, a degradation made the more apparent by the Friend's concluding response:

Alas! alas! pray end what you began,
And write next winter more *Essays on Man.* (ll. 254–55)

In spite of the overpowering force of Pope's arguments, the Friend refuses to change and, instead, exhorts Pope to write generalizing poems which threaten no one. His "Alas! alas!" is directed at Pope's consistent moral stand rather than the world that stand portrays.

The degree to which the adversary speaks is also a sign of his power. The meager response of Bathurst, Arbuthnot, and Fortescue functions on a metaphorical as well as literal level: in the light of Pope's arguments a "pagan" or prudent but well-meaning and rational man can offer little defense. Significantly, the adversary is far more vocal in the *Dialogues*, and not only in his own but in "Pope's" voice as well, for in the first *Dialogue* in particular Pope ironically speaks lines with which the Friend entirely agrees. The more the adversary says, the more his strength increases; he ignores or rejects the voice of wisdom, and he represents a world of inverted values and mindless intolerance. There is, in short, a direct relationship between how much the adversary says and how satiric the poem is.

Pope's use of the image of a hunting bird also characterizes certain aspects of poems on either side of the satiric spectrum. In *Arbuthnot*, Pope says of himself:

. . . not in Fancy's Maze he wander'd long,
But stoop'd to Truth, and moraliz'd his song. (ll. 340–41)

"Truth" in *Arbuthnot* is something which the epistolary satirist-bird hunts out and shows to an audience awaiting correction; the image is clear and unambiguous. In the second *Dialogue* a similar image portrays satire in a far more complex and frightening way. After the censurer has urged him to "Spare . . . the Person, and expose the Vice" (l. 12), Pope cries:

Come on then Satire! gen'ral, unconfin'd,
Spread thy broad wing, and sowze on all the Kind. (ll. 14–15)

Pope thus ironically embraces general satire which avoids mention-
ing specific villains; even the Friend realizes how absurd this is when
he replies to Pope's mention of "Rev'rend Atheists": "Scandal! name
them, Who? (l. 18) But the first *Dialogue* has made clear, and the
second *Dialogue* reiterates, that virtually "all the kind" do in fact
need to be satirized. On the one hand the satiric satirist-bird regards
the "sowze" as foolish; on the other he regards it as necessary. Moreover, the hunted "Truth" which was to correct the rational audience
in *Arbuthnot*, here "stands trembling on the edge of Law" (l. 249),
since, as Pope states in his final comment on this *Dialogue*, "bad
men were grown so shameless and so powerful, that Ridicule was become as unsafe as it was ineffectual."[36] A satiric bird huge enough to
prey on all of Britain is nevertheless incapable of amending any of
the manners it hunts out; it can only punish.

Certain kinds of imagery, the degree to which the adversary speaks,
and the role of the adversary are good guides to the poem's place
on the satiric spectrum. If we review for the moment the adversary's
concluding remarks in each of the four poems, we can see how far
along the satiric spectrum we have moved. In *Bathurst* a rational man
has been persuaded to return to an orthodox Christian position, and
his final word is "Agreed." In *Arbuthnot* a distinguished Doctor sees
that Pope's medicinal satire is necessary, helps to destroy the chief
enemy and, in so doing, becomes a satirist himself. Though this poem
is harsher than *Bathurst*, we again see the rational man siding with
the satirist: "Thus far was right, the rest belongs to Heav'n." In *Fortescue* we have moved firmly onto the satiric side; here the adversary
can only give conditional acceptance to Pope's moral pleas, and agrees
that "the case is alter'd" only when it seems that Pope has won
the approval of established power. Then he will see that "My Lords
the Judges laugh, and you're dismiss'd." By the time of the two *Dia-*

36. The entire statement is important: "This was the last poem of the kind
printed by our author, with a resolution to publish no more; but to enter
thus, in the most plain and solemn manner he could, a sort of PROTEST
against that insuperable corruption and depravity of manners, which he
had been so unhappy as to live to see. Could he have hoped to have
amended any, he had continued those attacks; but bad men were grown so
shameless and so powerful, that Ridicule was become as unsafe as it was
ineffectual" (*Imitations of Horace*, Butt, p. 327).

logues this tenuous alliance, or fantasy regarding one, has collapsed. In each of the epistles and the more moderate satire the adversary represented a presumed audience of reasonable men; if he is convinced, supposedly we are as well. In the *Dialogues* no such rational man exists. In the first part the impertinent Censurer concludes his remarks with a corrupt vision of a heaven in which Court sycophants thrive, while Pope is forced to speak lines which, properly, belong to his enemy, and to offer his own feeble affirmation in rebuttal. And in the second part all common ground is gone, and Pope must find his solace in Heaven not Britain. Both rational man and, presumably, rational audience have disappeared, and Pope is the "Last of Britons"; the dialogue, a metaphor for human communication, has broken down. As we move along the satiric spectrum, from *Bathurst* to the second *Dialogue*, the poems get progressively grimmer, and the relationship between satirist and adversary signals that change. The shape, strategy, and tone of each of these poems, I suggest, is affected by Pope's knowledge of the distinction between epistle and satire. As use of the image of a spectrum denotes, that distinction is not a rigid one; but knowledge of its presence and influence can help to clarify the poet's particular satiric aims in particular satiric poems, and force us to use the terms *satire* and *epistle* with greater precision.

I have discussed only a few of the characteristics of the verse epistle; there is obviously a great deal more that can be said about these poems, particularly since the form has so many other attributes: among them are an intimate, casual tone, an apparent artlessness, a pose of absolute sincerity appropriate to a "private" conversation among friends, and the use of the recipient as part of the rhetorical structure of the poem. Similarly, my remarks apply primarily— though not exclusively—to satiric epistles like *Arbuthnot* and satiric ethic epistles like *Bathurst*; other forms—the common arts of poetry, cookery, or architecture, elegiac epistle, or epistles regarding morality or theology—have somewhat different demands. As I have shown in chapter 3, however, part of Pope's literary heritage included a conception of formal verse satire as composed of both praise and blame; each satire or epistle would generally include its relevant share of either quality. But Pope was also aware that poems called *satires* usually included more blame, and *epistles* more praise, and that their tone, content, and poetic strategy would vary accordingly. Whether this distinction came to him from Scaliger, Casaubon, Heinsius, Dacier, numerous other commentators on Horatian satire, Horace's practice itself, or some combination of these, we cannot precisely say; in any case, Pope as a satirist and Pope as an epistolary writer is doing different, if related, things. The Muse of Satire wears many masks.

7

London and the Proper Grounds
of Satiric Failure

1 Biography and History: The Improper Grounds

Johnson's *London* (1738) was an immediate success; Pope enquired after its anonymous author and said that he would soon be *deterré*;[1] it went into a second edition within a week, and throughout much of the century was regarded as Johnson's finest poem. But when its political passion no longer seemed relevant, readers began to view it with dissatisfaction. In 1802 William Mudford observed that the *Vanity* "is by far more energetic, and more pleasing than London," and "it certainly contains more masterly touches, more spirited delineations, more rigour of sentiment, and compression of language than his London."[2] It is "manifest how far superior" the *Vanity* is to *London*, he continues. While the latter "contains nothing that is remarkable," the *Vanity* "frequently presents striking lines and paragraphs, and is often laboured into dignity; the language is more pure, the ideas more vivid, and the versification more harmonious."[3] In 1809 Nathan Drake similarly urged the superiority of the *Vanity*,

1. *Boswell's Life of Johnson*, ed. G. Birkbeck Hill, and rev. L. F. Powell (Oxford: Clarendon Press, 1934–50), 2: 129. Thomas Gray also offered spontaneous praise for *London*. Early in 1747 he wrote to Horace Walpole regarding the appearance of *London* and the *Prologue Spoken at . . . Drury Lane* (1747) in Dodsley's *Miscellanies*: "and (I am sorry to differ from you, but) London is to me one of those few imitations that have all the ease and all the spirit of an original. The same man's verses at the opening of Garrick's theatre are far from bad" (*Correspondence of Thomas Gray*, ed. Paget Toynbee and Leonard Whibley [Oxford: Clarendon Press, 1935] 1: 295).
2. *A Critical Enquiry into the Writings of Dr. Samuel Johnson*, 2d ed. (London, 1803), p. 73.
3. *Ibid.*, p. 79.

claiming that its "calm and dignified philosophy" was "more pleasing to the mind, and certainly much more consonant to truth, than the party exaggeration" of the earlier satire.[4] Most readers since then have felt a certain uneasiness regarding *London*. Most critics, too, have concurred in this judgment and have tried to determine the causes of the poem's relative failure; their conclusion seems to me the right one, but their methods of procedure are not relevant to the work at hand. *London* should be read both as an Imitation, and as a formal verse satire demanding examination of the speaker's *ethos* and of the necessary pattern of praise and blame. But *London*, the argument generally runs, fails because the portrait of the city is not historically accurate, or because the beliefs Johnson expresses are not his own. T. S. Eliot, for example, thinks that Johnson's indignation is feigned, since he must have exaggerated the dangers and discomforts of eighteenth-century life: "Johnson utters generalizations, and the generalizations are not true."[5] Similarly, Joseph Wood Krutch insists that Johnson did not believe that "luxury was destroying the

---

4. *Essays, Biographical, Critical, and Historical, Illustrative of the Rambler, Adventurer, & Idler* . . . (London, 1809), 1:135.
5. "Johnson as Critic and Poet," in *On Poetry and Poets* (London: Faber and Faber, 1957), p. 179. Eliot praises *London* in his Introduction to *London: A Poem, and The Vanity of Human Wishes* (London: Haslewood Books, 1930), reprinted in *English Critical Essays: Twentieth Century*, ed. Phylis M. Jones (London: Oxford University Press, 1947), pp. 301-10. Eliot's remarks regarding Johnson's apparently dubious generalizations have been quoted, largely with approval, by Vincent Buckley, in "Johnson: The Common Condition of Men," *The Melbourne Critical Review*, 6 (1963): 18. The reader of Johnson's *London* and *The Vanity of Human Wishes* will also want to see the following: Wallace Cable Brown, *The Triumph of Form: A Study of the Later Masters of the Heroic Couplet* (Chapel Hill: University of North Carolina Press, 1948), pp. 67-86; Donald Davie, *Purity of Diction in English Verse* (London: Chatto and Windus, 1952), pp. 45-47, 82-90; MacDonald Emslie, "Johnson's Satires and 'The Proper Wit of Poetry,'" *Cambridge Journal*, 7 (1954): 347-60; Chester F. Chapin, *Personification in Eighteenth-Century English Poetry* (New York: Columbia University Press, 1955), pp. 98-115; Susie I. Tucker and Henry Gifford, "Johnson's Poetic Imagination," *RES*, n. s., 8 (1957): 241-48; Rachel Trickett, *The Honest Muse: A Study in Augustan Verse* (Oxford: Clarendon Press, 1967), pp. 224-94. Further references may be found in James L. Clifford, *Johnsonian Studies, 1887–1950* (Minneapolis: University of Minnesota Press, 1951), pp. 93-95, and Clifford and Donald J. Greene, "A Bibliography of Johnsonian Studies, 1950–1960," in *Johnsonian Studies*, ed. Magdi Wahba (Cairo, Egypt: Oxford University Press, 1962), pp. 319-21.

nation," that "Britons were languishing in slavery," or that the country was superior to the city.[6] Remarks like these, however, not only ignore altogether the fact that Johnson carefully revised the poem in both 1748 and 1750—unlikely acts if the poem was, in fact, foreign to his mature thinking; they also ignore the demands of formal verse satire and do not even accurately represent Johnson's surroundings and character in 1738.

Examination of contemporary newspaper accounts, for example, makes clear that Johnson was among an intelligent and vocal anti-Administration group,[7] that his attacks on the city's evils are selective, and ignore large areas of urban danger,[8] and that his friends and

6. *Samuel Johnson* (New York: Henry Holt & Co., 1944), p. 63. For similar remarks, see David Nichol Smith, "Johnson and Boswell," *The Cambridge History of English Literature*, ed. Sir A. W. Ward and A. R. Waller, vol. 10, *The Age of Johnson* (Cambridge, 1913), p. 169; Louis I. Bredvold, "The Literature of the Restoration and the Eighteenth Century 1660–1798," in *A History of English Literature*, ed. Hardin Craig (New York: Oxford University Press, 1950), p. 419; Walter Jackson Bate, *The Achievement of Samuel Johnson* (New York: Oxford University Press, 1955), pp. 18-22; Patrick O'Flaherty, "Johnson as Satirist: A New Look at *The Vanity of Human Wishes*," *ELH*, 34 (1967): 88-89.

7. For some contemporary discussions of the Spanish maritime "depredations," see *London Evening Post*, October 6 and 8, 1737; *Craftsman*, January 28 and February 25, 1738 (as in *Gentleman's Magazine*, 8 [1738]: 39-40, 90-91); *Gentleman's Magazine*, 8 (1738): 163-64; *London Magazine*, 7 (January, 1738): 50; *ibid.* (February, 1738): 89-90; *ibid.* (March, 1738): 112-15, and *passim.* Johnson's anger regarding the "silenc'd [or licens'd] stage" was also shared by other opponents of the Licensing Act, Lord Chesterfield among them, who insisted that restraint of the stage was like "putting the *Press* under a Licenser." For remarks concerning Johnson's change of "silenc'd" to "licens'd," see *Samuel Johnson: Poems*, The Yale Edition of the Works of Samuel Johnson, vol. 6, ed. E. L. McAdam, Jr., with George Milne (New Haven: Yale University Press, 1964), p. 51, n. 59, and Donald J. Greene, *The Politics of Samuel Johnson* (New Haven: Yale University Press, 1960), p. 308, n. 19. For Chesterfield's remarks, see *GM*, 7 (1738): 409-11. For other complaints about this act and the threat to the freedom of the press, see *Common Sense*, June 4, 1737 (as in *GM*, 7: 358-59); *ibid.*, January 7, 1738 (as in *GM*, 8: 28-29); *Craftsman*, July 2 and September 17, 1737 (as in *GM*, 7: 430, 557); *ibid.*, January 21 and April 8, 1738 (as in *GM*, 8: 35-36, 198-201). *The Craftsman* for March 11, 1738, also attacked London as being (in Johnson's words) "The common shore of Paris and of Rome"; this essay was reprinted in *London Magazine*, 7 (March, 1738): 123-25, and *GM*, 8: 150-51, the issue in which Johnson's "*Ad* Urbanum" appears. For other attacks upon foreigners, see *London Evening Post*, May 21, December 8 and 15, 1737.

8. James L. Clifford, *Young Sam Johnson* (New York: McGraw-Hill, 1955), pp. 175-77. For information regarding falling houses, see also John R. Moore,

commentators regarded the poem as faithful to its historical setting and to Johnson's attitudes towards London in 1738: Boswell, Garrick, Joseph Warton, Percival Stockdale, and Nathan Drake reinforce this view.[9] Similarly, in his conversation and writings in later, admittedly "sincere," works, Johnson reiterates many of *London's* attacks on the British electorate and on foreigners,[10] while Donald J. Greene has demonstrated that the principles expressed in Johnson's political pieces of 1738 and 1739 do not contradict anything found in his later political writing.[11] Finally, we should recall that it was the secure and settled Johnson who said: "Sir, when a man is tired of London, he is tired of life,"[12] whereas in 1738 Johnson was insecure and newly transplanted from the country which, as *London's* favorable mention of the Trent (l. 211) suggests, was still in his mind. If we are to be biographical in our approach, it is wiser to regard *London* as evidence for Johnson's genuine state of mind rather

"Johnson as Poet," *Boston Public Library Quarterly*, 2 (1950): 161; *idem.* "Johnson's 'falling houses,'" *N&Q*, 195 (1950): 342; *London Evening Post*, April 12, 1737; and *London Magazine*, 7 (January, 1738): 45. On fires, see *London Evening Post*, January 4, 6, 8, March 17, April 5, 9, 19, May 6, 31, June 11, October 27, December 4, 1737; and for a few of the many examples of widespread robbery, see *London Evening Post*, May 14, July 9, and October 11, 1737. (Throughout, the date for *London Evening Post* is taken from the first part of the newspaper's time-span; *e.g.* "From Tuesday July 19, to Thursday July 21, 1737," is considered "July 19.")

9. For Johnson's own remarks and the comments of others regarding the poem, see Boswell, *Life*, 1:164, 193; Garrick, in Boswell's *Life*, 1:194; Sir John Hawkins, *The Life of Samuel Johnson, LL.D.*, 2d ed. rev. (London, 1787), pp. 56, 60-61, 72; Arthur Murphy, *Essay on the Life and Genius of Samuel Johnson* (London, 1792), reprinted in *Johnsonian Miscellanies*, ed. G. Birkbeck Hill (Oxford: Clarendon Press, 1897), 1:371; Clifford, *Young Sam Johnson*, pp. 210-11; Warton, *The Works of Alexander Pope* (London, 1797), 4:299, 309; Stockdale, *Lectures on the Truly Eminent English Poets* (London, 1807), 1:451; Drake, *Essays, Biographical, Critical, and Historical* (London, 1805), 1:131.

10. See *The Vanity of Human Wishes* (1749), ll. 93-98, and the Preface to the *Dictionary* (1755), sigs. B1ᵛ, C2ᵛ.

11. Greene, *Politics of Samuel Johnson*, pp. 106-7. Johnson's other political writings of this period were: *The State of Affairs in Lilliput* (probably Johnson's, 1738), *Marmor Norfolciense* (1739), *A Compleat Vindication of the Licensers of the Stage* (1739).

12. Boswell, *Life*, 3:178. Boswell records Johnson as saying this on "*Saturday 20 September 1777.* Aetat. 68." It seems less than fair of Professor Krutch (*Samuel Johnson*, p. 63) to judge the sincerity of *London*, written in an entirely different context, by a remark of this sort made almost forty years later.

than call it names because it does not fit our preconceived notions of what Johnson should have been thinking at the time.

We must admit, however, that Johnson—like Pope and Juvenal—has probably exaggerated his own anger and the evils of his surroundings. He did not literally believe that Britons were "languishing in slavery," nor, in fact, does he say so in the poem; but he and many others did believe that British liberty was threatened. Exaggeration is essential to the satiric art, and differs in degree only from simile and metaphor, "untruths" which, if denied to the poet would destroy poetry. Literal truth is rarely found in satire for, in Bredvold's words, "like caricature [it] presents a truth by means of a distortion."[13] When Johnson, or the critic of a modern city, announces that one cannot leave his home at night without being set upon by thieves or murderers, he is not making a statement which demands statistical verification; he hopes that his conscious exaggeration will shock the reader, point out that the crime rate is abnormally high, and that the city streets are dangerous after dark.[14]

Presumably, once the onus of "lie" or "insincere" has been removed from *London* the hostile reader should approach it with new expectation and leave it with new pleasure. I suspect, however, that neither alternative is likely, since the initial criteria of historical and biographical verisimilitude are irrelevant,[15] and tell us little about how literary pleasure is produced; they lead us into significant historical research rather than literary analysis. Accordingly, the critic of satire need not ask whether the speaker of the poem accurately mirrors the author's temper at the time; instead, he should ask whether the

13. "The Gloom of the Tory Satirists," in *Eighteenth-Century Critical Essays,* ed. James L. Clifford (New York: Oxford University Press, 1959), p. 15.
14. For other critical remarks on satire's use of fiction and distortion, see Elder Olson, "Rhetoric and the Appreciation of Pope," *MP,* 37 (1939–40) : 22; Maynard Mack, "The Muse of Satire," *Yale Review,* 41 (1951) : 85; Gilbert Highet, *Juvenal the Satirist* (Oxford: Clarendon Press, 1954), pp. 162-63; Alvin Kernan, *The Cankered Muse* (New Haven: Yale University Press, 1959), p. 23; A. R. Heiserman, *Skelton and Satire* (Chicago: University of Chicago Press, 1961), p. 299; Edward W. Rosenheim, Jr., *Swift and the Satirist's Art* (Chicago: University of Chicago Press, 1963), p. 17 and *passim; Satire Newsletter,* 2 (1964) : *passim.*
15. Though it may be rather late in the day, such a reminder is still necessary: see Thomas A. Maresca's remark regarding Johnson's lapse from historical veracity, on p. 80, above, as well as Eliot and Buckley, n. 5, above.

speaker himself presents a convincing image of a man who may justifiably criticize others. The problem of the soundness of the speaker's *ethos* is essential in judging formal verse satire, and was so recognized by the contemporary reader. The (unknown) author of *The Tears of the Muses* puts it this way:

> there is another Particular [in addition to the need for "praise" in satire], that calls aloud for the Regard of the *Satirist*: and That is, a Reflexion, how far Decency may make it a *Duty*, to abandon his personal Self, and insinuate Opinions, with *Modesty*. I mean from the Mouth of some *figurative Speaker*, whom He ought to *suppose* of more Consequence; and whose Sentiments the Reader will *be sure* to receive with less Scruple.
>
> There is a Meaning, in the very *Name*, of a *Poet*, that shou'd seem to prescribe us this Duty: And the Use and Necessity of *Invention* can never be more manifest, than where the Subject is so invidious, as *Satire*.
>
> Who is there, to say Truth, so unguilty of the Follies of Life, that he dares, in his own proper Person, stand out and *justify* the Right he assumes, of reproaching the Conduct of Others?
>
> Reproof is too bitter a Potion, to be welcome from our Sense of its *Use*. And the administring Hand shou'd be *dear*, not *disgustful*, if it would incline us to taste it, with Pleasure.[16]

In what way, let us ask, is the speaker in *London* "*dear*" and in what ways "*disgustful*"? Here, as in the later discussion of the satiric structure of the poem, some comparison with Juvenal's Third Satire will be useful.

II Ethos *and Structure: The Proper Grounds*

Johnson's Thales attempts to give the impression of being a man of modesty, virtue, tolerance, and essential good nature, who is roused to righteous indignation because of decadent surroundings and a desire to right contemporary wrongs. He is a "true Briton" (l. 8) aware

16. Second ed. (London, 1738), p. viii (italics and Roman type inverted).

of the past greatness of his country, pays homage to England's golden age, and "call[s] Britannia's glories back to view" (l. 26). Thales, like Umbricius in the parent-poem, helps to define his own good qualities through what he will not do in order to prosper:

> Here let those reign, whom pensions can incite
> To vote a patriot black, a courtier white;
> Explain their country's dear-bought rights away,
> And plead for pirates in the face of day;
> With slavish tenets taint our poison'd youth,
> And lend a lye the confidence of truth. (ll. 51–56)

He will neither carry a paramour's message, nor seduce virgins and, therefore, is forced to "Live unregarded, unlamented die" (l. 82). The wealth of the rich and corrupt cannot induce him to give up his peace of mind, and so he turns from a bribe in order to preserve his "Unsullied fame, and conscience ever gay" (l. 90). Thales is not a mere railler, not a malcontent without constructive criticism, and so he offers a solution to a life of misery: he will withdraw to "Cambria's solitary shore" (l. 7), and he advises his friend to retreat to the country and its inexpensive but elegant home, its pleasant surroundings, and small plot on which to grow one's own food (ll. 210–23). He is also a true friend and permanent enemy of vice, for in his final words he says that he will be glad to help his companion when he leaves London and also writes satire against the crimes of the city (ll. 256–63).

But Thales' *ethos* has several flaws which weaken *London*. For example, though we twice hear that he is going to Wales (ll. 7–8, 261), Thales still speaks only in general terms about the place of his retreat. He asks "kind heaven" for "some happier place,/ Where honesty and sense are no disgrace" (ll. 43–44) and again implores: "Some secret cell, ye pow'rs, indulgent give" (l. 49). If Thales does in fact know his destination, he should also know that it supplies the environment within which he can live peacefully; the conventional appeal to the gods therefore appears gratuitous. Moreover, his request for a "cell," probably, according to the *Dictionary*, "any small place of residence," contradicts his later description of the "elegant retreat" of a "hireling senator," which includes an extensive prospect, walks, brooks, and bowers (ll. 212–17). Though it is true that Thales is poor, will grow his own vegetables, and reject "the dainties of a venal lord" (l. 219), this normative section of the poem implies neither poverty nor a desire for it; indeed, Thales was apparently once wealthy, and has decided to leave London while he can still salvage some of his fortune. He "waits the wherry that contains/ Of dissipated wealth the small remains" (ll. 19–20). One thinks that with wealth—whether riches or even modest means—London might be more tolerable for Thales, and so his plea for a "secret cell" not only contradicts the picture he later draws, but seems insincere as well.

One also notices an occasionally self-pitying tone in Thales' speeches which, when added to his "surly virtue"[17] (l. 145) and his repetition of the word "me," detract from the credibility of his character:

> But what, my friend, what hope remains for me,
> Who start at theft, and blush at perjury? (ll. 67–68)
>
> . . . .
>
> The cheated nation's happy fav'rites, see!
> Mark whom the great caress, who frown on me! (ll. 91–92)

These remarks, I believe, are self-righteous rather than righteously indignant. Perhaps this flaw in Thales' image is partially due to his generalized character. We see him only when he reacts to the major public and private problems of the city, or to his status as a result of those problems. Juvenal's Umbricius, on the other hand, creates sympathy for the poor plebeian who is literally crushed under a mass of marble and makes us react in a similar way to the speaker himself,[18] the *vir bonus* who, metaphorically, is also crushed; he wins

17. Unfortunately, "surly virtue" is a fitting description for Thales. In the *Dictionary* Johnson defines "surly" as "gloomily morose; rough; uncivil; sour; silently angry." In other, admittedly later, writings, Johnson also uses the term in a pejorative sense. Milton's "political notions were those of an acrimonious and surly republican" (Boswell, *Life*, 4: 42, n. 3), and Johnson himself says that he was not "much plagued" by authors sending him "their works to revise" because "I have been thought a sour, surly fellow" (*ibid.*, 4: 121).

18. All citations from Juvenal are in *Juvenal and Persius*, Loeb Classical Li-

our sympathy by showing other persecuted men and his response to them. Thus in the Third Satire we see and react to crimes inflicted upon the individual, the family, the virtuous members of the "lower" class, and the city. In *London* we see little concerning the domestic life of the city or nation; we are forced to rely, instead, on Thales' assertions—on his telling rather than showing—of his own virtue and the sins that abound in London. Johnson eliminates all of the particularized homely scenes of family life in the Third Satire, so that our attention remains upon Thales' character and his indignation.

Now a poem which attacks a specific political administration in a specific city must have several highly specific details if it is to be at all effective. Hence Johnson clearly announces the crimes of Walpole, of his "pension'd band," of the population of London, and of its French and Frenchified inhabitants: the presence of Walpole, Henley, *The Gazeteer*, the Strand, falling houses, the Severn, the Trent, the Ways and Means, the King, and his mistress, all attest to the occasional nature of *London*. Accordingly, the generalized nature of Thales' character, and elimination of Juvenal's homely scenes are both the more apparent, and suggest that they are part of another aspect of Johnson's plan—that is, his portrayal of Thales not merely as a member of a virtuous minority but as almost the only virtuous man in a depraved world. In contrast, Juvenal provides three extended portraits of the glories of the old Roman life now extinct in the city but thriving in the country. In the first, he insists that modesty of dress, the simple life, love of mother and child, and respect of the judge for his people, are all preferable to extravagant living and persecution of the poor in the city (ll. 171–89). In the second he stresses the solidity of the homes, pleasant climate, and freedom from fire in rural areas (ll. 190–98) ; and in the third, he mentions economy of living in many Italian homes (ll. 223–31). In these portraits he discusses three different levels of society and six towns, and implies that the latter are representative of the abodes of virtue. For instance, Umbricius asks:

Who at cool Praeneste, or at Volsinii amid its leafy hills, was

brary, trans. G. G. Ramsay (London: Wm. Heinemann, 1930) ; for this quotation, see p. 52, ll. 260-61.

ever afraid of his house tumbling down? Who in modest Gabii,
or on the sloping heights of Tivoli? (ll. 190–92)

The method of naming several towns suggests the preponderance and
accessibility of good outside of Rome,[19] and it also shows Umbricius'
thorough knowledge of the country and of areas of old Roman values.
But Johnson adapts only Juvenal's final scene—the description of
the economical country home—eliminates the scene of a frightened
baby nestling against his mother's coarse tunic (ll. 175–76), and nowhere suggests that this kind of gentle and good family life is possible. Since mankind has deserted Thales, the Heavens are the only
ally left for him. This rage in isolation creates a tone of indignation
that is higher pitched than Juvenal's and, ultimately, is less convincing. Thales asks:

> Has heaven reserv'd, in pity to the poor,
> No pathless waste, or undiscover'd shore;
> No secret island in the boundless main?
> No peaceful desart yet unclaim'd by Spain?
> Quick let us rise, the happy seats explore,
> And bear oppression's insolence no more. (ll. 170–75)

Though the final couplet—and the friend's introduction—suggests
that there are others like Thales, throughout the poem he considers
himself the sole virtuous man in the world; thus, instead of turning
to man for help, he calls upon the Heavens, an ally which, we will
see, is hardly more powerful than Thales himself. Thales emphasizes
his isolation in the phrases "pathless waste," "undiscover'd shore,"
"secret island," and "peaceful desart," for, it is logical to suppose,
in all of these Thales would be alone; to be safe from corruption
virtue must be out of the reach of all except Thales. This impression
is confirmed when, after he laments the loss of "your little all" (l.
189), he represents man's inhumanity as universal:

19. William S. Anderson discusses the importance of this device in "Studies in
    Book I of Juvenal," *Yale Classical Studies*, vol. 15, ed. Harry M. Hubbel
    (New Haven: Yale University Press, 1957), pp. 56-68. For other useful com-
    ments on both the Third and Tenth Satires, see Anderson's "Anger in Ju-
    venal and Seneca," *University of California Publications in Classical Philol-
    ogy*, vol. 19 (Berkeley and Los Angeles: University of California Press,
    1964), pp. 131-48, 174-95.

Then thro' the world a wretched vagrant roam,
For where can starving merit find a home?
In vain your mournful narrative disclose,
While all neglect, and most insult your woes. (ll. 190–93)

Moreover, it is a "deserted seat" (l. 213) to which Thales advises his friend to retreat, and a "solitary shore" (l. 7) to which he himself will go.

Johnson further isolates the good man by suggesting that rich, powerful, and evil men may even defy the Heavens themselves. When fire ravages the poor quarter of town, "th' affrighted crowds tumultuous cries/ Roll thro' the streets, and thunder to the skies" (ll. 182–83). But this thunder is unheard in Heaven, for, as we have seen, the poor man is neglected and insulted. The fire in Orgilio's palace, on the other hand, comes "When publick crimes inflame the wrath of heav'n" (l. 66), and stems from "heaven's just bolts" (l. 194); but "publick mournings pacify the skies" (l. 197), and Orgilio's pensioned bands distort the situation, making their master appear to be the virtuous man wronged by the malign gods:

> The laureat tribe in servile verse relate,
> How virtue wars with persecuting fate. (ll. 198–99)

The crowd assumes the functions of Heaven as they "The price of boroughs and of souls restore" (l. 204), and are able to *bless* Orgilio "with all the baubles of the great" (l. 206). Heaven hopes to "confound" Orgilio's wealth, but his parasites restore it and more. Instead of new poverty and an angry Orgilio, we have new riches and an "angry heav'n":

> Orgilio sees the golden pile aspire,
> And hopes from angry heav'n another fire. (ll. 208–9)

Similarly, the poor good man whom the Heavens should protect is killed in the apparent sanctity of his home where he hopes for "the balmy *blessings* of repose." The murderer, "daring with *despair*,/ . . . bursts the *faithless* bar;/ Invades the *sacred* hour of silent rest" and kills the humble, betrayed man (ll. 236–41 [italics added]).

This perversion of God's purposes and of religion fits into a larger pattern depicting London's perversion. For example, normal sexuality and love seem impossible in a city where "warbling eunuchs" (l. 59) sing, and one must either carry a licentious lover's note or "bribe a virgin's innocence away" (ll. 77–78); similarly, vice is so powerful that the virtuous are considered rebels (l. 63); the English Parliament defends Spanish piracy of English ships (l. 54); the French use "industry" to escape from honest work (l. 113); officers in the army kill their own people (ll. 225–27) and—in short—black is white (l. 52). It is not surprising that, in such a context, the elements themselves should be corrupted. We have already seen that the rich and the vicious turn the purging power of fire into a source of evil, whereas the same fire destroys even the meager comforts of the poor. But we also see that the "fiery fop" (l. 226) attacks the poor man in the streets, whereas he shuns "the flambeau" (l. 234) of the rich. The air has also been corrupted: the friend says that Thales must "breathe in distant fields a purer air" (l. 6). The English air of freedom has been replaced by the slavish air of the French, for, "Their air, their dress, their politicks [they] import" (l. 110). The Thames was once a "silver flood" (l. 22), and the ocean bore Britannia's "cross triumphant on the main" (ll. 26–27), whereas now London is a great sewer,[20]—"The common shore of Paris and of Rome"—

20. The use of *shore* is probably another example of what Johnson is never supposed to do—pun. *Shore* is not only a sewer, but a prostitute; London is thus reduced to the role of a dishonored, corrupted, and—as the rest of the poem makes clear—diseased woman. See Benjamin Martin's *Lingua Britannica Reformata: Or, A New English Dictionary* (London, 1749): "*A Common Sewer*, 1. a common shore, as 'tis vulgarly pronounced, or drain to carry away water, filth, &c. 2. a prostitute, or common whore." (I am indebted to Professor Paul K. Alkon for this reference.) Johnson does not define *shore* in this way, but he was certainly aware of its association with *prostitute*. Under his second definition of *whore*, he cites Dryden's translation of the parallel passage from Juvenal's Third Satire:

Orontes

Conveys his wealth to Tiber's hungry shores,
And fattens Italy with foreign *whores*.   *Dryden.*

Johnson's use of "flambeau" (l. 234) may be another pun. According to Johnson's *Dictionary* a *flam* is a deception or lie. The rich who carry flambeaus are thus false beaux, mere Frenchified and corrupt English dandies ("Behold the warrior dwindled to a beau" [l. 104]). Indeed, throughout the poem fire and water when in or near London suggest decadence; when in the country or the past, however, water suggests purity and English grandeur.

that "With eager thirst, . . . / Sucks in the dregs of each corrupted state" (ll. 94–96), the fleet is dishonored, and a German on the British throne crosses the seas to visit his mistress. Finally, the "consecrated earth" of Elizabeth (l. 24) has given way to a "sinking land" (l. 245) whose fields can no longer supply enough hemp for the gallows and the King's adulterous convoy. London, then, is a world deserted by a defeated God, a world of destructive and negative values, a world of chaos and, in Thales' terms, a world of dead people existing within "curs'd walls" and "degen'rate days" (ll. 37, 35); one can find both God's blessing and the proper world order only in the country.

Thales, we have seen, is not content to berate London alone, since he assumes that people throughout the world share London's cruelty. But surely the overstatement of the case suggests its own weakness. Now this is not the same kind of exaggeration in, say, Juvenal's Sixth Satire. As Dryden noted about that poem, the very strength of the condemnation urges the reader to avoid women of the sort described; but the reader who hopes to avoid London apparently can go nowhere but to a "pathless waste," or a "peaceful desart." The repetition of desert imagery is significant, for it suggests an alternative which, for the reasonable man of the presumed audience, is no alternative at all, and one which Thales himself finally rejects in favor of more amiable country prospects. Both the quasi-atheistic women of Young's Sixth Satire, and the withdrawn God of Pope's second *Dialogue* are different from Johnson's vision. In the former Caroline's benevolent qualities restore a prelapsarian innocence to the world (6:156), and in the latter Pope carefully preserves the image of an all-powerful God who rewards and protects the virtuous and, through Pope's satire, punishes the vicious. The terrors of *London* are too extreme to be believable even in a genre of extremes. But—it should be clear—this is not the same as the simplistic belief that Johnson's generalizations are not true, for Johnson is not using satiric hyperbole but totally condemning everything and everyone— but himself. Thales forgets—as Juvenal's Umbricius did not regarding Rome—that the reader will doubt whether London is entirely evil, that all men in all places are evil, that total seclusion will bring happiness to the good man, and that God Himself has virtually been dethroned. Even if we were to agree that Thales' evaluation of the world is just, his self-portrait does not convince us that he is as virtuous as he pretends.

In addition to his occasional contradictions and self-righteousness, we see his character suffer in the attack upon French dominance in London. The portrait of the Frenchman is intended to contrast with Thales' own good character and to emphasize his isolation in the French metropolis. Thales, for instance, is a reliable friend and confidant, whereas the Frenchman will "soon your ill-plac'd confidence repay" (l. 156); Thales is a free-born Englishman in danger of being enslaved, whereas the Gaul is a slave dangerous because free (ll. 145–47); Thales honestly gives his opinion, whereas the foreigner can "lye without a blush, without a smile" (l. 147); and Thales is among the last of the true Britons, while the preying Frenchmen "Their air, their dress, their politicks import" (l. 110), and thus are able to "Behold the warrior dwindled to a beau" in imitation of the French import (ll. 104, 106). Accordingly, Thales' virtuous posture demands that he reject all French values and condemn flattery of any kind; instead, he is angry because the superior foreign flatterer supplants the crude native flatterer. Thales' indignation seems to be based merely upon the versatile Gaul's success while, in this instance, he overlooks the Briton's equal corruption:

> In ev'ry [French refugee's] face a thousand graces shine,
> From ev'ry tongue flows harmony divine.
> These arts in vain our rugged natives try,
> Strain out with fault'ring diffidence a lye,
> And get a kick for auwkward flattery. (ll. 127–31)

Finally, in his concluding speech, Thales appears arrogant in his pose of what may be called "satiric superiority." He leaves London a poor but healthy and energetic man, in whose veins "life still vig'-rous revels" (l. 42). However, he assumes that his friend lacks the intelligence to quit the city before it destroys him: he will leave only with his "youth, and health, and fortune spent" (l. 256). Moreover, whereas Umbricius, in a similar position, promises to visit his friend

and modestly help him write his satires, Thales implies that his
friend—apparently an inferior poet—*must* accept his aid in learning
to write properly indignant satire:

> Then shall thy friend, nor thou refuse his aid,
> Still foe to vice, forsake his Cambrian shade;
> In virtue's cause once more exert his rage,
> Thy satire point, and animate thy page. (ll. 260–63) [21]

In drawing Thales' character Johnson has ignored a prime rule
of rhetoric which he knew well. In a letter to Charles Burney he says:

21. Johnson's interpretation of the final line of the poem depends upon an important textual crux. The text he uses, the translations of Holyday, Stapylton,
and Dryden, and the Latin editions of Rigaultius and Petreus, all use the
word *adjutor* in the final line of Juvenal's Third Satire: "satirarum ego, ni
pudet illas,/adjutor gelidos veniam caligatus in agros." Though *auditor* was
then a variant for *adjutor*, it was not fully accepted until the late nineteenth
and early twentieth centuries. The Loeb text thus portrays Umbricius visiting
his friend and *listening* to his satires "if they think me worthy of that honor,"
whereas Johnson puts Thales (who, after all, is addressing an unnamed
speaker rather than the satirist Juvenal) into the role of *helper*. In his prose
gloss of this line Prateus uses the phrase "Satyrarum auxiliator," and in his
note to the passage observes that "Nonnulli codices habent, *auditor*" (*D.
Junii Juvenalis et A. Persii Flacci Satyrae*, ed. Ludovicus Prateus [London,
1699], p. 62; see also *D. Junii Juvenalis & Auli Persii Flacci Satyrae cum
veteris scholiastae & variorum commentariis*, of Graevius and N. Rigaultius
[Amsterdam, 1684], p. 106). Dryden used the Prateus text and the translations of Robert Stapylton and Barten Holyday (*The Poems of John Dryden*,
ed. James Kinsley [Oxford: Clarendon Press, 1958], 4: 2006). The text and
the relevant manuscripts are discussed by A. E. Housman, *D. Junii Juvenalis
Satyrae*, 2d ed. (Cambridge, 1931), pp. v-lvii.
  Even among those using the term *adjutor*, Johnson's lines are extremely
assertive. Sir Robert Stapylton merely says:
>   To your moist fields, if us *this* do not shame,
>   I'le come in *tases*, and more *Satyrs* frame.
(*Juvenal's Sixteen Satyrs, or A Survey of the Manners and Actions of Mankind* [London, 1647], p. 46.) Barten Holyday is even more moderate:
>   And if thy Satyrs blush not to give room,
>   To your cold fields a Booted Aid I'le come.
(*Decimus Junius Juvenalis, and Aulus Persius Flaccus* [Oxford, 1673],
p. 43.) And even Dryden does not go so far as Johnson in pressing the
speaker's superiority:
>   Then, to assist your Satyrs, I will come:
>   And add new Venom, when you write of *Rome*.
*The Satires of Decimus Junius Juvenalis . . . . Together with the Satires
of Aulus Persius Flaccus* [London, 1693], p. 52.) As an Imitation, *London*
need not adhere to the original's scheme, but this seems to me an instance
where Johnson would have been wise to imitate Umbricius' more modest
stance.

"We must confess the faults of our favourite, to gain credit to our praise of his excellencies. He that claims either for himself or for another the honours of perfection, will surely injure the reputation which he designs to assist."[22] The flaws which we have found in Thales are not "confessed"—rather, they are weaknesses claiming to be strengths and, therefore, "injure the reputation which" the poet "designs to assist." As a result, the "administring Hand" of reproof is not sufficiently *"dear"* and is too often *"disgustful."* We must remember, however, that these are traits of Thales the speaker and not of Johnson the man.

At this point it might be best to anticipate a possible objection to the case I have been stating: does not the discrepancy between Thales' appearance and his reality argue for Johnson's skill rather than his lack of it? Does not Johnson stand behind Thales, consciously and ironically undercut him and, thereby, point out that a truly virtuous man would *not* leave the city and would continue to fight? There are, I think, several objections to this view, not the least of which are that no one in over 225 years has committed it to print, that Johnson's contemporaries regarded the poem as "straight," and that Johnson himself never suggests irony toward Thales. Indeed, he tries to remove any stigma from the departure when he has the friend insist:

> Yet still my calmer thoughts his choice commend,
> I praise the hermit, but regret the friend. (ll. 3–4)

Similarly, Johnson revised the first edition's reading of line 5 in order to emphasize Thales' long and thoughtful decision to leave; hence he changed the couplet which began "Who now resolves, from vice and London far" to "Resolved at length, from vice and London far/ To breathe in distant fields a purer air."[23] If Johnson had been ironic we would have known it at once; his genius lent itself to obvious ironic structures like *Marmor Norfolciense* and not the subtle interplay of man and mask. Furthermore, there is usually little dis-

22. R. W. Chapman, ed., *The Letters of Samuel Johnson* (Oxford: Clarendon Press, 1952), 1: 178.
23. *Poems of Samuel Johnson*, McAdam and Milne, p. 48, n. 5.

crepancy between Johnson himself and his "mask." His remark in the *Rambler*, no. 208 (1752), applies to his other works as well. A mask, he says, following Castiglione, allows even a known author "a right of acting and speaking with less restraint." Hence the reader should not force him "to justify those sallies or frolicks which his disguise must prove him desirous to conceal." But, he continues, he has committed this "offence" infrequently. "I have always thought it the duty of an anonymous author to write, as if he expected to be hereafter known."[24] As I will show in the following section, the relationship between the poet and his mask in *London* is indeed a close one.

We recall that Dryden's concept of formal verse satire was widespread throughout the Restoration and the eighteenth century, that Johnson knew the theory well, that he took "Dryden's Juvenal" with him to Oxford in 1728, and that he probably reclaimed these volumes in 1735 when he wished to establish his own school. On May 18 of that year he asked Gilbert Repington at Oxford to send his books to "the Castle [Inn] in Birmingham Warwickshire"; and on June 25 he wrote to Richard Congreve, thanking him for his "very important kindness," evidently in helping Repington to collect and forward his library.[25] According to Reade, on Johnson's Oxford library "must largely have been founded his immense knowledge of ancient and modern literature."[26] Now I cannot prove that Johnson consciously said: "I will attempt to write a formal verse satire on the pattern described by Dryden"; but the evidence presented above cer-

24. *Works of Samuel Johnson* (Oxford, 1825), 3: 463.
25. Allen Lyell Reade, *Johnsonian Gleanings* (London: Privately printed for the Author by Percy Lund, Humphries, & Co., 1928), 5: 225; Chapman, *Letters of Samuel Johnson*, 1: 5–6. Reade (5: 117), Chapman (1: 6n.), and Clifford, *Young Sam Johnson*, p. 157, agree that the kindness refers to Congreve's aid in the dispatch of Johnson's books. Similarly, Reade (5: 115) and Clifford (p. 156) agree that the books were intended for use at Edial.
26. Reade, *Johnsonian Gleanings*, 5: 214. Reade is probably right, for the three works of Dryden in Johnson's Oxford library are also those works of Dryden which he cites most frequently in the first volume of the *Dictionary*: the translation of the *Aeneid* (843 times), Ovid's *Fables* (526 times), and the satires of Juvenal and Persius (471 times, including citations from the "Discourse"): see Lewis Freed, "The Sources of Johnson's *Dictionary*" (unpubl. Ph.D. diss., Cornell University, 1939), p. 57.

tainly makes defensible a reading of *London* using the criterion of satiric unity. Hence, if we ask what *London* praises and what it blames, we will see that, unlike its parent-poem, it attacks two kinds of evil: it is both a "social" poem which berates private vice, and a "political" poem which criticizes the public acts of the Walpole Administration.[27] It seems likely, because of the demands of formal verse satire, the pattern of Juvenal's own poem, and, most important, certain evidence in *London* itself, that Johnson attempts to relate these two kinds of vice and to select one virtue to offset them. In fact, however, he inculcates two virtues: on the one hand he exhorts the reader to return to the peace and security of the country; on the other he exhorts him to return to the courage, strength, and political wisdom of the old Briton. The unsuccessful attempt to unify the two virtues blurs the satire's focus.

Thales' friend begins the attack on London with complaints about private or social evils, and contrasts them with the austere pleasures of the country. Who, he asks, would "change the rocks of Scotland for the Strand?"

> There none are swept by sudden fate away,
> But all whom hunger spares, with age decay. (ll. 10–12)

The grimness of this retreat may make one think that Johnson is being ironic, that he is undercutting the country itself. But the succeeding attack on the city, with its heavily stressed repetition of *here*, implies that the apparent barrenness of Scotland is normative: there at least the natural order is preserved; one knows what to expect, and death is due to natural, not unnatural, causes. The rocks of Scotland are stable; the "rocks" of the Strand—the word itself suggests instability—are shifting and unstable, and may, in fact, be from falling houses: "Here falling houses thunder on your head" (l. 17).

27. The political attacks are Johnson's; there is no precedent for them in Juvenal. Ramsay remarks: "Juvenal was no politican; he never casts an eye on political conditions of his day . . . . He is essentially the moralist of private life; perhaps the only distinctly political observation that can be discovered in his satires is when he declares that Rome was free in the days when she called Cicero the 'Father of his Country'" (*Juvenal and Persius,* p. xxxvii). See also *The Poems of Samuel Johnson,* ed. David Nichol Smith and Edward L. McAdam (Oxford: Clarendon Press, 1941), p. 2.

Similarly, instead of the anticipated death which Scotland offers, we are surprised to find that "here a female atheist talks you dead" (l. 18).

Thales himself follows a similar pattern of attack on the city and praise of the country. He begins his own speech by berating "those curs'd walls, devote to vice and gain" (l. 37), and then asks the Heavens for a retreat at "Some pleasing bank where verdant osiers play," or "Some peaceful vale with nature's paintings gay" (ll. 45–46). Many of his subsequent complaints are not political in nature; they are directed against the social life of the city, against, as it were, man's inhumanity to man. We see Johnson's anger regarding this evil in the famous lines:

> This mournful truth is ev'ry where confess'd,
> SLOW RISES WORTH, BY POVERTY DEPRESS'D:
> But here more slow, where all are slaves to gold,
> Where looks are merchandise, and smiles are sold;
> Where won by bribes, by flatteries implor'd,
> The groom retails the favours of his lord. (ll. 176–81)

England's greatness, we may infer, was partially due to her foreign trade and respect for the humble poor. In Walpole's decadent age, however, the old standards are perverted: poverty is now incompatible with worth, and the oceanic commerce that extended Britain's borders is turned into an unnatural commerce in human attributes within those borders, where gold rather than a good man is master. Hence the favors (l. 181) are probably looks and smiles of the patron toward present or prospective clients. The groom, who knows the "stock," will sell his information for money or flattery. The virtuous poor man, who will not flatter, cannot buy information from the groom; thus his natural worth is depressed by lack of opportunity to see and benefit from the wealthy patron.

The remedy for these several evils of the city, says Thales with his "rustick tongue" (l. 79), is a life in the country, where one may still find blessings rightfully apportioned:

> Could'st thou resign the park and play content,
> For the fair banks of Severn or of Trent;

There might'st thou find some elegant retreat,
Some hireling senator's deserted seat;
And stretch thy prospects o'er the smiling land,
For less than rent the dungeons of the Strand;
There prune thy walks, support thy drooping flow'rs,
Direct thy rivulets, and twine thy bow'rs;
And, while thy grounds a cheap repast afford,
Despise the dainties of a venal lord:
There ev'ry bush with nature's musick rings,
There ev'ry breeze bears health upon its wings;
On all thy hours security shall smile,
And bless thine evening walk and morning toil. (ll. 210–23)

Presumably, Thales is addressing his friend and, through him, the remaining audience of reasonable men; by extension the norms of this section must also apply to Thales. Furthermore, we have already seen that he explicitly asks for "Some pleasing bank" and "Some peaceful vale," which suggest the country retreat described above. Thales is probably exhorting his friend to find an English equivalent for what he expects to find in Wales. But there is also biographical and geographical evidence that demonstrates the speaker's own association with the retreat he recommends to others. The friend, Thales says near the end of the poem, will go to "the wilds of Kent"; but here he urges him to settle near the "banks of Severn or of Trent." Neither river flows through Kent, but the Severn, in Shropshire, flows near Johnson's home city of Lichfield, and the Trent flows directly through it; Johnson has temporarily and, I believe, unintentionally, lowered Thales' mask, allowing us to see the poet behind the poem, and to see that the "thou" of line 210 applies not only to Thales advising his audience, but Johnson—"unconsciously," let us say—urging himself to ignore the charms of the decadent city and return to his home. Speaker and audience briefly become one, thus making explicit what had already been implicit—in spite of the apparent dissociation intended by the word "thou,"—that the values of the satire's central affirmation are the values and desires of the speaker-poet himself.

The speaker, then, firmly endorses the country's goodness, and opposes it to the city's evil. Attacks upon this evil, however, account for only about sixty percent of the satire; frequent references to London's political decadence punctuate the poem, raise it to an attack upon national policy, justify its reception as another example of "patriot" literature, and remind us that, unlike Juvenal, Johnson is turning back to a golden political rather than peculiarly "pastoral" age. For instance, his friend calls Thales a "true Briton," praises the "consecrated earth" (l. 24) of Greenwich, Elizabeth's birthplace, and recalls Britain's past splendor:

> Behold her cross triumphant on the main,
> The guard of commerce, and the dread of Spain,
> Ere masquerades debauch'd, excise oppress'd,
> Or English honour grew a standing jest. (ll. 27–30)

In other parts of the poem, Thales attacks the power of Orgilio, a rich member of Walpole's Administration (ll. 194–209), heavy taxes (ll. 58, 64–65), corrupt holders of pensions (ll. 200–5), and perjury (ll. 68, 250–52). He also frequently invokes a past golden age—like Elizabeth's—to contrast with the present. Edward III reigned over "The land of heroes and of saints" (l. 100), but can no longer see in the "British lineaments" either the "rustick grandeur, or the surly grace" (ll. 101–2) which once characterized not Londoners merely, but his countrymen in general:

> But lost in thoughtless ease, and empty show,
> Behold the warrior dwindled to a beau;
> Sense, freedom, piety, refin'd away,
> Of France the mimick, and of Spain the prey. (ll. 103–6)

Similarly, he invokes his "Briton's right" of liberty which was taught to him as he lisped the tale of Henry V's victories (ll. 119–20) and, finally, he praises Alfred's reign, during which a single jail could hold half the nation's criminals, and justice, rather than today's "special juries" (l. 252) triumphed. Thales concludes: "Blest age! but ah! how diff'rent from our own!" (l. 253)

In order to be successful as a formal verse satire on Dryden's—

and Juvenal's—pattern, all vices but the chief "should only be transiently lashed, and not insisted on, so as to make the design double." The satirist must "inculcate one virtue and insist on that." Now Juvenal's Third Satire deals with both the difficulty of the virtuous poor man's rise in Rome, and the dangers of the city itself; it thus requires deft handling, else the design will in fact seem "double." Boileau, for one, was aware of this problem, for according to Brosette and Saint Marc, he originally imitated all of this satire in his own First Satire.

> *Juvénal* y décrit encore les embaras de la même ville; & à son exemple, M. *Despréaux* avoit fait ici la description des embaras de Paris; mais il s'apperçut que cette description faisoit un double sujet. C'est ce qui l'obliga à l'en détacher, & il en fit une Satire particulière, qui est la sixième.[28]

Boileau thus divides the poem and avoids having to show how the country retreat solves both problems posed in the satire. Johnson was more courageous and less skillful than Boileau, and so *London* includes two objects of praise and two of blame, neither of which can be considered the "chief." The evidence suggests that this double effect was due to accident not art, that Johnson probably hoped to show a relationship between social and political vice, and to hold up the long country scene quoted above, as an answer to both related forms of evil.

The portrait of the French in *London* is the longest single section in the poem, and deals primarily with their unhappy social effects upon native Britons. We have seen, for instance, that the supple Gauls not only adapt themselves to any situation and perform any low task ("They sing, they dance, clean shoes, or cure a clap" [l. 114]) but

---

28. *Oeuvres de Boileau Despréaux, . . .,* ed. M. de Saint-Marc (Paris, 1747), 1: 24. In his Amsterdam, 1772 edition, Saint-Marc adds that the "embaras de Paris . . . étoit comme hors d'oeuvre" (1: 15). In general, Saint-Marc is following Brosette (*Oeuvres de Boileau . . .* , ed. Charles Brosette [Amsterdam, 1717], 1: 11, 87). Brosette's edition first appeared in Geneva, 1716, and Saint-Marc's in Paris, 1747. Brosette's notes were reviewed by Boileau himself: see the former's edition of *Satyres et autres oeuvres de Regnier* (London, 1733), p. vi. For a slightly different account of Boileau's division of his First and Sixth Satires, see the reference to Pierre Le Verrier's *Commentaire,* chap. 2, p. 41, n. 30, above.

have also induced the English to imitate their ways. Thus when Thales complains that the French—a nation of slaves (ll. 117, 146)—"Their air, their dress, their politicks import," he is also complaining that this influx of corrupt values will lead to loss of English liberty. Immediately after the first attack on the French, Thales therefore introduces a political comment which praises Henry's conquests and laments their subsequent reversal:

> Ah! what avails it, that, from slav'ry far,
> I drew the breath of life in English air;
> Was early taught a Briton's right to prize,
> And lisp the tale of Henry's victories;
> If the gull'd conqueror receives the chain,
> And flattery subdues when arms are vain? (ll. 117–22)

Earlier he criticized the principles of Walpole's Administration: its "slavish tenets taint our poison'd youth" (l. 55), and those who prosper under it,

> With warbling eunuchs fill a licens'd stage,
> And lull to servitude a thoughtless age. (ll. 59–60)

Apparently, a nation ready to be corrupted by Walpole's politics of "servitude" is also ready to be subdued to "slav'ry" to French *mores* and politics; English slaves to gold easily become slaves to the French who, ironically, are already slaves themselves. Similarly, the tainted youth are probably among those who "taint the heart" (l. 76) of a virgin. But this attempt at relating the social and political vices is faltering and obscure as, indeed, is the attempt to use the country vignettes to unite the political and rural rational plans for betterment. In Thales' opening speech he declares:

> Grant me, kind heaven, to find some happier place,
> Where honesty and sense are no disgrace;
> *Some pleasing bank where verdant osiers play,*
> *Some peaceful vale with nature's paintings gay;*
> *Where once the harrass'd Briton found respose,*
> And safe in poverty defy'd his foes. (ll. 43–48)

The lines I have italicized associate the early "harrass'd Briton" with Thales, an equally harrassed "true Briton"; they also place the early Briton near a quiet river with peaceful country scenes similar to those described near the modern Severn or Trent. Later in the poem Thales says that he possesses a "rustick tongue," and thereby aligns himself with the early Briton of "rustick grandeur" (l. 102). The same mode of association—using similar phrases to describe Thales and the early Briton—is used again where Thales' "surly virtue" (l. 145) connects him with the "surly grace" (l. 102) eminent in the old British values now lost because of political and social crimes; he is to leave London for the country, where he will not be tormented by such London dangers as falling houses, fires, and ruffians. Since the hireling senator —now one of the "Senatorian band" in London (l. 244)—has left the country, which here includes the mythic Wales, it is, presumably, free of political corruption and is fit for the antique British values. The country, then, should be clearly related to both the social and political vices of London.

However, the values presented in the rural scene (ll. 210–23, above), are not those of the early Briton, who is poor, a guardian of commerce, a brave sailor, and the embodiment of rustic grandeur and surly grace. Thales describes an eighteenth-century country estate, an "elegant retreat" on the banks of a small inland river;[29] there is no suggestion of maritime activity, and the associations of *breeze*, *rivulets*, and *fair banks*, are distant from any image of commerce on the Spanish Main. Though Thales does not disparage commerce, an activity essential to the Briton, it is clear that he advocates growing enough food only for himself, without concern for feeding the hundred guests whom Juvenal's Umbricius is willing to entertain (ll. 229–30). Commerce to satisfy his own material or "human" needs, or to enhance English honor and wealth by expansion across the seas does not seem necessary for his country life; he is willing to abandon "Britannia's cross [once] triumphant on the main," and in so doing abandons the right to be considered the vestigial

---

29. See Mary Lascelles' remark in "Johnson and Juvenal," *New Light on Dr. Johnson*, ed. Frederick W. Hilles (New Haven: Yale University Press, 1959), p. 43.

Briton. If, as the definitions in the *Dictionary* permit, we take "rustick grandeur" to mean simple, unadorned, but stately and magnificent in appearance, Thales' vignette again shows little relation to the qualities of the archetypal Briton. It is charming rather than artless, and implies nature methodized and improved upon rather than nature rustic or grand:

> There prune thy walks, support thy drooping flow'rs,
> Direct thy rivulets, and twine thy bow'rs. (ll. 216–17)

Another couplet evokes the images of repose and gentility in both man and nature and is hard to reconcile with "surly grace":

> There ev'ry bush with nature's musick rings,
> There ev'ry breeze bears health upon its wings. (ll. 220–21)

Finally, as I have observed in the discussion of Thales' *ethos*, this "elegant retreat" is foreign to the old British trait of poverty. Thus the lack of clear correlation between the values of the antique Briton and the present English countryside, and the social and political vices in London, foils what I believe was Johnson's plan to imitate Juvenal's unified pattern by finding one virtue to offset two related kinds of vice; since it inadequately suggests the political solution, the beautiful country functions largely as an idyllic foil to the grim city. In *London* Johnson is unfaithful to Dryden's *"ex-officio"* rule—a rule based on successful practice—that the satirist must "give his reader some one precept of moral virtue, and . . . caution him against some one particular vice or folly" which is the opposite of the virtue inculcated.

This essay has been primarily addressed to the weaknesses of *London*, and so I should emphasize that the poem includes vivid portraits, passionate and indignant response to injustice, and skillful handling of the couplet form. The friend's introduction and Thales' opening remarks are particularly fine (ll. 19–45). His "dissipated wealth" is stored in a small wherry in which he will cross the Thames; this contrasts with the massive and rich British trading and battle ships formerly "triumphant on the main"; the smile of Greenwich, the "seat" of Elizabeth, gives way to the "contemptuous frown" of Thales as he looks at modern London, the seat of Walpole; the humility of Thales as he kisses "the consecrated earth" and recalls "the blissful age" (whose ships carried the "cross") changes to the "degen'rate days" and "curs'd walls" of the city before him; the "pleasing dreams" of Elizabeth surrender to "awaking" to the reality of vice, distress, and persecution because of "honesty and sense"; former "English honour" is now "a standing jest." Johnson compresses and contrasts then and now, dream and reality, expansion and limitation, bliss and degeneracy, happiness and misery, real and false material and spiritual wealth, and country and city. This section, I believe, is superior to Juvenal's, as is one aspect, at least, of Johnson's fire-scene. Juvenal's Codrus is surely a pathetic, victimized creature; but Johnson's unnamed character gains in immediacy by being labelled "you." It is not Codrus but the reader himself who is engaged in the destructive, preying, world of London: "Aghast you start," and "Swift from pursuing horrors take your way,/And leave your little all to flames a prey." You will fruitlessly tell "your mournful narrative" and receive insults, not succour, for "your woes" (ll. 186–93).[30]

For many readers these and other qualities of distinction, some of which I have discussed obliquely, will adequately compensate for *London*'s flaws; but the poem is nevertheless not as successful a for-

30. Further discussion of the poem might offer conjecture regarding Johnson's change of the name of the chief speaker from Umbricius to Thales. Thales was one of the seven wise men of Greece; he travelled in quest of knowledge and held that all things had their origin in water. Might this relate to the emphasis upon water in *London*? Johnson would have found the relevant information in the dictionaries of Louis Moréri and Pierre Bayle; both were immensely popular and were in Johnson's library at his death (*A Catalogue of the Valuable Library of Books of . . . Samuel Johnson* [London, 1785], pp. 12, 16). Moreover, Moréri (but not Bayle) adds a second Thales relevant to Johnson's choice of name: "a Lyrick Poet of the Isle of *Crete* or *Candie*, whom *Solon* sent to *Sparta* to excite the People to the love of honest things, and dissuade them from the Seditions and Enmities that reign'd amongst them, so that it was he that prepared the way for *Lycurgus* to bring the *Lacedomians* to their *Duty*" (*The Great Historical, Geographical and Poetical Dictionary* [London, 1694]). The first edition of Moréri's dictionary appeared in Lyons, 1674; the first edition of Bayle's in Rotterdam, 1697. For an extensive study of Bayle's relationship with England, see Léo Pierre Courtines, *Bayle's Relations with England and the English* (New York: Columbia University Press, 1938).

mal verse satire as *The Vanity of Human Wishes*. The reasons, however, must be traced to Johnson's improper use of the poem imitated and the satiric form rather than to his lack of verisimilitude in portraying his city or his opinions at the time. Furthermore, unlike the character of Juvenal's Umbricius, the character of Johnson's Thales is marred by contradictions, suggestions of insincerity, self-pity, self-righteousness, and arrogance: it is hard for us to believe in a person who exhorts us both to retreat to the country and to declare war on Spain. The satiric focus of the poem is also blurred: *London* consists of two alternating and only occasionally interlocking parts, rather than one satiric whole in which the objects of attack and praise are intimately related. Johnson has neglected or improperly imitated two of the central and successful aspects of Juvenal's poem; in these respects, *London* fails not because it imitates too closely, but not closely enough.

8

The Vanity of Human Wishes
and the Satiric Structure

Most modern critics view *The Vanity of Human Wishes* as "pessimistic" from beginning to end, and see no change of tone between the body and the twenty concluding lines of the poem. The *Vanity*, so the argument generally runs, shows man consistently defeated by his own fulfilled wishes; it is bitter, "tragic," as somber as the Book of Job, and penetrated throughout with classical resignation.[1] This interpretation, however, ignores both the "optimistic" eighteenth-century reading and the difference between the body of the poem and its conclusion.

For example, in his *Life of Dr. Samuel Johnson* (1787) Sir John Hawkins briefly describes the entire poem, but reserves his praise for the final section:

> The poem concludes with an answer to an enquiry that must necessarily result from the perusal of the foregoing part of it, viz. what are the consolations that human life affords? or, in other words, in whom or on what is a virtuous man to rest his

1. For some of these remarks see Bertrand H. Bronson, Introduction to *"The Vanity of Human Wishes" and Two "Rambler" Papers*, Augustan Reprint Society publication no. 22, series 6, no. 2 (Los Angeles, 1950), p. v; Ian Jack, *Augustan Satire* (Oxford: Clarendon Press, 1952), pp. 135-45; Francis G. Schoff, "Johnson on Juvenal," *N&Q*, 198 (1953): 293-96; Mary Lascelles, "Johnson and Juvenal," in *New Light on Dr. Johnson*, ed. F. W. Hilles (New Haven: Yale University Press, 1959), pp. 35-55; Robert Voitle, *Samuel Johnson the Moralist* (Cambridge, Mass.: Harvard University Press, 1961), pp. 40-46; Vincent Buckley, "Johnson: The Common Condition of Men," *The Melbourne Critical Review*, 6 (1963): 29; Patrick O'Flaherty, "Johnson as Satirist: A New Look at *The Vanity of Human Wishes*," *ELH*, 34 (1967): 90-91; John Wiltshire, "Dr. Johnson's Seriousness," *Critical Review* (Melbourne and Sidney), 10 (1967): 73.

hope? the resolution of this question is contained in the following lines [343–68], which for dignity of sentiment, for pious instruction, and purity of style, are hardly to be equalled by any in our language.[2]

In his own *Life of Johnson* Boswell insists that the *Vanity* is "as high an effort of ethick poetry as any language can shew," and that it "must ever have our grateful reverence from its noble conclusion; in which we are consoled with the assurance that happiness may be attained, if we 'apply our hearts' to piety."[3] Moreover, in a letter to Johnson dated April 22, 1775, Boswell says: "In your 'Vanity of Human Wishes,' and in Parnell's 'Contentment,' I find the only sure means of enjoying happiness; or, at least, the hopes of happiness."[4] Similarly, in his *Life of Dr. Samuel Johnson* (1795) Robert Anderson echoes Boswell's remarks and insists that "in some instances" Johnson surpasses Juvenal, "particularly in the pious and consolatory conclusion of the satire."[5]

2. Second ed. rev. (London, 1787), p. 202. See also John Courtenay, *A Poetical Review of the Literary and Moral Character of the Late Samuel Johnson,* 3d ed. (London, 1786), p. 28; and Arthur Murphy's remarks in *Monthly Review* (August, 1787), 68: 131. This article is attributed to Murphy by the publisher of the periodical, Ralph Griffiths: see Benjamin Christie Nangle, *The Monthly Review, First Series, 1749–1789: Indexes of Contributors and Articles* (Oxford: Clarendon Press, 1934), p. 134. For modern interpretations which suggest "optimism," see R. C. Churchill, *English Literature of the Eighteenth Century* (London: University Tutorial Press, 1953), p. 158; an unsigned note on *"The Vanity of Human Wishes.* Lines 15-20," *N&Q,* 202 (1957): 353-54; Donald J. Greene, "Johnson as Stoic Hero," *Johnsonian News Letter,* 24 (June, 1964): 7-9; Frederick W. Hilles, "Johnson's Poetic Fire," in *From Sensibility to Romanticism: Essays Presented to Frederick A. Pottle* (New York: Oxford University Press, 1965), pp. 67-77; Edward A. Bloom, *"The Vanity of Human Wishes*: Reason's Images," *Essays in Criticism,* 15 (1965): 182, 191-92. For other essays relating to the *Vanity,* see n. 5 in chap. 7, above, and Clarence R. Tracy, "Democritus Arise! A Study of Dr. Johnson's Humor," *Yale Review,* 39 (1949): 294-310; Henry Gifford, *"The Vanity of Human Wishes,"* *RES,* n. s., 6 (1955): 157-65; Paul Fussell, *The Rhetorical World of Augustan Humanism* (Oxford: Clarendon Press, 1965), pp. 155-62; and Bruce King, "Late Augustan, Early Modern," *Sewanee Review,* 76 (1968): 139-42 (see especially King's remark regarding Democritus, p. 141).
3. *Boswell's Life of Johnson,* ed. G. Birbeck Hill, and rev. L. F. Powell (Oxford: Clarendon Press, 1934–50), 1: 194-95.
4. *Ibid.,* 3: 123, the conclusion of n. 1 beginning on p. 122.
5. Third ed. (Edinburgh, 1815), pp. 123-24. This passage is not included in the first edition.

In spite of its recognition by these readers, most modern critics fail to discuss this important key to "the hopes of happiness." One reason for an excessively "pessimistic" reading lies in modern neglect of the *Vanity* as a formal verse satire which embodies the classical Roman concept of attack on a particular vice and praise of its opposing virtue. Thus read, the title and the final lines are intimately related, for the final lines represent a positive statement about the virtue set against the vice attacked.

We know that this notion of satire was most clearly stated in Dryden's "Discourse concerning the Original and Progress of Satyr," a work which Johnson used during the period of writing the *Vanity* and the *Dictionary.* Here he read about "the design of satire," and, accordingly, read that "Juvenal exhorts to particular virtues, and they are opposed to those vices against which he declaims." This concept made a lasting impression on Johnson's mind, since in Sermon 6 he says: "every argument against any vice is equally an argument in favour of the contrary virtue; and whoever proves the folly of being proud, shows at the same time, 'that with the lowly there is wisdom.' "[6]

This evidence suggests that modern readers of the poem are mistaken in ignoring the satiric pattern of praise and blame; its presence lends supportive evidence for one answer to a central question regarding the *Vanity.* Is it an unrelieved assault upon man's condition, or does it offer a source of hope which counter-balances the apparent gloom? Of course this question is genuine whether or not we are aware of Dryden and Juvenal; but the answer to it is more convincing if we see not only that the poem's Christian framework implies hope, but that the satiric conventions within which it exists demands an affirmation and that, as well, the convention of Imitation demands comparison with its pagan and ethically inferior source. This is not to say that because of Johnson's knowledge of Dryden's dictum the final lines of the poem *must* be read as embodying its "one precept of moral virtue"; it is to say that Johnson's intimate knowledge of that

6. See *The Essays of John Dryden,* ed. W. P. Ker (Oxford: Clarendon Press, 1926), 2: 84; and *The Works of Samuel Johnson* (Oxford, 1825), 9: 349. Maurice J. Quinlan places this sermon "in the last ten years" of Johnson's life (*Samuel Johnson: A Layman's Religion* [Madison, Wis.: University of Wisconsin Press, 1964], p. 97.

pattern while writing the poem, makes it possible, if not likely, that he had it in mind. And it places substantial new weight behind the "optimistic" reading, particularly since the desired contrast with Juvenal would be clearer. We must now determine not only what Johnson praises and blames in the poem, but also how he goes about doing this and, in part, how he imitates certain aspects of his original, Juvenal's Tenth Satire.[7]

Johnson uses several poetic methods in the *Vanity*: he subtly makes clear to the reader that his own experience and wisdom let him speak with authority and understanding; he attempts to give the impression of being exhaustive; through explicit exhortation and the linking of different portraits through the same metaphor, he forces the reader to look to the world and see the results of vain human wishes; he brings the characters before us like actors on a stage, so that we can see them the better; he suggests reasons for man's present misery; and, consistent with the satiric pattern, he offers a rational solution for that misery. For instance, Johnson's tone throughout is one of inclusion in universal folly, for he refers to man, fate, destiny, and the human condition. His castigation includes pity and understanding, and so, when the opportunity arises, he suggests that he shares man's weakness. When describing the reaction to a statesman out of office, he says: "now no more *we* trace in ev'ry line/ Heroic worth, benevolence divine" (ll. 87–88 [ital. added]). This pose enhances

7. For comparison of the two poems, see the essays by professors Jack, Schoff, Gifford, Lascelles, Voitle, Buckley, and O'Flaherty cited in n. 1, above, and H. A. Mason, "Is Juvenal a Classic?" in *Critical Essays on Roman Literature: Satire*, ed. J. P. Sullivan (London: Routledge & Kegan Paul, 1963), pp. 118-21. Dryden's "Argument of the Tenth Satyr" may also be useful: "The Poet's Design in this Divine Satyr, is to represent the various Wishes and Desires of Mankind; and to set out the Folly of 'em. He runs through all the several Heads of Riches, Honours, Eloquence, Fame for Martial Atchievements, Long-Life, and Beauty; and gives Instances in Each, how frequently they have prov'd the Ruin of Those that Own'd them. He concludes therefore, that since we generally chuse so ill for our selves; we shou'd do better to leave it to the Gods, to make the choice for us. All we can safely ask of Heaven, lies within a very small Compass. 'Tis but *Health of body and Mind*—And if we have these, 'tis not much matter what we want besides: For we have already enough to make us Happy" [italics and Roman type inverted in text] (*Juvenal and Persius*, Loeb Classical Library, trans. G. G. Ramsay [London: Wm. Heinemann, 1930], p. 190).

rather than vitiates the *ethos* suitable for the poem, for it suggests a wisdom won only through battle and defeat of the world on its own terms. Observation and history have reinforced the speaker's estimate of the world; hence when we reach the satire's final paragraph we are likely to feel that such a speaker—one who has been so right, gentle, and forgiving thus far—is bound to be right again. Moreover, the opening question of that paragraph, "Where then shall Hope and Fear their objects find?" (l. 343) immediately engages the reader by forcing him, as well, to ask *where?* and by evoking a response of anxious expectation. Johnson has the answer, and it is to him that we must turn.

Johnson also castigates what he considers the most universal wishes, those for fame, fortune, long life, and beauty, and shows that they all lead to bitter disappointment and human misery. He discusses, with some overlapping of classes, the court, church, academy, field of battle, young and old, the beauty of the *gaie-monde*, private life and public life. Wolsey, a powerful figure in the church, state, and court, first enjoys public power and then falls into ignominy and death. The young scholar wishing for recognition of his learning faces the doom of poverty and failure or, like the public figure Laud, success and death. Similarly, the warrior of each century, the aged man, and the beautiful woman are all destroyed by satisfaction of their earthly desires. By using general classes and particular examples which span several centuries and the world, Johnson gives the impression of being both inductive and exhaustive. Much of the generalizing weight of the poem thus comes from its organization into attacks on the different classes, as Johnson tends to move from universal to more limited wishes.[8]

The wishes also contrast with one another, so that the pretensions to public power by Wolsey immediately precede the scholar's wish merely to spread his labors "O'er Bodley's dome" (l. 139), and the image of Swift expiring "a driv'ler and a show" (l. 318) is neatly

8. The poem's attack begins with the "gen'ral cry" (l. 45) for money, and ends with the poor mother's desire for beautiful daughters; hence only the broad movement of the poem is from general to particular, since the common wish for long life follows the undoubtedly less popular wish to be a great general.

placed before "The teeming mother, anxious for her race" (l. 319). Whether we see youth or age, desire for preferment or knowledge— misery results.

Much of the power of this evaluation stems from the linking of different character portraits with similar metaphors. Images of falling buildings or falling men appear, among other places, in the discussion of the statesman (l. 79), Wolsey (ll. 127, 245), and the female beauty (l. 341). Similarly, the notion of life as a battle is implicit in the section on Laud (ll. 165–74) and all of the martial portraits, and is made explicit in the discussion of the old man and the young beauty: in the former "Unnumber'd maladies his joints invade,/ Lay siege to life and press the dire blockade" (ll. 283–84), and in the latter the attack on chastity also includes siege imagery: "Against your fame with fondness hate combines,/ The rival batters, and the lover mines" (ll. 331–32). Like the siege image, sickness and discomfort are also applicable to several classes: "Unnumbered suppliants" are "Athirst for wealth, and burning to be great" (ll. 73–74), Wolsey's "Grief aids disease" (l. 119), the young scholar suffers "the fever of renown [which]/ Burns from the strong contagion of the gown" (ll. 137–38), and the mature scholar must hope that "no disease [his] torpid veins invade" (l. 153).

In addition to the constant variation on the theme of unhappiness because of vain human wishes, Johnson frequently reminds us to examine the world, and shows the consequences of false evaluation of it.[9] The poem begins, for example, with the unhappy results of ob-

9. William Law's influence on Johnson is well known. See Boswell, *Life*, 1: 68; Katherine C. Balderston, "Doctor Johnson and William Law," *PMLA*, 75 (1960) : 382-94; Balderston, "Dr. Johnson's Use of William Law in the Dictionary," *PQ*, 39 (1960) : 379-88; Quinlan, *Samuel Johnson: A Layman's Religion*, pp. 3-26, and Paul K. Alkon "Robert South, William Law, and Samuel Johnson," *SEL*, 6 (1966) : 499-528. Law's remarks in his *Serious Call* often sound like a gloss of the *Vanity*. The appeal to look to the world, for example, appears frequently: "If we look into the world, and view the disquiets and troubles of human life, we shall find that they are all owing to our violent and irreligious passions"; "look into the world, and observe the lives of those women"; "for as great as the power of the world is, . . . we need only open our eyes, to get quit of its power" (*A Serious Call to a Devout and Holy Life* [cited hereafter as Law] [London, 1729], pp. 165, 198, 311). Of course Law is in the orthodox Augustinian tradition; both he and Johnson express commonplaces. For a brief account of the essentials of

servation's extensive view of mankind from China to Peru, from East to West. Shortly thereafter (l. 29) Johnson invites history to "tell" what it knows about human vanity. Democritus, who is borrowed from Juvenal, and who can now "See motly life in modern trappings dress'd" (l. 51), laughs at modern man, but Johnson insists:

> How just that scorn ere yet thy voice declare,
> Search every state, and canvass ev'ry pray'r. (ll. 71–72)

He then asks us to "see Wolsey stand" (l. 99) in all his power, and then to see him "sink beneath misfortune's blow," and to hear the sound of his fall into "ruin to the gulphs below" (ll. 127–28). The young scholar, whose "views" are to surpass Roger Bacon in wisdom, is told to turn his eyes "on the passing world" and "pause awhile from letters, to be wise" (ll. 157–58). Johnson tells him to "mark" (l. 15) and "See" (l. 167) the true state of the scholar's life. To the viewer "All times their scenes of pompous woes afford" (l. 223), while the old man, who foolishly wishes for extended life, is punished because he

> Hides from himself his state, and shuns to know,
> That life protracted is protracted woe. (ll. 257–58)

The beautiful young girl also falls because she does not properly evaluate the world: "Pleasure keeps [her] too busy to be wise" (l. 324).

Since both the readers and the characters in the poem must learn to see more clearly, Johnson provides a series of stage images which frame individual scenes of the extensive view before us. Hence, among the "busy scenes of crouded life" (l. 4) we see Democritus, who is able to "pierce each scene with philosophic eye" (l. 64). For the laughing philosopher, life is merely a "farce" (l. 67) which maintains his scorn of man. The reader, however, must evaluate the justness of

Augustinian theology, see W. Norman Pittinger, "Augustinianism," in *A Handbook of Christian Theology* (New York: Meridian Books, 1958), pp. 22-23. For some aspects of Augustinian theology in Johnson's thought, see Donald J. Greene, "Dr. Johnson's 'Late Conversion': A Reconsideration," in *Johnsonian Studies*, ed. Magdi Wahba (Cairo, Egypt: Oxford University Press, 1962), pp. 61-92.

Democritus' view: he sees that for the politician "On ev'ry stage the foes of peace attend" (1. 77) ; that "All times their scenes of pompous [martial] woes afford" (1. 243) ; that "Superfluous lags the vet'ran on the stage" (1. 308) ; and that "In life's last scene" (1. 315) even the formerly great might die in terrible sickness and become a mere "show" (1. 318). Many of the characters, then, are before us, acting out their previously fated roles; the audience must decide whether it is in fact viewing a "farce" worthy of scorn, or whether the drama is of a different sort. The entire final paragraph, and final couplet in particular, imply that the pagan, bitter, Democritan view must give way to the Christian. "Scorn . . . fill'd the sage's mind" (1. 69), but love, patience, and faith are the lot of the properly religious Christian, as "celestial wisdom calms the mind,/ And makes the happiness she does not find" (ll. 367–68). The stage images thus help us to see more clearly both by forcing us to look at the world before us and, therefore, look up and reject the notion that we are really actors in a despicable farce rather than in a divine comedy.

The reasons for man's blindness and largely self-induced anguish are presented at the start of the poem, for observation's survey reveals the disastrous quality of man's pride. Our "hope and fear, desire and hate" (1. 5) lead us away from the proper path and into dangerous traps. Man is betrayed by pride—the same sin that led to the initial fall of angel and of man—into thinking that he can walk the "maze of fate" (1. 6) without a guide, that is, without God.[10] Moreover, it would seem that pride also subverts man's use of reason as a guide to his wishes, for we see

How rarely reason guides the stubborn choice,
Rules the bold hand, or prompts the suppliant voice. (ll. 11–12)

Significantly, however, after introducing the theme of man's pride, Johnson emphasizes an equally non-Juvenalian element, the presence

10. An interesting essay concerning the pride of Satan appeared in *Gentleman's Magazine* for March, 1738; see especially p. 119. This is the same issue in which Johnson's poem "*Ad* Urbanum" appeared (p. 156). Law remarks about earthly pride: "Pride is only the disorder of the *fallen world*, it has no place amongst other beings; it can only subsist where *ignorance* and *sensuality*, *lies* and *falsehood*, *lusts* and *impurity* reign" (p. 301). See also Johnson's Sermon 6.

of fate in man's life. It is fate that "wings with ev'ry wish th' afflictive dart,/ Each gift of nature, and each grace of art," and it is with "fatal heat" that "impetuous courage glows," and "With fatal sweetness" that "elocution flows" (ll. 15–18). Even if man wishes wisely or innocently he is ordained to fall, for every human wish leads to destruction. This is clear both in the portraits of the scholar, whose desire for knowledge brings him death or poverty, and the virtuous old man, who deserves happiness but is punished with decay and loneliness. Similarly, even such great men as Marlborough and Swift (ll. 317–18) are reduced to dotage or insanity. Hence any *human* wish, any wish aimed at attaining success on earth through man's own efforts, leads to misery. The "fated" reasons for this unhappiness seem to be the human condition (originally induced by pride) and the further operation of man's "vent'rous pride" (l. 7) within that condition. Though it is the nature of things that man's life on earth can never be perfectly happy, still the pride which causes him to refuse God as a guide destroys any chance for the good life on earth. Life in Heaven is infinitely better than any form of life on earth; but life here is made unnecessarily painful by vain wishes.[11] Indeed, the association of *pride* with man's vain wishes and literal or moral fall from heights is consistent throughout the poem, whereas absence of pride connotes happiness. Man is "betray'd by vent'rous pride"; however in the good old days of political virtue, "scarce a sycophant was fed by pride" (l. 56). When Wolsey falls "At once is lost the pride of aweful state" (l. 113); just before discussing the defeat of Swedish Charles, Johnson asks: "On what foundation stands the warrior's pride"? (l. 191); Xerxes' pride (ll. 225, 230) causes his bloody battle against the Greeks; female "Pride" is susceptible of "Flatt'ry" (l. 340) and so the beauty falls. The word *pride* does not appear in the final, affirmative, section of the poem.[12]

11. For Law's discussion of man's foolish use of reason, see pp. 297 ff. He also remarks that the rules of religion will render life "full of content and strong satisfactions." Moreover, "he that is endeavouring to subdue and root out of his mind all those passions of *pride, envy,* and *ambition,* which religion opposes, is doing more to make himself happy, even in this life, than he that is contriving means to indulge them" (pp. 163-64).

12. There is only one point at which *pride* is used with any ambiguity. In the application of the portrait of Wolsey to the reader, Johnson says:

The discussion of *pride* and vain *human* wishes suggests that at no point prior to line 343 does Johnson offer an affirmation, a rational plan to offset the vice attacked. Since the virtue in the "praise" section of the satire is the opposite of the vice attacked, Johnson avoids offering any ordinary human wish as a remedy for the evils of an-

> Speak thou, whose thoughts at humble peace repine,
> Shall Wolsey's wealth, with Wolsey's end be thine?
> Or liv'st thou now, with safer pride content,
> The wisest justice on the banks of Trent? (ll. 121-24)

It might at first seem that we here see both an affirmation of retirement and obscure virtue, and a new use of *pride*, one related to Johnson's fourth definition of the word in the *Dictionary*: "generous elation of heart." The Trent was also the river of peace and retirement in *London*, and it is the river that flows near Johnson's home town of Lichfield. Yet even in this line, I suggest, Johnson subtly satirizes the position apparently favored, since all those who sought wisdom—the young scholar, Lydiat, Galileo, and Laud—met unpleasant ends. This satiric intention was, perhaps, more evident in the first edition's reading: "The richest landlord on the banks of Trent?" Here the line is ironically directed against the rich landlord, for Johnson had already shown that with Wolsey's wealth comes Wolsey's end; hence, once wealthy, the former vassal may be attacked by "confiscation's vulturs" (l. 36). Moreover, we are told of the needy but serene traveller: "Increase his riches and his peace destroy" (l. 40), and even this wise justice is not "safe," but merely "safer" than Wolsey. It is unlikely, then, that "safer Pride" is a description of moral character which we are to emulate in order to gain peace and security; the best that we can say about it is that it is a mitigated form of human sin. Furthermore, even though moderate in its aims, "wisest justice" is a human wish and therefore necessarily "doomed" to failure.

The line also represents a little discussed textual crux. In the first edition, l. 124 reads: "The richest landlord on the banks of Trent?" In the second edition, revised perhaps by Johnson, for Dodsley's *Collection of Poems* (London, 1755), the line is changed to "The Wisest Justice. . . ." However, in Johnson's manuscript of the poem, for a facsimile of which I am indebted to Mr. and Mrs. Donald Hyde (The Hyde Collection, Somerville, New Jersey), "Wisest Justice" is the original reading and is crossed out; "wealthiest Landlord" is substituted for it. Since wealthiest contains too many syllables for the line, Johnson (probably) changed it to *richest* in the published version. The sequence of correction, then, is from (1) *wisest justice*, to (2) *wealthiest landlord*, to (3) *richest landlord* (all 1749), and once again (if Johnson is responsible for the revision) to (4) *wisest justice* (1755). Though one cannot be sure what to make of these changes, it is clear that Johnson was indecisive and perhaps careless in selecting the best word for the passage; hence, in this case, we may have an exception to the usual rule that the author's revisions improve his poem and clarify his intention. Johnson may also have been indecisive because for his purposes, and in this context, he regarded the phrases *richest landlord* and *wisest justice* as being nearly synonymous.

other human wish. Thus he devotes the first 342 lines of the poem to attack and sympathetic denigration.

This view of the body of the *Vanity*, however, runs counter to that of a recent commentator in the main-stream of thought regarding the poem. Miss Mary Lascelles notes a tragic sense, one that is not found in Juvenal, where one loses nothing but "worthless counters." "The people of tragedy," she continues, "are playing for high stakes; and it is real money." Throughout his poem Johnson is sympathetic towards his satiric victims. Indeed, a "sense of a greatness whose authenticity is manifest in the very agony of *going off* underlies Johnson's treatment of downfall and defeat." Her subsequent remark is correct, but does not follow from her assumption that the agony which results from man's previous vain wishes shows greatness. The explicitly Christian conclusion, she says, "is consistent with the course of his argument in this poem."[13]

It seems to me, however, that though the people of tragedy may play for stakes worth having, the people of the *Vanity* do not; Johnson never implies that it is "real money" the characters fall and die for. If the stakes were real, the wish for them would not be vain, and the entire poem would lose its satiric point. Wealth is one stake, but it is described as a "pest" that kills and induces madness (ll. 23, 25, 30). In his disgrace Wolsey's "remember'd folly stings" (l. 119); though Johnson does say that "Truth" has a "throne," he does not suggest that learning is either "real" or worth dying for; instead, he states that the scholar must "pause a while from letters, to be wise." The military characters desire irrational objects, for "Reason frowns on War's unequal game" (l. 185); indeed, these men are such threats to order that "the steady Romans shook the World" (l. 180). Charles of Sweden, perhaps, is a tragic character, but his "hopes" are not "just" (l. 192), Xerxes becomes mad and "The bold Bavarian" (l. 241) is a man of "hasty greatness" (l. 252). There is nothing tragic in the wicked old man who disowns his children in favor of a sycophant, and the few virtuous old men are not subjects of tragedy but of the deepest pathos. Finally, the beautiful girl gains little stature in the resistance to her fall and hardly communicates

13. *New Light on Dr. Johnson*, Hilles, pp. 52-54.

dignity in *"going off."* Johnson's point throughout the poem is that the stakes these characters play for are *not* "real money," that they are in fact counterfeit. Nor, we have seen, can he present the opposite of each particular human wish as a way of betterment.

Only the portrait of Charles, then, leaves any doubt about whether it is intended as tragic. As analysis of his "character" will show, however, Charles is super-human but inhuman, heroic but common, and kingly but "gothic." Johnson's opening statement—"On what foundation stands the warrior's pride"—immediately suggests a foundation too weak to support his "frame of adamant" and "soul of fire" (l. 193). The word *pride*, by this point in the poem, implies disaster, and the word *foundation* is likely to recall a central question and answer concerning Wolsey:

> For why did Wolsey near the steeps of fate,
> On weak foundations raise th' enormous weight?
> Why but to sink beneath misfortune's blow,
> With louder ruin to the gulphs below? (ll. 125–28)

Charles' exclusion of women from his life was well-known,[14] so he includes conquests not only over his normal fears and fatigues, but "O'er love" as well. As "Unconquer'd lord of pleasure and of pain" he rejects the needs of mere humanity, and fixes his mind solely on martial glory. The degree of negatives in the portrait is therefore extraordinary. *"No* dangers fright him, and *no* labours tire"; *"Unconquer'd* lord of pleasure and of pain"; *"No* joys to him pacific scepters yield"; "Peace courts his hand, but spreads her charms *in vain;/* 'Think nothing gain'd, he cries, till *nought* remain.' " This series of negations makes the final line of the portrait's opening (fourteen line) sentence the more impressive: " 'And *all* be mine beneath the polar sky' " (ll. 194–204 [italics added]). Charles rejects peace, love, and joy, and defines his pleasure as complete possession of "all" the north under his "Gothic standards." Of course "Gothic" means Swedish, but other common meanings of the word were *rude, barbarous,* and *uncivilized;* it was a term associated with the destruc-

---

14. See, for example, Percival Stockdale, *The Memoirs of the Life and Writings of Percival Stockdale* (London, 1809), 1: 253-60.

tion of Rome and the encroachment of darkness, and reminds us that in spite of the force of Charles' personality, his destructive and vain wish for military supremacy threatens civilization.[15]

But his conquest proceeds, now over nature herself, since "He comes, not want and cold his course delay." Johnson takes us to the peak of Charles' fame and power, describes him with epic grandeur and diction, and immediately drops him into "the gulphs below." Formerly a leader, the Swede now deserts "his broken bands"; formerly used to having kings "capitulate" or "resign," he is now "Condemn'd a needy supplicant to wait"; formerly the master of women, he now hears "ladies interpose" on his behalf (ll. 209–14).[16] The word *supplicant* again associates the ends of Charles and Wolsey; the latter's "suppliants scorn him, and his followers fly" (l. 112).

15. Nathan Bailey observes that "the *Goths* and *Vandals* . . . demolished the greatest part of the antient *Roman* Architecture," and that the Goths "brought into Subjection and Barbarism a great Part of the Christian World" (*Dictionarium Britannicum* [London, 1730]). Johnson does not define the word. For an earlier allusion to the "Gothic" destruction of civilization, see *Paradise Lost*, 1: ll. 347-55, and Swift's "*Ode to the Athenian Society*" (1692), *Poems of Jonathan Swift*, ed. Harold Williams, 2d ed. (Oxford: Clarendon Press, 1958), 1: 25. Note, too, that this ambiguous term was used to describe Charles in at least one other place. The unnamed author of "A Letter To the Right Honourable the Lord * * * * * , Giving a description of the Person, Behaviour, &c. of the King of *Sweden*, King *Augustus*, and King *Stanislaus*," is generally unfavorable to Charles, whom he regards as "this *mighty* and *dirty* Monarch." He says: "I did venture the other day to ramble into *Saxony*, to satisfy my curiosity, in seeing those different Kings there, and penetrating as far as I could how matters stood there, and how our fate is like to be determined by that *Gothick* Hero, who with a handful of men makes himself dreaded and courted by all the powers of *Europe*" (*The History of Charles XII. King of Sweden. By Mr. De Voltaire*, 2d ed. [London, 1732], pp. 371, 367).

16. "Ladies interpose" may simply mean that the Sultan's female favorites thrust themselves in "To mediate: . . . . To put in by way of interruption" (Johnson's *Dictionary*) to Charles' or his minister's visits to the Sultan. It is more likely that Johnson is here referring to the Sultana's intervention on his behalf, and that the word means "to offer as a succour or relief" (*Dictionary*). She "took the King's part openly in the *Seraglio*, she called him by no other name than that of her Lion: And when will you, said she sometimes to the Sultan her son, help my Lion to devour this *Czar*?" (*History of Charles XII . . . De Voltaire*, p. 201). For a French text, see *Oeuvres Complètes de Voltaire* (Paris, 1785), 23:197-98. Both the context of the lines and the *History* make it unlikely that Charles is referring to Catherine of Russia: for this view see *The Poems of Samuel Johnson*, ed. D. Nichol Smith and E. L. McAdam (Oxford: Clarendon Press, 1941), p. 41; and *Poems*, McAdam and Milne, p. 102.

Like the ecclesiastic who desired everything, Charles finally receives six feet of land; by denying his humanity, Charles is forced bitterly to realize it all the sooner.

Through association with the earlier portrait of Wolsey, through showing that Charles is most inhuman when most superhuman, and through the speed of his collapse, Johnson makes clear that Charles is far from being worthy of emulation. He is, admittedly, more attractive than Hannibal, his original, whom Juvenal burlesques and treats like a slightly daft one-eyed elephant driver; scorn, after all, motivates Juvenal's portrait. At the center of Johnson's we find extreme pity for the misguided man rather than the more typically tragic emotion of admiration for the defeated hero. Unlike the tragic hero, Charles has learned nothing from his fall, and so he is not even allowed the dignity of the noble death which each of the four questions below raises and then rejects.

> But did not Chance at length her error mend?
> Did no subverted empire mark his end?
> Did rival monarchs give the fatal wound?
> Or hostile millions press him to the ground?
> His fall was destin'd to a barren strand,
> A petty fortress, and a dubious hand;
> He left the name, at which the world grew pale,
> To point a moral, or adorn a tale. (ll. 215–22)

Even Charles, then, does not play for "real money," and so, up to its last section the poem is consistently "pessimistic." Obviously, however, the poem does not end before its conclusion and, since formal verse satire as Johnson understood it demanded an affirmation, it is unlikely that the poem's final line is "bitter," or that, according to Johnson, our only hope for any kind of happiness is after death.[17] On the contrary, Johnson specifically tells us that we may be safe, secure, calm, and happy if we sincerely look upward towards God. Consequently, the closing couplet is consoling and positive:

17. Francis G. Schoff maintains this in "Johnson on Juvenal," p. 296; for a similar view, see John Wiltshire, "Dr. Johnson's Seriousness," p. 73.

. . . celestial wisdom calms the mind,
And makes the happiness she does not find. (ll. 367–68)

Part of the consolation comes from the source of celestial wisdom: God and religion. "Nor deem religion vain" (l. 350) in giving man hope for happiness, Johnson says in the *Vanity*; and shortly before and shortly after writing the poem he also said that only religion can lead us to earthly happiness and point the way to eternal happiness.[18] In *The Vision of Theodore* (1748) we read that reason is a poor choice as man's sole guide up the mountain of life, for there are "asperities and pitfals, over which Religion only can conduct you." If man looks upwards he will see "a mist . . . setled upon the highest visible part of the mountain; a mist by which," Reason says, "my prospect is terminated." This mist is "pierced only by the eyes of Religion." Though it is clear that one can reside in "the temples of Happiness" beyond the mist only after death, it is equally clear that "those who climb the precipice by [Religion's] direction" have the solace of piercing the mist, of knowing that the temples exist, and of knowing that by having followed Religion, "after the toil of their pilgrimage, [they may] repose for ever" in them. Thus the ultimate happiness comes after death, but if man will "Look upwards" he can still attain his share of happiness on earth.[19]

Johnson's periodical essays also suggest that religion offers happiness to man. The *Rambler*, no. 44 (1750), was written by Johnson's

18. For Law's similar remark, see n. 11 above. Note also that though "the *strict rules* of religion . . . relieve our ignorance, save us from tormenting ourselves, and teach us to use *every thing* about us to our proper advantage" (pp. 175-76), religion also teaches man that there is a happier world "reserved for him to enter upon, as soon as this short life is over" (p. 177).

19. *Works of Samuel Johnson*, 9: 168-69. D. Nichol Smith notes: Johnson "told Percy that he thought this fable the best thing he ever wrote. It states the part which he assigned to religion in the conduct of life, and should be read as a supplement to *The Vanity of Human Wishes*" (*The Cambridge History of English Literature*, ed. Sir A. W. Ward and A. R. Waller, vol. 10, *The Age of Johnson* [Cambridge, 1913], p. 170). See also, Boswell, *Life*, 1: 192, 537. Persius' Second Satire should also be read as a supplement to the *Vanity*. In his Argument to the poem, Dryden remarks: "This Satyr, contains a most Grave, and Philosophical Argument, concerning Prayers and Wishes. Undoubtedly it gave occasion to *Juvenal's Tenth Satyr*" (Dryden, *Juvenal and Persius*, p. 20 of "Persius" [italics and Roman type inverted in text]).

friend Elizabeth Carter, but must be in tune with his own thoughts on the matter. She distinguishes between religion, "the offspring of truth and love, and the parent of benevolence, hope, and joy," and superstition, "the child of discontent," whose "followers are fear and sorrow." Though we hope for a better life hereafter, religion leads to some happiness in this world, to the grateful enjoyment of the true pleasures of earth placed here by a beneficent author:[20]

> The happiness allotted to man in his present state, is, indeed, faint and low, compared with his immortal prospects and noble capacities; but yet whatever portion of it the distributing hand of heaven offers to each individual, is a needful support and refreshment for the present moment, so far as it may not hinder the attaining of his final destination.[21]

In the *Rambler*, no. 118 (1751), Johnson once more affirms that to be happy on earth we must lift our gaze and, in the words of Africanus, "raise our eyes to higher prospects, and contemplate our future and eternal state, without giving up our hearts to the praise of crowds, or fixing our hopes on such rewards as human power can bestow."[22] Shortly thereafter, in the *Rambler,* no. 180 (1751) he again asserts: if "the candidates of learning fixed their eyes upon the permanent lustre of moral and religious truth, they would find a more certain direction to happiness."[23]

Johnson's sermons also insist upon the happiness that religion brings. In the sermon on his wife's death (1752), for example, he observes that it is "the privilege *only* of revealed religion" to *"cheer* the gloomy passage . . . , and to *ease* . . . anxiety . . . . [and] give *comfort* to misery, or *security* to enjoyment."[24] Without the "peculiar excellence of the gospel of Christ," he continues, there is ". . . no other remedy than obdurate patience, a *gloomy* resignation to that which can not be avoided." With the Gospel, however, "so much is

20. *Works,* 2: 215.
21. *Ibid.,* 217.
22. *Ibid.,* 3: 64.
23. *Ibid.,* 345. See also the *Idler,* no. 41 (1759), written a few days after the death of Johnson's mother.
24. *Works,* 9: 516-17 [italics added].

our condition *improved* . . . , so much is the sting of death rebated, that we may now be invited to the contemplation of our mortality, as to a pleasing employment of the mind, to an exercise *delightful* and recreative."[25] Shortly thereafter he stresses: "to show that grief is vain, is to afford very little comfort, yet this is all that *reason* can afford; but *religion,* our only friend in the moment of distress, in the moment when the help of man is vain, . . . religion will inform us, that sorrow and complaint are not only vain, but unreasonable and erroneous," and that the infinite mercy of God will extend to the departed.[26]

Such is the power of the term *religion* for Johnson; but he has also supplied us with a prose gloss of what he means by "the vanity of human wishes." In his Sermon 12, on Ecclesiastes I, 14, he says:

> When we examine, first, in what sense we are to understand that all is vanity; we must remember, that the preacher is not speaking of religious practices, or of any actions immediately commanded by God, or directly referred to him; but of such employments as we pursue by choice, and such works as we perform in hopes of a recompense in the present life; such as flatter the imagination with pleasing scenes, and probable increase of temporal felicity; of this he determines that all is vanity, and every hour confirms his determination.[27]

Indeed, man's often unhappy state on earth is an argument for the attainment of happiness hereafter and—with that thought in mind—of man's proper happiness in this world. After examining man's present state he says:

25. *Ibid.,* 520 [italics added].
26. *Ibid.,* 522 [italics added]. In Sermon 5 Johnson says that no man can have his "tranquility . . . interrupted, who places all his happiness in his prospect of eternity." Accordingly, "it appears, that by the practice of our duty, even our present state may be made pleasing and desirable" (9: 341). See also Sermon 14: "He, therefore, that trusts in God will no longer be distracted in his search after happiness, for he will find it . . . ; by staying his mind upon the Lord, he will be kept in peace" (9:421). Johnson is quite orthodox in these remarks. For a relevant observation by Pope, see his *Correspondence,* ed. George Sherburn (Oxford: Clarendon Press, 1956), 3: 400, Pope to Caryll, January 1, 1734.
27. *Works,* 3: 397.

it is natural to wish for an abiding city, for a state more constant and permanent, of which the objects may be more proportioned to our wishes, and the enjoyments to our capacities; and from this wish it is reasonable to infer, that such a state is designed for us by that infinite Wisdom, which, as it does nothing in vain, has not created minds with comprehensions never to be filled. When revelation is consulted, it appears that such a state is really promised; and that, by the contempt of worldly pleasures, it is to be obtained. We then find, that instead of lamenting the imperfection of earthly things, we have reason to pour out thanks to Him who orders all for our good.[28]

We must remember that man is "to pour out thanks" at this moment; paradoxically, to the religious mind earthly unhappiness is its own argument for earthly happiness.

In the *Vanity*, then, as in the rest of Johnson's religious thought, the turn towards God and religion brings man his proper happiness on earth. Accordingly, it would seem that those who detect a dominant pessimism and tragic sense in the poem consider only the "blame" section of the satire—the first 342 lines—and ignore the essential "praise" section—the conclusion. Without both parts *The Vanity of Human Wishes* is incomplete as a formal verse satire. If we look at the final lines in general, and one of the key lines in particular, we will see that in his concluding remarks Johnson assures us that all is not vanity, that wishes should rise and may be answered:

> Where then shall Hope and Fear their objects find?
> Must dull Suspence corrupt the stagnant mind?
> Must helpless man, in ignorance sedate,
> Roll darkling down the torrent of his fate?[29]

28. *Ibid.*, 403. The most recent study of Johnson's Sermons is in Paul K. Alkon, *Samuel Johnson and Moral Discipline* (Evanston: Northwestern University Press, 1967), pp. 180-214. Certain aspects of Johnson's religious thought are also discussed in Arieh Sachs, *Passionate Intelligence: Imagination and Reason in the Work of Samuel Johnson* (Baltimore: Johns Hopkins Press, 1967), *passim*.

29. Johnson's revision of this line indicates his intention. The manuscript and the 1749 edition read: "Swim darkling down the current of his fate." It was revised for Dodsley's *Collection* in order to make clearer man's helpless state unless he looks towards God.

Must no dislike alarm, no wishes rise,
No cries attempt the mercies of the skies?
Enquirer, cease, petitions yet remain,
Which heav'n may hear, nor deem religion vain. (ll. 343–50)

Even in these few lines—which clearly reject a "stoical" interpretation of the poem[30]—there is a perceptible upswing from man's wretched condition because of wishes addressed to men for earthly success, to a more hopeful condition because of wishes addressed to God for spiritual success. In the lines concerning man in his present condition, we read: *must, suspence, corrupt, stagnant, helpless, ignorance, sedate, darkling, down, torrent, fate.* After the caesura of the fifth line, and particularly in the final couplet, the tone and the corresponding images change: *wishes rise, attempt, mercies, skies, enquirer, petitions, heav'n, may hear, religion.* Man need not wallow in his helpless state if he shifts his role. Johnson emphasizes this point in the important line "nor deem religion vain." Like the word *pride, vain*—or a derivative of it, or puns upon it—is placed at

---

30. Ian Jack, for example, insists that "the similarity between Juvenal's ethical position ["Stoicism"] and [Johnson's] own," made Juvenal's Tenth Satire "a perfect model" (*Augustan Satire*, p. 136); this position unfortunately forgets that "Christian stoicism" is a contradiction in terms. A similar logical fallacy may be found in Carey McIntosh's essay, "Johnson's Debate with Stoicism," *ELH*, 33 (1966): 327-36 (p. 331 in particular). There is a long list of anti-Stoical Johnsonian writing, several of which Professor McIntosh himself cites: the lines above in the *Vanity* should be added to it. Furthermore, Johnson includes this illustrative quotation under the term "Stoick" in the *Dictionary*:

> While we admire
> This virtue, and this moral discipline,
> Let's be no *stoicks*, nor no stocks, I pray.   *Shakespeare.*

And under *apathy* he offers this quotation from *An Essay on Man*, 2:101-4. Significantly, the final couplet of this paragraph is: "Nor God alone in the still calm we find,/ He mounts the storm, and walks upon the wind" (ll. 109-10):

> In lazy *apathy* let stoicks boast
> Their virtue fix'd; 'tis fixed as in frost,
> Contracted all, retiring to the breast;
> But strength of mind is exercise, not rest.

The pun upon "breast" suggests that stoicism is unworthy of the mature adult. For a well-balanced view of Johnson's similarity and differences from stoicism, see Robert Voitle, "Stoicism and Samuel Johnson," *Essays in English Literature of the Classical Period presented to Dougald MacMillan*, *SP*, extra series, no. 4 (1967), pp. 107-27.

strategic points throughout the poem; it always reminds us of the satire's title and almost always exemplifies it. Even in Democritus' days the philosopher laughed at those "whose griefs are vain" (l. 68); the seasons pour their their gifts "In vain" (l. 261) on the old man; in a punning parallel to Juvenal's Lucretia, Johnson observes that "Vane could tell what ills from beauty spring" (l. 321); shortly thereafter he castigates the nymphs "Who frown with vanity, who smile with art" (l. 327). The other uses of *vain* and, often, the relevant rhyme words are also important. The sickness of the young student, for example, is nicely communicated in this pun on *vein* which has the power of metaphor:

> Through all his veins the fever of renown
> Burns from the strong contagion of the gown. (ll. 137–38)

The older scholar hears this couplet regarding the dangers of the world:

> Should tempting Novelty thy cell refrain,
> And Sloth effuse her opiate fumes in vain . . . . (ll. 149–50)

Perhaps to associate the young and old scholars, Johnson then repeats the earlier pun in the line "Should no disease thy torpid veins invade" (l. 153). Finally, he rhymes *in vain* and *remain* (ll. 201–2) in the portrait of Charles, and *reign* and *in vain* (ll. 335–36) in the portrait of the young beauty.

There have been nine uses of *vain* so far; all have overtly negative denotations, and their rhyme words have overtly temporal connotations. If *pride* is conspicuous by its absence from the final section, *lack* of vanity due to religion is conspicuous by its presence in this positive couplet, the importance of which cannot be overstated:

> Enquirer, cease, petitions yet *remain,*
> Which heav'n may hear, *nor deem religion vain* [italics added].

Associating *remain* with *nor . . . vain* contrasts with the earthly non-religious direction of, for example, *reign, in vain*. Johnson is quietly stressing that there is no vanity in sincere spiritual wishes.

In the "attack" section of the poem man—like Wolsey and Charles

—had been imaged as a suppliant to other men for earthly favors; he must now address petitions to God and rest in His wisdom:

Still raise for good the supplicating voice,
But leave to heav'n the measure and the choice. (ll. 351–52)

Earlier in the poem man would temporarily rise and then fall; he was surrounded by mist, unable to see clearly and unable to withstand defeat; but in the conclusion we hear that man is "Safe in his pow'r, whose eyes discern afar" (l. 353). Similarly, at first no one is secure in his physical possessions as, "confiscation's vulturs hover round" (l. 36) but everyone can "secure" gifts of God, just as we can avoid the "restless wishes" (l. 105) that induce Wolsey's fall:

Implore his aid, in his decisions rest,
Secure whate'er he gives, he gives the best. (ll. 355–56)

Johnson warns us against the "specious pray'r" (l. 354), but hastily counsels that when we feel God's presence, when our devotion is addressed to the Heavens, then we may properly pray for a healthy mind, obedient passions, resignation, faith and "love, which scarce collective man can fill" (l. 361).[31] That is, we are enjoined to pray either for God's love, which is so great that all of mankind cannot absorb it, or, perhaps, for the abstract quality of love for all of one's brothers.[32] With this love will come the faith that contrasts with the "last sighs" of Wolsey, who reproached "the faith of kings" (l. 120).

The final section mentions "Heaven" three times, and refers to

31. Law remarks about prayer: "If we are to pray often, 'tis that we may be often happy in such secret joys as only prayer can give; in such communications of the divine presence, as will fill our minds with all the happiness, that beings not in heaven are capable of" (p. 180).

32. Bertrand H. Bronson (Introduction to *"The Vanity . . . ,"* p. v) believes that l. 361 "has perhaps never been satisfactorily explained by any commentator (The eighteenth paragraph of Johnson's first sermon might go far to clarify it.)" These lines from Law are also useful: "If religion commands an *universal charity,* to love our neighbour as ourselves, to forgive and pray for all our enemies without any *reserve;* 'tis because all degrees of love are degrees of happiness, that strengthen and support the divine life of the soul, and are as necessary to its health and happiness, as proper food is necessary to the health and happiness of the body" (p. 178). Donald J. Greene discusses this section of the poem in "Augustinianism and Empiricism," and observes that "ill" in l. 362 "is not repressed or removed; it is alchemically transmuted to something else" (*ECS,* 1 [1967]: 65).

God or Heaven obliquely in terms like "skies," "sacred presence," "happier seat," and "he grants the pow'r to gain." Man, in return for proper prayer, receives the unstoical but very Christian traits of faith, hope, love, devotion, and celestially inspired happiness. Moreover, this section breaks the pattern of destructive water-images. Since "Fate wings with ev'ry wish th' afflictive dart" (l. 15) man is miserable as long as he wishes unwisely. Hence "the stream of honour flows" (l. 103) from Wolsey but soon dries up and causes his ruin; the triumphant Britons "stain with blood the Danube or the Rhine" (l. 182) but impoverish subsequent generations; Xerxes returns to Persia "Through purple billows and a floating host" (l. 240); and from the elderly "Marlb'rough's eyes the streams of dotage flow" (l. 317). Johnson then asks: "Must helpless man, in ignorance sedate,/ Roll darkling down the torrent of his fate?" (ll. 345–46); he images man as being swept along "a violent and rapid stream" (*Dictionary*) by the strength of his own folly. "Enquirer, cease, petitions yet remain" thus not only induces proper sight but proper movement as well; man is neither "stagnant" nor uncontrollably rolling, but in the right path towards "a happier seat." Thus the final paragraph begins with a "stagnant mind," moves to "a healthful mind," and ends with a calm and happy mind.

The concluding lines of the poem again contrast with the insecurity portrayed earlier, for with the wishes granted by Heaven man has "goods" of permanence, goods ordained to be man's by the just and immutable laws of Heaven:

> These goods for man the laws of heav'n ordain,
> These goods he grants, who grants the pow'r to gain. (ll. 365–66)[33]

33. The couplet is based upon a subdued metaphor of trade. Note a similar use in the *Rambler*, no. 182 (1751): "It has been observed in a late paper, that we are unreasonably desirous to separate the goods of life from those evils which Providence has connected with them, and to catch advantages without paying the price at which they are offered us" (*Works*, 3: 350). Of course the famous section of *London* beginning with "SLOW RISES WORTH BY POVERTY DEPRESSED" is based upon another mercantile image. Donald J. Greene has discussed some aspects of Johnson's imagery in " 'Pictures to the Mind': Johnson and Imagery," in *Johnson, Boswell and their Circle: Essays Presented to Lawrence Fitzroy Powell* (Oxford: Clarendon Press, 1965), pp. 137-58. See also Bloom's essay, n. 2, above.

With these spiritual goods man may have, *on earth, at this moment,* what does not exist in the world of human wishes. Thus in his final couplet Johnson returns to his method of viewing the world, but now sees what human eyes could not see before:

> . . . celestial wisdom calms the mind,
> And makes the happiness she does not find.

In spite of certain clear similarities between the satires of Johnson and Juvenal, it is in their conclusions that they are furthest apart. Ultimately, Juvenal's poem is about how to be safe in a difficult world; Johnson's is about how to be virtuous. Hence for the modern poet man must not merely be inconspicuous, but must actively pursue the good life and actively reject the bad; he must both petition to God and look at his own state. If he performs both of these acts properly his resignation will be the ability to experience a "refreshed" wait for greater happiness; he will not merely accept this world's misery or the fact of death, for he will no longer maintain earthly vain wishes or fear death as an end to earthly happiness. The concept of active and positive—as opposed to "gloomy"—resignation is made explicit in the Prologue to *Irene* (1749), where Johnson tells his audience that they will:

> Learn here how Heav'n supports the virtuous mind,
> Daring, tho' calm; and vigorous, tho' resign'd. (ll. 9–10) [34]

34. Johnson probably wrote the Prologue shortly after finishing the *Vanity* in November of 1748: it seems likely that a Prologue would not be attempted until other revisions were finished and a date for production settled—in this case February 6, 1749; lines 9-14 epitomize the *Vanity*; and l. 31 includes one of the basic images of the poem: "He scorns the meek address, the suppliant strain." Johnson coupled resignation and vigor in the *Rambler*, no. 32 (1750): "Patience and submission are very carefully to be distinguished from cowardice and indolence. We are not to repine, but we may lawfully struggle; for the calamities of life, like the necessities of nature, are calls to labour and exercises of diligence" (*Works*, 2:159). Similarly, on August 12, 1784, Johnson wrote: "Let me rejoice in the light which thou hast imparted, let me serve thee with active zeal, and humble confidence, and wait with patient expectation for the time in which the soul which Thou receivest, shall be satisfied with knowledge. Grant this, O Lord, for Jesus Christ's sake. Amen" (*Samuel Johnson: Diaries, Prayers, and Annals*, The Yale Edition of the Works of Samuel Johnson, vol. 1, ed. E. L. McAdam, Jr., with Donald and Mary Hyde [New Haven: Yale University Press, 1958], p. 384).

Nevertheless, even with Heaven's support, the victory over the world is a difficult one; this difficulty may explain both the sense of battle in the *Vanity*, the many martial images, and the sense of earned resolution towards which the virtuous man must strive. Once achieved, however, today's victory over the world implies tomorrow's victory over death and, ultimately, the type of Christ's victory over Satan. The Juvenalian vision is far narrower: Johnson's man is subject only to the "measure and the choice" (l. 352) of a benign and omnipotent Heaven, whereas Juvenal's is limited in space, time, and joy by anthropomorphic gods who demand the "entrails and presaging sausages from a white porker"[35] (ll. 354–55). For the Roman once man achieves earthly victory over his passions he is safe, has slain a false god, and can rest, since the divinity of Fortune is merely a function of man's stupidity. Worldy *virtu* is all that matters for one poet; spiritual *virtu* all that matters for the other.

The true "optimism" of the *Vanity* can also be seen if we compare its tone and vision to *London*'s. The earlier poem shows a world in which villains thrive, frustrate the wishes of Heaven, and carry evil principles of perversion to the elements themselves. God has abandoned man and can be found only in the barren desert; accordingly, the structure of the family, the city, and the state, have collapsed and —like their defeated God—the few remaining good men must leave for a pathless waste. In *London* man is alone and suffers with no recourses but flight, surly virtue, and harsh satire. In the *Vanity*, however, one everywhere sees defeated man accompanied by regenerate man; behind the melancholy tones of the narrator one always senses a body of received and impregnable truth. If there is sadness in man's fall, there is also joy in his resurrection; the exhortations of the narrator insist that one can be engaged in the world, engaged in the battle for one's soul, and win because of the presence of a beneficent God's grace. The final couplet of *London* images one defeated man helping another to exert his rage in satire; the final couplet of the *Vanity* shows the calm which celestial wisdom makes within a man who will accept the proven alternative. *London* points towards Gehenna, the *Vanity* towards the city of God and a paradise within.

35. *Juvenal and Persius*, Ramsay, p. 219.

Most of *The Vanity of Human Wishes*, then, attacks wishes related to pride and the denial of God's help. As a formal verse satire, however, the poem includes an affirmation praising the virtue opposed to the vice attacked. To counteract our cloudy vision and fallen state, we must accept the Heavenly Guide and change our wishes in accordance with His wise dictates. Thus guided, man possesses the only lasting happiness available to him in this world, and prepares himself for greater happiness in the next. Perhaps this is not what the modern reader would call happiness, but it is surely what Hawkins called the answer to the question "in whom or on what is a virtuous man to rest his hope"; it is also what Boswell regarded as "the only sure means of enjoying happiness; or, at least, the hopes of happiness," and it is what Anderson insisted was "consolatory." Of greatest importance, it is Johnson's satiric affirmation in *The Vanity of Human Wishes*; the poem explicitly offers a source of hope which can offset the earlier account of man's misery. In this respect the poem represents the kind of satire that Dryden prescribes; it is likely that Johnson had that doctrine in mind. In any case, the *Vanity*'s affirmative qualities are a function not only of its Christian *ethos*, but of its role as formal verse satire and Imitation of a classical poem.

9

Some Implications

The preceding chapters have several implications for students of Augustan poetry: the formal Imitation which requires close knowledge of the parent-poem is largely a post-Restoration form; but the roots of the period's literary theory and practice are planted on both sides of 1660 and on both sides of the Channel; we need to speak with greater precision regarding the discrimination of Imitations and satires; the "Romantic" (and, alas, later Johnsonian) notion of Imitation as unoriginal and limiting must be discarded. The evidence suggests that the opposite was the case, and lends support to two of Pope's remarks in the *Essay on Criticism*:

> The winged Courser, like a gen'rous Horse,
> Shows most true Mettle when you *check* his Course. (ll. 86–87)[1]

And shortly thereafter we hear that: "those move easiest who have learn'd to dance" (l. 363). In many cases it is the formal aspects of the work—the "checking" and only apparently restrictive movements—that can supply imaginative bursts, revivification of commonplaces, new insights, and comparisons or contrasts with other cultures that may have had a variety of similar "experiences." The Imitation is thus not a restrictive but a liberating form which enlarges the poet's possibilities for metaphor and insists that the reader be aware of his moment in history and its relationship to other moments; the Imitation is internationalist not isolationist. The expansion of con-

1. *Alexander Pope: Pastoral Poetry and An Essay on Criticism*, The Twickenham Edition of the Poems of Alexander Pope, vol. 1, ed. E. Audra and Aubrey L. Williams (London: Methuen, 1961), p. 249.

sciousness encouraged in Imitation is extraordinarily overt in these remarks by Peter Motteux, editor of *The Gentleman's Journal*:

> Mr. *R.D.* sent me seven Lines by *Jovianus Pontanus*, the *Italian* Poet, in reference to our two Lovers, as not being extreamly distant from the question. They partly seem the reverse of a short Epigram, in the 7th Book of the *Anthologia*, . . . which *Greek* Epigram itself seems borrow'd from those inimitable Verses of *Sappho*, commended and cited by *Longinus*. I have seen a merry Version of the *Greek* Epigram in *French*, and he that made it, as well as the *Italian* Poet, and the *Greek* Epigramatist, very civilly give it as their own. But as for the *Italians*, they all have taken so much freedom in owning the thoughts of the ancients, that it would seem a severity like that of indicting a man about a Magpy, should we quarrel with *Jovianus Pontanus* about a small Epigram. And to say the Truth, as well as *Virgil*, and the rest of the Ancients, many of the best Authors of our Age, as *Boileau*, &c. can hardly be said to be freer from Plagiarism, than many a charitable dull Fellow in our Age, who like a famous *English* Poet, still chuse to give a Melon of their Neighbor's rather than a Pumpkin of their own.[2]

Though Pontanus' poem is not a formal Imitation, the imitative conception of his seven lines—followed by "a Paraphrase of it made over a Glass, by Mr. *W. Pittis*"—has evoked an immense range of Greek, Roman, Italian, French, and English literary culture. Johnson would have regarded this reaction as possible only in the man of learning's "artificial state of mind." Perhaps this is true, but surely the clear rewards of such a state make it desirable; and surely modern students trained to examine the varied, learned, and difficult works of poets like Blake, Yeats, and Eliot would not object to reclaiming information which can enhance their pleasure when reading the works of other major poets. Indeed, there is evidence to suggest that modern poets themselves have rediscovered the value of imitative forms. T. S. Eliot, for instance, used a method of imitation as borrow-

2. 2 (June, 1693): 189.

ing—as discussed in chapter 1—which is similar to Imitation as a separate genre. He remarked: "I gave the references [to Dante] in my notes [to *The Waste Land*], in order to make the reader who recognizes the allusion, know that I meant him to recognize it, and know that he would have missed the point if he did not recognize it."[3] This makes clear that older poems and cultures are still alive for practicing poets,[4] and that by incorporating earlier critical and creative modes of thought, the reader enhances his understanding not only of earlier poems, but of certain aspects of creative thought in general and metaphor in particular. Hence, though I have dealt with the more "learned" poets, critics, and audiences, we should not limit the context of Imitation to them only or, for that matter, to poetry only. Defoe, for instance, admitted that in his *Present State of the Parties* (1712) "he might have provided marginal references to the passages he was parodying, but that then no one would have been tricked."[5] Comparison with the original is necessary, but he erroneously thought that his audience would surely be able to make the comparisons without his help. Even Pamela, with her mixed audience of country gentry, noble families, and a Parson (and, therefore, Richardson with his largely "middle-class" audience) turns to Imitation as a generously evocative form. We recall that Bolingbroke told Pope "how well that [*First Satire of Horace's Second Book*] would

3. "What Dante Means To Me," in *To Criticize the Critic and Other Writings* (New York: Farrar, Straus & Giroux, 1965), p. 128.
4. Robert Lowell's recent volume, *Imitations* (New York: Farrar, Straus, 1961), again shows the versatility and modernity of the form. His approach does not demand awareness of the original ("This book is partly self-sufficient and separate from its sources" [p. xi]) and is a form of what he calls "poetic translation" or "imitation" (p. xii). As he sees it, this demands great freedom, since he has "tried to write alive English and to do what my authors might have done if they were writing their poems now and in America" (p. xi). Since Mr. Lowell mentions Dryden's criticism on the next page, perhaps it is no accident that he is here "imitating" Dryden's observations on translating Ovid and Virgil: see Dryden's *Essays*, ed. W. P. Ker (Oxford: Clarendon Press, 1926), 1:239; 2:228, and n. 41, chap. 1 above. Mr. Lowell's "The Vanity of Human Wishes (*After Juvenal's Tenth Satire*)" clearly borrows its title from Johnson (*Encounter*, 27 [December, 1966]: 91-94).
5. Maximillian E. Novak, "Defoe's Use of Irony," in *The Uses of Irony: Papers on Defoe and Swift Read at a Clark Library Seminar, April 2, 1966*, Novak and Herbert J. Davis (Los Angeles: William Andrews Clark Memorial Library, 1966), p. 23.

hit my case, if I were to imitate it in English." Similarly Pamela, Mr. B. reports, "recollected, that the cxxxviith psalm was applicable to her own case; Mrs. Jewkes having often, . . . in vain, besought her to sing a song: . . . thereupon she turned it more to her own supposed case; and believing Mrs. Jewkes had a design against her honour, and looking upon her as her gaoler," she thus gives her version of this psalm. "But pray, Mr. Williams, do you read one verse of the common translation, and I will read one of Pamela's."[6] The audience consciously compares and contrasts Pamela in "prison" with the Hebrews in Babylon, and comments accordingly; the characters of Pamela and Mr. B. are thus played off not only against one another, but against the resonance of the Biblical psalm. Parson Williams, for example, begs "to have the rest read; for I long to know whom you make the Sons of Edom, and how you turn the Psalmist's execrations against the insulting Babylonians" (p. 337). Mr. B. himself responds and observes that his very Christian Pamela has transcended the Old Testament ethics she is imitating: "Poor Mrs. Jewkes stands for Edom's Sons; and we must not lose this," he says, "because I think it one of my Pamela's excellences, that, though thus oppressed, [unlike the Hebrews] she prays for no harm upon the oppressor" (p. 337).

Imitation, then, in any of its several forms, may be a valuable mode of discourse for seventeenth and eighteenth-century learned poets, biographers, less learned party-writers, or middle-class novelists, as well as major modern poets like Eliot and Lowell, or, in fact for, modern political satirists of the stage or cinema.[7] I suspect that

6. *Pamela: or Virtue Rewarded*, intro. William M. Sale, Jr. (New York: Norton Library, 1958), p. 334. Subsequent references are cited in the text. (This exchange may also be found in *The Works of Samuel Richardson: Pamela*, intro. by Leslie Stephen [London, 1883], 1: 360-67.) One finds a form of Imitation—again related to parody—in eighteenth-century biography as well: see Donald A. Stauffer, *The Art of Biography in Eighteenth Century England* (Princeton: Princeton University Press, 1941), pp. 465-66.

7. Barbara Garson's unfortunate travesty *MacBird* relies heavily upon the conventions of Imitation, as does the final scene of the film *The Billion Dollar Brain*, which virtually replays the ice-battle scene of Eisenstein's *Alexander Nevsky*. Many modern novels also take their places on the imitative spectrum, among them James Joyce's *Ulysses* (Odyssey Press: Paris, 1922), Vladimir Nabokov's *Pale Fire* (Putnam: New York, 1962), and John Barth's *Giles Goat-Boy* (Doubleday: Garden City, New York, 1966).

Some Implications

it is more accurate to say that the genre of Imitation is not so much the product of the learned as of the active mind. And so, even more than in most other forms, the reader cannot be lazy if he is to read an Imitation properly. To do so, one might ask (among others) overlapping questions of this sort: what is the relationship of the original to the imitated poem? What kind of Imitation is this? In what ways is the modern poem like or unlike the parent-poem, and why does the poet want us to be aware of these similarities and differences? Perhaps in this way we can begin to approach what Pope called "the first principle of Criticism, which is to consider the nature of the piece, and the intent of its Author."[8]

"The nature of the piece" necessarily includes more than Imitation alone, and requires further refinements in terminology since, of course, a poem that imitates a lyric is likely to differ from a poem that imitates a satire. One danger in discussing satire is the passion to define what is actually a single species, or certain central *differentiae* of it, and without any warrant on historical grounds, to assume that all satire shares these traits. Such discussions generally tell us that there are "standard procedures of satire;" or "satire consists of" certain traits; or "satire is a work organized so that" specified things happen; or "satire is the genre most preoccupied with" a few selected themes; or, "the satiric form is anything that" includes what the critic observes that it should include.[9] Any "satire" that does not fit the definition or description should, logically, be

8. Postscript to *The Odyssey, Works of Alexander Pope*, ed. Joseph Warton (London, 1797), 4: 425.
9. For the full context of these remarks, see Bernard N. Schilling, *Dryden and the Conservative Myth* (New Haven: Yale University Press, 1961), p. 11; Edward W. Rosenheim, Jr., *Swift and the Satirist's Art* (Chicago: University of Chicago Press, 1963), p. 31; Paul Fussell, *The Rhetorical World of Augustan Humanism* (New York: Oxford University Press, 1965), p. 112; Sheldon Sacks, *Fiction and the Shape of Belief* (Berkeley and Los Angeles: University of California Press, 1964), p. 26; Ronald Paulson, *Satire and the Novel in Eighteenth-Century England* (New Haven: Yale University Press, 1967), p. 4; Paulson, *The Fictions of Satire* (Baltimore: John Hopkins Press, 1967), pp. 6-7. Leonard Feinberg notes that, however brilliant a critic might be, his attempt to define "satire" is likely to fail, since satire "offers so many varieties of structure that by careful selection one can prove almost anything he sets out to prove" ("Satire: The Inadequacy of Recent Definitions," in *Genre*, 1 [1968]: 32. See also Patricia Meyer Spacks, "Some Reflections on Satire," *ibid.*, 13-30).

banished forthwith. Ian Jack believes that "satire and the sympathetic feelings are absolutely incompatible";[10] and Northrop Frye is convinced that satire "breaks down when its content is too oppressively real to permit the maintaining of the fantastic or hypothetical tone."[11] However well these remarks fit particular types of satire, exceptions arise at once and neutralize a too limited but harmless description of all satiric art. The danger in such synoptic views emerges when the descriptive becomes normative. For instance, one recent writer asserts that *The Vanity of Human Wishes* is "ill-advised"[12] because Johnson abandons the mask of "the aloof, cynical observer" (p. 84), abjures laughing at his victims and, instead, mistakenly shows so much compassion towards them (p. 87) that the poem "lacks one of the essential ingredients of satire: an object of attack" (p. 88). Moreover, "the reader who is alive to poetry" (p. 88; later called the "sensitive reader," p. 91) will surely concur "that the poem . . . must be judged finally a failure" (p. 91).

This is precisely the kind of criticism we should mistrust: it presents a monolithic notion of satire that distorts the poem,[13] is based

10. *Augustan Satire*, (Oxford: Clarendon Press, 1952), p. 23.
11. *Anatomy of Criticism* (Princeton: Princeton University Press, 1957), p. 224.
12. Patrick O'Flaherty, "Johnson as Satirist: A New Look at *The Vanity of Human Wishes*," ELH, 34 (1967) : 88. Subsequent references are cited in the text.
13. O'Flaherty totally ignores the final section of the poem, in which man is comforted and celestial wisdom makes happiness in the world. This selective quotation is typical of other serious misrepresentations of Johnson's thought. Many of these statements, for example, cry out for refutation: "Now Johnson's vision of human life [as opposed to that of Pope, Swift, and Dryden] is too dark, too sorrowful, to encourage any kind of humanistic hope in a brighter, more rational civilization for man. To Johnson misery and vice are the inevitable lot of man, and the only possibility for redemption lies in God. As he says in *The Vanity of Human Wishes*, the civilizations of the past, the 'rapid Greeks' and 'heady Romans,' were corrupt; present civilization is corrupt; and hope for the future is vain. No great improvement is possible for man. With such an overpowering sense of the inevitability of human misery, the impetus of the satirist to correct and provoke reform becomes pointless" (pp. 90-91). O'Flaherty to the contrary, it is curious how one can say that Johnson's vision of life is darker than Swift's. It is also curious to imply that Pope, Swift, or Dryden, would conceivably disagree that "the only possibility for redemption lies in God"; could the Dean of St. Patrick's believe that man alone might redeem himself? In the *Vanity* Johnson specifically denies that "hope for the future is vain," and in several other works he insists that, given the limitations of man's fallen state,

on a conception foreign to Johnson's and is, therefore, mistaken, or, at least, beside the point. "The criterion of generic appropriateness," E. D. Hirsch reminds us, "is relevant only so far as generic conventions are possessed and accepted by the author."[14] So far as I know, there is nothing in classical Roman or Augustan English satiric theory that demands consistent aloofness or cynicism and prohibits sympathetic censure; *Mac Flecknoe* pillories its victim, the *Vanity* pities him. Different kinds of satire demand different masks, and one may even see different masks from one part of the poem to the next, as in both *Arbuthnot* and *Fortescue*. Analysis of varied satiric modes may help us to avoid the snares of the omnibus definition; after all, when we have said that satire attacks, and that *London* is a satire, we may be constructing a nice syllogism, but have not said very much about the poem. We may have said more when we answer several questions, including some like these: in what ways, toward what ends, and with what language does the satire attack? What alternatives (norms, or "praise") does the satire offer? How important —and how overt—are these alternatives in the satirist's apparent scheme? The answers will probably be different for different forms of

---

"progress" is nevertheless an achieved fact. The English language, the Preface to the *Dictionary* makes clear, reached its peak during the Renaissance; the *Idler*, no. 4, praises modern, Christian, charity, as opposed to ancient insensitivity; the Preface to *Shakespeare* (1765) calls upon readers hostile to Shakespeare to understand that "the English nation, in the time of Shakespeare, was yet struggling to emerge from barbarity" (*Works of Samuel Johnson* [Oxford, 1825], 5: 124) ; and there are numerous remarks in the *Journey to the Western Islands* (1775) that show Johnson's sense of demonstrable "progress": this, for one, attacking the primitive social system at Ostig in Sky: "He, therefore, who is born poor never can be rich. The son merely occupies the place of the father, and life knows nothing of progression or advancement" (*Works*, 9:98). This is not the place to analyze Mr. O'Flaherty's article, but one should doubt much of its method and major points. There are similar misunderstandings of the Christian views in the poem in Vincent Buckley, "Johnson: The Common Condition of Men," *Melbourne Critical Review*, 6(1963) : 29, and John Wiltshire, "Dr. Johnson's Seriousness," *Critical Review* (Melbourne and Sidney), 10(1967) : 73.

14. "Objective Interpretation," *PMLA*, 75 (1960) : 478. Hirsch also observes "that objectivity in textual interpretation requires explicit reference to the speaker's subjectivity" (p. 475). Hirsch discusses some aspects of "The Concept of Genre" in *Validity in Interpretation* (New Haven: Yale University Press, 1967), pp. 68-126; "Objective Interpretation" is reprinted as "Appendix I," pp. 209-44.

satire. If those forms cannot be found in current theory, and if that theory is not based upon historical evidence, then the theory, not the poem, is the failure. As the previous remarks have shown, the critic's job is complicated and enriched by the blending of the traditions of Imitation and formal verse satire; through awareness of this union we may, however, come closer to "the first principle of Criticism."

INDEX

Adversary: Arbuthnot, 152; as audience of reasonable men, 163; points towards harsh end of satire spectrum, 157–58; Pope's voice in *Dialogues*, 161; role of, 149; won over, 154
Aenid, 26, 65, 90, 181
Aeschylus, 3, 7
Alkon, Paul K., ix, 176n, 198n, 210n
Anderson, Robert, 194
Anderson, William S., 174n
Arbuthnot, John. *See* Pope
Auditor: variant of *adjutor* in Juvenal, 179n

Bailey, Nathan, 70n, 205n
Bayle, Pierre, 190n
Beattie, James, 29
Bentley, Richard, 135
Birch, Thomas, 70
Blackmore, Sir Richard, 68
Blair, Hugh, 128n
Blount, Sir Thomas Pope, 68
Boileau-Despréaux, Nicolas: anonymous Imitation of his satires, 47n; compared with Rochester, 46–48; Eighth Satire imitated by Oldham, 21, 48–49; and Rochester, 21–22, 47–49; First Satire imitated by Etherege, 20, 46; imitates Juvenal, 41–46, 186; imitates Horace, 46–47; Imitations different from Cowley's, 41; Imitations noted in England, 20, 42–43; translated Longinus, 9; translated by Butler, 46; on Vauquelin, 133–34n. *See also*, Horace, Imitation, Johnson, Juvenal, Oldham, Rochester
———— works cited: *L'Art poètique*, 54–55; *Epistles:* Ten, 42–43; Eleven, 43; translation of Longinus, 9; *Le Lutrin*, 9, 32n, 55, 127n;

Ozell translation of Boileau, 9, 32n, 43, 55, 127n; *Satires:* First, 41, 43–46, 186; Second, 47n; Third, 46; Fourth, 47n; Sixth, 41, 43–46, 186; Seventh, 47n; Eighth, 21, 47–49.
Bolingbroke, Henry St. John, 20, 140–41, 143, 148, 221
Boswell, James: accuracy of *London*, 168; Johnson's method of Imitation, 1; praises Dryden's "Discourse," 68; praises *Vanity*, 194, 217; other references to *Life of Johnson*, 71, 165, 168n, 172n, 207n
Bouhours, Pére Dominique, 69n
Boyce, Benjamin, 109
Britain. *See* English nation
Brome, Alexander, 39–40
Brooks, Harold F., 15n, 39n–56n *passim*
Brossette, Claude: on Boileau, 41–42; on Regnier, 42n, 132n, 186n
Brower, Reuben, vii, 15n
Brown, John, 72
Brown, Tom, 9, 51n
Burlesque: similarities to Imitation, 23–30
Burnet, Sir Thomas, 23–24
Burnet, Bishop Gilbert, 40
Burney, Charles, 179
Butler, Samuel, 46–47
Butt, John, 15n, 77, 138n, 140, 162n

Caricature: truth by means of distortion, 169
Caroline, Queen, 98, 107–8, 125
Carter, Elizabeth, 208
Casaubon, Isaac, 21n, 69, 129–30, 135n
Characters: treatment of in Pope and Young, 108–13
Charles of Sweden, 203–6, 210
Christianity: in conclusion to *Vanity*, 195, 203, 206–17; in Pope's *Bath-*

Index

Fiske, George Converse, 6, 7n
Flambeau: defined in Johnson's *Dictionary*, 176n
Florio: character in Young, 109–11; inferior to Pope's florist, 111–12
Formal verse satire (*see also* Satire): defined, 59, 86, 91–94
———— pattern of praise and blame in, 91–94; known to Dacier, 60–64; Dryden, 65–68; Johnson and others, 68–75
———— use of pattern of praise and blame to distinguish other kinds of satire: comic and punitive, 87; Horatian epistle and satire, 129–38; in Pope, 138–48
Fortescue, William. *See* Pope, *The First Satire of the Second Book of Horace*
Freed, Lewis, 69n
Frenchmen: corrupt values in *London*, 173, 176, 178, 186–87
Fresnay, Vaquelin de la, 129, 133, 134n

Garrick, David, 168
General nature, 2–6
Gentleman's Journal; on Dacier's *Horace*, 135n; on Dryden's *Juvenal and Persius*, 65n; on Imitation by by Pontanus, 220. *See also* Motteux
George I, 93, 98, 108, 113, 123
Giacomini, Lorenzo, 8
Gifford, William, 68
Gildon, Charles, 61–62n *passim*, 64–65
God: in Pope's satires and epistles, 142–43, 148–50, 158–59
———— in *London*: His blessings only in the country, 177; dethroned, 178; perversion of purposes, 175
———— in *Vanity*: prayed to, 213–16; refused by pride, 201; security and happiness with, 206–7, 219n, 210–11
Goths: subjected Christian world, 205n
Gray, Thomas, 14, 85, 165n
Greene, Edward B., 21n, 73
Greene, Donald J., ix, 25n, 88n, 96n, 166n, 167n, 168, 194n, 213n, 214n
Guardian, The, no. 12, 6n

Hannibal, 206

Harte, Walter, 71
Hawkins, Sir John, 101–2, 168n, 193, 217
Heinsius, Daniel, 65, 67n, 131, 134, 135n, 164
Higden, Henry, 3, 4, 19, 53
Hill, Aaron, 71–72, 74, 96
Homer: emulated, 11; parodied, 16, 23–24, 26; translated, 16, 85
Horace (Horatius Quintus Flaccus): edition by Dacier, 60–64 (*see also* Dacier); demands recognition of original, 7, 9; distinction between satire and epistle, 129–38, 138–64 *passim*; follows and differs from Lucilius, 6–7; imitated by Boileau, 41–43, 46–47; Brome, *et al.*, 19, 39–40; Cowley, 35–40; Oldham, 4, 19, 53–55; Pope, 1, 3–5, 16–17, 20, 78, 80–86, 92, 138–64 *passim*, 221–22; Rochester, 20, 46–47; Swift, 28, 50–51, 57; improper use of satiric pattern, 65; praised by Young, 68, 100; refines original, 9
————works cited (*see also* Pope, *for his* Imitations): *Ars poetica*, 4, 7, 9n, 20–21, 24, 30, 53–54, 125; *Epistles* i. 1, 80, 136; *Epistles* i. 5, 28, 57; *Epistles* i. 7, 50; *Epistles* i. 14, 43; *Epistles* ii. 1, 3n, 81; *Epode* ii. 38–39; *Odes* i. 5, 37, 38n; *Odes* i. 27, 39; *Odes* iii. 2, 51; *Odes* 4.2, 36–37; *Odes* 4.9, 51; *Satires* i. 6, 57; *Satires* i. 9, 31, 39; *Satires* i. 10, 6n, 40; *Satires* ii. 1, 20, 82, 138, 221–22; *Satires* ii. 2, 25, 138; *Satires* ii. 4, 39; *Satires* ii. 6, 39, 51; *Satires* ii. 8, 46
Hurd, Richard, 3, 12
Hyde, Donald and Mary, 202n, 215n

Imagery: of desert, 177; falling buildings and men, 198; hunting bird, 161–62; man as suppliant, 213; martial, 155; mercantile, 214; repose and gentility, 189; stage scenes, 199
Imitation: before the Restoration, 31–32; defined by Johnson, 14–15; Johnson's objections to, 82–85, 219–20; dual nature of, 57; early modes of, as modernized translation faith-

229

Index

by Johnson, 69–71; not a politician, 182n; translated by Dryden, 65–67, 179n; Holyday, 179n; Gifford, 68; Greene, 21n, 73; Owen, 68, 73n; Stapylton, 2, 179n. *See also* Boileau, Imitation, Johnson, Oldham

—— works cited: First Satire, 27–28, 44, 55, 67; Third, 28, 41–46, 78–79, 165–91 *passim*; Sixth, 66, 67, 124, 177; Seventh, 44–45, 55; Eighth, 67; Tenth, 19, 55, 56, 193–217 *passim*; Thirteenth, 2–4, 55.

King, William, 28
Kolb, Gwin J., ix, 70n
Krutch, Joseph Wood, 166–67, 168n

Lascelles, Mary, 78–79, 188n, 203, 206
Laughing Satire, 99
Law, William, 198n, 200n, 201n, 207n, 213n
Le Verrier, Pierre, 41, 186n
Liberty: in *London*, 166–68, 176, 178, 185, 187; in Pope's *Epilogue to the Satires*, 144–45, 149, 157–64 *passim*
London, city of: contrasted with country, 189; crimes of, 171, 173; deserted by God, 177; perversion, 176; political decadence, 185; portrait thought innacurate in *London*, 166–67; viewed by Thales, 190
Longinus, 9–12
Lowell, Robert, 221n
Lucilius, 6, 7n, 63, 130

Man of Ross: central norm of *Ethic Epistles*, 148; in *Bathmat*, 148, 150
Maresca, Thomas E., 16, 62n, 80–81n, 154, 169n
Martin, Benjamin, 176n
Mask: Johnson, 180–81; Pope, 225; Swift, 50
Misery: induced by vain human wishes, 197–99, 201
Modernization: as Imitation in Brome, 39–40; Cowley, 35–36; Denham, 33–35; Dryden, 54–55; Etherege, 46; Oldham, 32, 48–49, 52–56, 78–79; Elizabethan theory of translation, 32–33. *See also* Imitation
Moréri, Louis, 61n, 190n
Motteux, Peter: ed. of *Gentleman's Journal*, 65n, 135n, 220

Mudford, William, 165
Murphy, Arthur, 25, 168
Muse: expansion of term in Pope, 160

O'Flaherty, Patrick, 193n, 196n, 224n–25n
Oldham, John: admired Rochester, 48–49; cited by Johnson, 82; concept of general nature, 4, 19; influence of Dryden, 52–54; influences later imitators, 54–56, 82; imitates Boileau, 21; Horace, 4, 19, 53–54; Juvenal, 78–79; method of Imitation, 4, 19, 21, 31–32, 52–55; compared with Pope and Johnson, 77–79; paraphrases Ovid, 52–53

—— works cited: Horace's *Ars poetica*, 4, 19, 21, 53–55; "*Bion:* A Pastoral* . . . bewailing . . . the Death of . . . Rochester*," 49; "The Eighth Satyr of Monsieur Boileau, Imitated," 48–49; Imitation of Juvenal's Third Satire, 78–79; "Passion of Byblis," 52; *Satyrs Upon the Jesuits*, 53
Oldmixon, John, 68, 69n
Owen, Edward, 68, 73n
Ozell, John, 9, 32n, 42, 55, 68, 127n

Panegyric, 65, 72, 93, 113, 115–16, 118, 120, 125
Parody: discussed, 25–30
Partial Imitation in Boileau, 41–46; Tom Brown, 51n; Cowley, 36–37, 38–39, 49; Hodgson, 52n; Swift, 50–51, 57
Paulson, Ronald, 88n, 149n, 223
Persius, vii, 31, 66–71, 74n, 86, 181n
Philips, Ambrose, 11
Phillips, John, 13–14, 23
Pope, Alexander: adapts Dacier, 136; author of *London* will be *deterré*, 165; awareness of original, 5, 11–12, 16–17, 21–22, 32, 56; awareness of satiric pattern, 71–74; criticized for neglect of it, 73–74; compared with Young, 95, 99, 109–12, 126–28; contrasted with Boileau, 43; distinction between satire and epistle, 138–64 *passim*; echoes Oldham, 56; first principle of criticism, 223, 226; general nature, 4; Imitations at-